119174

D1603479

LESSER
PARABLES
OF OUR LORD

WILLIAM ARNOT STUDY SERIES

LESSER PARABLES

OF OUR LORD

by

William Arnot

KREGEL PUBLICATIONS
Grand Rapids, MI 49501

Lesser Parables of Our Lord by William Arnot, published by Kregel Publications, a division of Kregel, Inc. All rights reserved.

Library of Congress Cataloging in Publication Data

Arnot, William, 1808-1875.
  Lesser Parables of Our Lord.

  Reprint of the 1884 ed. published by T. Nelson, London.
    1. Jesus Christ—Parables.   2. Bible. N.T.
Gospels—Criticism, interpretation, etc.   I. Title.
BT375.A7   1981   226'.806   80-8066
ISBN 0-8254-2121-7   AACR1

Printed in the United States of America

CONTENTS

LESSONS IN FIRST PETER

LIFE IN CHRIST

BIOGRAPHY

BIOGRAPHY

WILLIAM ARNOT was a remarkable man. He was a power in his time, and made himself felt as preacher, writer, lecturer, both on this and on the other side of the Atlantic. His life contains but few incidents, but is nevertheless well worthy of being related, partly by his own graphic pen in a short Autobiography, and partly by his daughter through a selection from his private papers and correspondence.

We have only to look at the portrait attached to the Autobiography and Memoir, and we know at once what manner of man he was. If the mind be written in the face, here we have a man simple yet strong-brained, earnest and true, full of humour, full too of " the milk of human kindness."

These traits all gradually become apparent as we read his story from childhood onward to manhood, and at last see him placed in an honoured grave, mourned not only by that branch of the Church to which he belonged, but by all who can estimate genius when sanctified by grace and devoted to the highest aims.

William Arnot was born at Scone in 1808. His father lived here for about twelve years, and here seven children were born ; and here his mother died when she gave him birth. While William was still an infant, his father removed with his family to the Boat of Forgan, on the river Earn, in the parish of Forgandenny, about four miles from Perth. This he always looked upon as his native place, as he never could feel an interest in the spot where he was born, since he never knew it as a home. This was the home of his youth. No other spot on earth was half so dear to him ; and to use the touching words of the Autobiography, " The love of it is fresh in my bosom yet, when many other emotions are fading." And again, when describing the place connected with his earliest recollections, he says, " There are three trees at the west end of the house, and two—a venerable plane and wide-spreading ash—at the edge of the garden, right behind the barn. Oh, the hum of bees in the top of that plane tree on a summer afternoon, when its blossoms hung from every twig ! I think I hear it now ; and it makes me weep to think that I shall never hear it as I was wont to hear it, with the fresh, buoyant, hopeful bosom of boyhood. I should like to sit beneath it again on a warm summer evening and hear that hum. I do not know whether it would gladden my heart again, or break it ; but I would like to try."

His parents lived in the faith and the fear of God. They were universally respected. The following is a characteristic anecdote of his father :—The small farm which he cultivated was rented from Lord Ruthven. He had obtained a verbal authority from his landlord to execute some building, and repay himself by retaining his rents. Lord Ruthven left home for the Continent, where he resided some seven years. The building was erected, and the cost was £49, 10s. Robert Arnot retained this sum ; but as he had no voucher, the factor could not give him a discharge. On Lord Ruthven's return, the factor sent Arnot a letter, stating that this sum stood on his book as arrear of rent, and advising him to get the necessary voucher. He carried the factor's letter to Lord Ruthven, and received one in return to the factor. " On presenting his lordship's letter to the man-of-law, my father observed him smiling as he read, and asked the cause of his merriment. Whereupon he read aloud the contents of the letter, which were as follows : ' I believe whatever this man says.' "

His mother was a woman who loved her Bible and walked with God. He notes down one very characteristic habit of hers which had reached him. "When employed in spinning, she was wont to have her Testament lying open upon the body or frame-work of the wheel, within sight, and would catch a verse from time to time without interrupting her toil. 'Diligent in business; fervent in spirit; serving the Lord.'" Though he had never seen his mother, he delighted to think that all his blessings came in answer to her prayers; and he felt it was very good for him to have grown up with the conception of his mother being a glorified saint. "Her company has often awed me out of evil, and encouraged me to good. Even yet, the thought of my mother's eyes fainting in death, taking a last look of me, her helpless infant, melts me as nothing else is able to do." So, although his birth was humble, and the scenes and circumstances which surrounded his childhood rude, he could with thankfulness take up the words of the poet Cowper,—

> " My boast is not that I deduce my birth
> From loins enthroned and rulers of the earth;
> But higher far my proud pretensions rise—
> The son of parents passed into the skies."

The glimpse which he gives us into his boyhood is interesting. His memory was so good that it retained a connected and continuous record of events from the time that he was four years old. This period was to him "like the era which divides the fabulous from the authentic history of a nation." He takes us to the village school, and paints the teacher in a few graphic touches. "He was an elderly man, lame in body, and of a most inoffensive and gentle disposition. His character penetrated right through the childlike, and stuck fast in the childish. He was, however, a good, conscientious, Christian man, of a most unblemished reputation." He describes the school, with its two stone steps outside the door leading to the floor, a little elevated above the level of the road. We see the little boy standing on the street, and looking through the opened door at the whole extent of the school-room, where his eye is arrested by "the rows of dangling feet and legs, whose owners were seated at the tables above, and not so directly in my view......I was soon introduced to the master and the alphabet. I had the credit of being a good scholar from the commencement."

That he had a lively imagination, may be gathered from the following incident :—" Somewhere about this time my brothers and sisters and companions began to persuade me that I had been enlisted, and that as soon as I should grow up they would take me away to be a soldier. The foundation of this dangerous joke was this : Some soldier, or perhaps a yeoman going to Perth for drill, took me up in his arms and gave me a shilling, when I was quite an infant. It was afterwards repeated, as I thought seriously, that I was enlisted and must be a soldier. I never spoke of it ; I was too much afraid even to mention it ; but it often imbittered my joys throughout the period of childhood. It was a grievous wrong that was done me. Why will not all mankind speak truth, and only truth, to children ?"

Arnot had no distinct remembrance of the dawn of religious impressions on his mind. He was sure, however, that the influence of prayer and the Bible at school was good. He had a very vivid recollection of the first prayer that he ventured to offer in his own words and thoughts, and he felt the emancipation from the trammels of prayers learned by rote to be very great. At seven years of age he was sent to school at Aberdalgie, the nearest parish on the other side the river. Its master, Mr. Peddie, was a teacher in advance of his age, and a fine specimen of an old gentleman. He used to give Scripture lessons with a vigour and a genius that made the Bible stories most attractive to his scholars. " I remember well the hearty laugh of the scholars when the worthy old gentleman, who was somewhat corpulent and very tall, enacted David throwing the stone at the Philistine. How he did swing his one arm round his white head, while the loose sleeve where the other arm should have been danced in the wind ; and what a race forward he took to give additional impetus to the stone when at last it was let off; and how earnestly he looked forward to see whether his missile had taken effect on the forehead of his adversary! The whole essence of the training system was there."

While at this school and other schools he did much as other boys do. He fought many a battle, played the truant, and proved the truth of the saying that "evil communications corrupt good manners."

His father married again when he was about eight or nine years of age. As the boy grew in years and strength he was kept at home in the summer to herd cows, and attended school only in the winter. He had but few books; but amongst them were "The Pilgrim's Progress," Brydone's "Tour through Sicily and Malta," "The Arabian Nights," and "Don Quixote." These were greedily devoured, and, whetting his appetite for mental food, contributed to his intellectual development. The historical parts of the Bible were an inexhaustible theme, and Watts' "Hymns for Children" became a part of memory itself. The first glimpses he obtained of the political world were connected with the trial of Queen Caroline. Robert Liddel, owner and master of a sloop trading from Perth, and married to Mary Laing, his cousin, often visited his father, and sometimes brought with him a newspaper; and in this way he first found out the existence and nature of government.

When about fourteen, his father sent him to a school in Perth; but he had not been there more than six or seven weeks when he was compelled to leave through illness. An attack of measles, and then of acute inflammation in the chest, was so severe that for two or three days his family were apprehensive for his life. He recovered, however, and from the period of convalescence in the summer he dates a most important era in his spiritual history. He was made to feel the reality of his sin and danger, and ardently to desire the safety of his soul. Baxter's "Saints' Rest," which he read at this time with great profit, gave reality and power and personal interest to all that he had previously known of divine things.

In the autumn of the same year, while he was still feeble, he was invited to reside with a cousin of his father, Mr. William Thompson, at Leadketty, in the parish of Dunning. Mr. Thompson was a farmer, and young Arnot was set to work on the farm, the horses being chiefly intrusted to his care. The open-air employment and the constant exercise were favourable to health, and he became strong and robust. The inward man did not prosper so much as the outward man. Evil influences were manifold. He was almost wholly in the society of ploughmen and other young persons employed on the farm. The moral tone was low. The conduct in many instances was most vicious. He was now fifteen years of age and far from his father's house. It was only on Sabbath evenings that he escaped from the society of the servants and farm-labourers, for on such occasions he was invited to drink tea with the family in the parlour.

A painful experience at this time of the truth that "the way of transgressors is hard" begat in him a resolution which coloured all his future days. At an annual fair in a neighbouring village, he went with Mr. Thompson's foreman and other men into several public-houses, where they gave him whisky-toddy. After he reached home, he became sick and giddy, passed a wretched night, and, gnawed by thirst, left his bed at three in the morning, and seeking a well at the bottom of the garden, drank of its clear, cool stream. He was not well for several days after ; and the sickness and disgust produced so great an effect upon his mind that for many years he could not endure the taste of whisky in any shape, and could not even remain in a house where toddy was emitting its fumes. The illness of that night, and the loathing of spirits which resulted from it, became a shield of defence to him from that time forth.

The reflective powers which were so prominent a feature of his character began now to put forth some faint buddings. " One hot summer day I was alone in a field, driving three horses in the harrows. The ground was soft and dry. The harrows raised the hot dust round my head, and my feet at every step sank heavily into the dry ground. It was a weary day ; it was fatiguing work. I had no human being to speak to. I betook myself to rhyme. I composed a poem on a snowdrop. It occupied my thoughts pleasantly, and diverted me from the oppressive exercise of my lungs and limbs." When the hour of release came, he unyoked the horses, leaped joyfully on the bare back of one, and, leading the other two, soon had the poor brutes in the stable. Hurrying to his sleeping-room, he committed the lines to paper. They were "sad doggerel," he says ; "they have long been lost, and not one could I now recall. But though the lines are lost, and would be of no value if found, the memory of the making of these lines, with the attendant circumstances, is still fresh and sweet. It is one of a number of little mental efforts which served to keep me from being entirely absorbed in the mass of coarse vulgarity."

That experience on the farm, hard as it was, he never regretted. "The rude contact with men and familiarity with horses rubbed off a good deal of my constitutional 'bairnliness,' and imparted a dash of manliness to my character, which I think is by no means to be despised. I certainly do not regret that I held the plough at sixteen years of age, or that I could throw myself on the bare back of a horse while he was in motion, or that I learned horsemanship at the expense of many a fall. It has helped, I think, to wring the womanhood out of a nature somewhat soft in its original contexture. It enables me to feel easy in many positions which are sufficient to annoy those who have been more tenderly cradled in their youth. I delight to notice every one, even the least, of the multifarious influences which during youth go to mould the character of the man."

About the year 1824 or 1825 he went home, and was called to occupy for a time the place of his brother, who had been apprenticed to the business of a gardener at Kilgraston, in the parish of

Dunbarney, and who was laid aside by illness. When he left Kilgraston he returned to his father's house, and became an apprentice to the gardener of Lord Ruthven at Freeland. His father was not favourable to this step, believing that a lawyer's office offered better prospects of remuneration; yet many influences combined to attract young Arnot to the occupation. A spice of the romantic in his nature, a strong desire to continue under his father's roof, and a decided contempt for money-making, made him prefer the open air and freedom of a garden to a desk in a county town. He entered joyfully on his duties at Martinmas (November 11th) 1824, when he was just sixteen years of age. His work was often heavy, but he was in good health, and lived in great happiness.

With regard to his religious impressions he thus writes:—
"My mind made some progress in spiritual understanding; but there was a great conflict between the claims of Christ and the claims of pleasure. One thing I ought to record with unmeasured thankfulness,—that the enemy in that conflict never got the advantage over me which results from actual indulgence in vice. I am well aware that there may be to a great extent the abstinence from vice where Christ is not permitted to dwell in the heart by faith; but I am most firmly convinced that every defilement of the conscience by actual guilt strengthens the adversary's hold, and diminishes the power of resistance. The conflict in my experience was hard enough; and I thank God now that elements were not permitted to enter which would have made it tenfold harder,—that such giant lusts as drunkenness and licentiousness were kept at bay without the camp, and never obtained the advantage of actual possession. One touch of defilement on the conscience corrodes the very sinews of the combatant's strength. The vain thoughts—the pleasures of sense—the dislike of seriousness,—these and a multitude of other sins maintained within me the conflict against the truth. But at this hour I rejoice with trembling that their power was not then reinforced by those lusts

which, besides presenting enticements to the spirit, lay hold of the body, and drag down the man by all the force of natural laws."

About this time he freed himself by a desperate struggle from the bondage of the recognized drinking usages of society. And though in doing so he had to run the gauntlet of sarcasm and scorn, yet his own strong common-sense prevailed, aided as he was by the support and counsel of his father, who not merely condemned excess, but was "opposed to the drinking customs root and branch."

"The great ruling event of my youth, the event which by sovereign wisdom was made the pivot on which my life and character turned, was the long illness and death of my only brother." This brother was obliged in the year 1825 to leave his employment finally, and to come home an invalid. He had grown up to manhood with many qualities fitted to gain the esteem of his fellows. His person was handsome, his manners refined, and he possessed a considerable amount of mechanical genius. From his frolicsome and social qualities, as well as from the purity of his conduct, he was a favourite in every circle, and greatly beloved. He came home to die from a disease of the spine, which gradually increased, paralyzing the limbs, and telling with effect on his general health.

The companionship of this brother became a turning-point in William Arnot's life. For his brother was a true Christian ; his faith was seen by its fruits, and the new life was manifested in his conversation. Communion with this brother, sometimes by the river-side, or in the woods, where William carried him in his arms "as a nurse takes a child ; " sometimes on a grassy bank, where they basked in the softened rays of the evening sun ; or sometimes on a bed in the sick-room,—was the training provided by his heavenly Father to break the power of the world over his heart. And when at last his brother died, and his "dearest earthly treasure was torn away," a new purpose was formed in his heart, and he wished to devote himself to the ministry.

He now commenced the study of Latin in right earnest, and

the account which he gives of his preparation for the work to which his after-life was to be consecrated is remarkable, and shows us the earnest, determined, noble character of the man :—

" Even during the hours of labour I continued to learn something. Digging, which was one of our most laborious occupations, became nevertheless, by a little management, a favourable occasion for learning a conjugation or a rule of syntax. The management was after this manner. When three or four persons were together digging a large plot of ground, we followed each other closely, each carrying a furrow across. When the first man reached the edge with his furrow, he stood aside and waited till the others completed theirs, and turned with each a new one in the opposite direction. Then he who had arrived first at this side struck in last when the motion began towards the other side. Thus at each round we obtained in turn two or three minutes to stand and change the position for the relief of the muscles. I latterly fell upon the plan of having my elementary books of Latin or Greek in my pocket. During the moments of rest I snatched the book, ran over a tense or a portion of whatever might be in hand, and put the book in my pocket again when it was time to move on again with a new furrow. While toiling across a field I kept conning and trying the portion I had read. At the next halting I corrected the errors, and took up a new portion. This was done without any prejudice to the work. I found in it a double benefit. The memory in these circumstances acted very freely ; the lesson was easily learned, and the employment of the mind on that subject acted as a diversion, greatly lessening the weariness of the toil."

Truly William Arnot was a man of mark, and one who proved himself able to rise above the circumstances which would have dragged a man of weaker nerve or infirmer purpose down.

He had now begun to save every penny of his wages that could be spared from necessaries. He earned nine shillings a week during the two latter years of his labour, and his father, thinking the discipline good for his son, charged him two and sixpence a week for his board. He had saved twenty pounds in November 1828. His father would fain have persuaded him to remain at home, and offered to take a farm and stock it for him ; but when he saw that his heart was set upon the work of the ministry, he fell in with his views, and encouraged him in every possible way. He now devoted all his time to study, preparatory to entering college. He went to Perth, and placed himself under a Mr. Thomas Scott, a probationer, lately licensed, who had begun to keep a school. Here he read the whole of the Æneid of Virgil, acquired some knowledge of the Greek grammar, and read portions of the New Testament and other selections from Sandford's "Extracts."

At the invitation of his uncle, Robert Fisher, who offered him lodging in his house free of expense during the first session, he went to Glasgow on the 8th of October 1829. On the 10th October he purchased a red gown, paid his matriculation fee at the library, and his tickets for the Greek and Latin classes, and was ready to commence work on the following day. And work he did,—obtained an honourable place in his classes,—carried off prizes, and enjoyed learning not only for its own sake, but for the enlargement of mind which it brought. The amount of his private teaching, which was needful for his support while at college, was no doubt a hindrance to his own studies, and prevented him from specially distinguishing himself as a student. He felt this necessity keenly at the time, and regretted it in after-years.

While at college he formed some life-long friendships. With two students especially he was intimate, and enjoyed with them a tender and hallowed brotherhood. They were both men of mark, and both entered into rest before him. He was the eldest of the three, and yet it was his singular lot to begin his own literary life-work by composing the Memoir of one of his friends, and to close it by composing the Memoir of the other. These friends were Halley and Hamilton ; and now, as the author of Arnot's

Memoir beautifully says, they three "who paced long ago the dingy quadrangle of Glasgow College, now pace the golden streets, praising together the Lord whom they all three loved and served so faithfully on earth."

"All the friends were earnest workers in the cause of Sunday schools. Some of them, including Mr. Arnot, were amongst the first promoters of the Glasgow Sabbath-School Union." He taught for four years an advanced Bible class for young women, in connection with the mission at St. Rollox. His work was much blessed, and many were the testimonies he received as to the good that was done.

His correspondence at this time with his intimate friends is very interesting, and throws much light on his character in all its phases. "Some letters overflow with playfulness, and sparkle with humour; others are full of serious thoughts on the most solemn subjects; in many the grave and the humorous lie side by side in very close contact, but never mingled so far as to jar on the strictest sense of propriety."

He was keenly alive to all that took place in the great city, and threw himself as far as he was able into the question of Negro Emancipation and of Reform, and into the other public movements of the day. Through the whole of his college life the love of home runs like a strong current through all his correspondence; and his love of flowers crops up in almost every letter; so that when a parcel has to be sent from home the invariable request is, "Be sure to send me a flower."

On the 4th of October 1837 Mr. Arnot was licensed as a preacher of the gospel by the Presbytery of Glasgow. Soon afterwards he was appointed assistant to the Rev. John Bonar, then minister of the united parishes of Larbert and Dunipace, and entered on his duties in November 1837. The year spent in the work at Larbert and with Mr. Bonar was both pleasant and profitable, and was a time which he always liked to look back to.

He had hardly been a year at Larbert when he received a call to St. Peter's Church, Glasgow. "He began his ministry here on the first Sabbath of January 1839; but before many weeks had passed, his health, already much enfeebled, broke down completely under the new strain. A severe illness ensued, which disabled him entirely for work during a period of about three months."

When he recovered from this illness, he very soon gathered around him a large and warmly attached congregation. His preaching had a peculiar attraction for young men, who, both in Glasgow and afterwards in Edinburgh, formed an important element in his congregation. Though his church became crowded, and his hearers eagerly drank in the Word as it fell from his lips, the preacher himself was far from satisfied with his work. His private journal and letters "show how strictly he scrutinized his work, with all its springs and motives; and how sternly he judged, and how unsparingly he condemned, when he himself was the prisoner at the bar."

He was truly at this time in labours abundant; and besides the duties more particularly connected with his own church and congregation, he began to take his share in more public work, and his name was announced in the prospectus of "a course of lectures on the physical, educational, and moral improvement of the people, especially of the great towns." Fully occupied with the laborious work of a city charge, he took no prominent part in the proceedings which led to the Disruption. But when the crisis came, he, with his whole congregation, left the Establishment, though they continued for some years in possession of their old place of worship.

On the 30th July 1844 he married the second daughter of Mr. Fleming of Clairmont, Glasgow; and although a stranger to all the family but the lady herself, he gradually gained their love, and exercised a growing influence for their good.

In the spring of the following year he was requested by the Colonial Committee of the Church to supply the newly-organized Free Church congregation in Montreal for some months. To this he agreed, and sailed from Liverpool on the 4th May, accompanied by his wife. During his absence he wrote some pastoral letters to his people, giving an account of his journey and his labours, and exhorting them to cleave with steadfast heart unto the Lord. He left for home in the end of September.

From his own letters we learn the number of calls he received to become the pastor of other churches, and to minister to other congregations. Now the call comes from Lerwick, in Shetland; now it comes from Canada; now it is to a professorship in the Presbyterian College in London. These different proposals to remove from Glasgow caused him considerable anxiety, and brought him to the throne of grace for guidance; but bound by the ties of strong affection to his flock, he refused them all, and for twenty-five years he continued to minister to the same people.

St. Peter's congregation was not, like many others, ejected from their place of worship immediately at the Disruption. The church belonged to the Church Building Society, and continued until the commencement of the year 1849 to be used by the Free Church congregation, they paying to the Society a yearly rent of £100. But in February 1849, by a decision of the Court of Session, the congregation, along with others similarly situated, were formally ejected from their place of worship, which was declared to be the property of the Established Church. A new church, however, had been building in Main Street for Mr. Arnot and his congregation. This was opened on the 26th May 1850, and Dr. Hamilton preached the opening sermon.

In 1851 he published his first volume of sermons. It was entitled "The Race for Riches, and some of the Pits into which the Runners Fall: Six Lectures applying the Word of God to the Traffic of Men." The first edition of one thousand was sold out within two months, and a second thousand printed. At the close of the next year a little book appeared with a fictitious signature, but which his friends at once ascribed to William Arnot. The title of this was, "The Drunkard's Progress: being a panorama of the overland route from the station at Drouth to the general terminus in the Dead Sea ; in a series of thirteen Views, drawn and engraved by John Adam, the descriptions given by John Bunyan, junior." He was a determined foe to drinking under all its forms during the whole course of his life. He entered heart and soul into the battle against it, and there can be no doubt that his manly and consistent protest against the evil did much to advance and strengthen the temperance cause.

During his long ministry in Glasgow, from the close of 1838 till October 1863, there are few striking events or great changes to be recorded to mark the progress of the years. To use his own words in describing a similar period in the life of James Hamilton: —" Where there are no battles, the history of a country is brief and dull ; but great are the happiness and progress of the people. It is the same with the work and sphere of a Christian minister, when he is faithful and his flock affectionate. The minister, loving and beloved, is felt everywhere as a rallying-point and centre of attraction. The beneficent machinery goes smoothly round, Christian charity lubricating every wheel ; and precisely because everything is going on well there is not much for the historian to tell." But his time is fully occupied. Now he is engaged on a new series of tracts ; now he prepares a paper for some periodical ; then he writes a warm letter of sympathy to a friend on the occasion of his mother's death, or he sends a kind farewell letter to a young man connected with the congregation going abroad. And many a proof do his letters afford of a rich affectionate nature, of ripe wisdom, of strong common-sense, of kindness toward man, and of love toward God.

His Autobiography and Memoir gives us pleasant glimpses of the writer, and lecturer, and preacher at home. We see him in his holiday time giving daily lessons to his two girls in the rudiments of Latin, or reading aloud to his children Longfellow's poem of " Hiawatha." " The peculiar rhythm of this poem took his fancy, and he would frequently improvise long screeds of mock-heroic verse in imitation of it. Any little incident at home or in his walks furnished a subject, and he would proceed as uninterruptedly as if reciting from a book. If a rhyme was wanted and did not immediately present itself, a word was coined to suit the emergency."

Amidst his busy life, Mr. Arnot found time to write and publish some works of lasting interest, great originality of conception, and remarkable freshness of thought. Amongst these may be mentioned lectures on the Book of Proverbs, entitled " Laws from Heaven for Life on Earth ; " a volume illustrating the Parables of our Lord ; a volume of sermons called " Roots and Fruits of the Christian Life ; " and " The Church in the House, or Primitive Christianity as exhibited in the Acts of the Apostles."

How active was this man of God, how energetic in body and mind, may be gathered from the fact that he spent six months in Canada in evangelistic work, that he paid several visits to the Continent, attended the meetings of the Evangelical Alliance at Geneva, and preached the gospel at the Salle Evangélique in the Paris Exhibition of 1867. Besides all this, he twice visited the United States,—going on the first occasion as one of "a deputation from the Free Church to the United Assembly of the Presbyterian Churches in America ; " and on the second occasion being invited to attend the meetings of the Evangelical Alliance at New York in the autumn of 1873. His two eldest sons were engaged in business in the United States, and this strongly influenced him to accept the invitation—which was further pressed upon him, in a personal interview, by Mr. G. H. Stuart of Philadelphia and Dr. Hall of New York. During this latter visit "he traversed the Pacific Railway to San Francisco and back—a great undertaking for one of his years, and alone ; indeed, the result proved that it was too great. A serious illness detained him some days in Salt Lake City ; and though he recovered so as to be able to complete the journey, the fatigue of it more than balanced the pleasure, and the very recollection of it was never anything but dreary to him."

It should have been mentioned that in 1863 he received a call to the Free High Church, Edinburgh, which he accepted, as believing it to be the leading of Providence, though it was directly opposed to his own inclinations at the time. Once settled in his new sphere, he soon began to feel at home, and enjoyed his work, rapidly filling a church which had been thinned during the long vacancy.

During Mr. Arnot's first absence in America the editorship of the *Family Treasury* became vacant, and the publishers proposed that he should undertake the conduct of the magazine. On his return it was definitely arranged that he should become editor, and his duties commenced with the beginning of the year 1871. It added considerably to his labours ; but he enjoyed the work, and entered upon it with all his might. He was now in his sixty-third year. So his life ran on quietly, happily, usefully. He had many blessings and some sorrows. He took both from his Father's hand, and both were made to work together for his good.

One of his great sorrows was the death of that eminent man Dr. Candlish. He heard the tidings on his return from his second visit to America. " At Queenstown, on Monday night, Irish newspapers came on board. I was listlessly glancing over paragraphs in one of them, when my eye fell on one of two and a half lines, thus :—' At the funeral of Dr. Candlish yesterday, in Edinburgh, the procession was nearly a mile long.' It blinded me like a flash of lightning in my face. It was the first intimation to me of our great bereavement. Edinburgh seems naked and empty since." And then Mr. Arnot adds : " Many beautiful things are told of his faith and love and childlike demeanour towards the close. I must tell you a thing that he said of myself, that I count a very precious legacy. His mind was wandering ; he thought he was in some meeting of Presbytery or Assembly. Suddenly and sharply, after a pause, he said, 'That's Arnot ; I want to hear what he is saying.' His son took occasion to say, ' Do you love Arnot ? ' ' Love him ! who would not love Arnot ? I love him as a brother.' These words have distilled like oil to soothe other rufflings ever since—all the more that they were spoken while the intellect was beclouded, and judgment not sitting on watch to restrain the expression of the heart's thoughts."

Towards the close of the year 1873 the two American evangelists, Moody and Sankey, paid their first visit to Edinburgh, and Arnot was one of the first to throw himself heart and soul into their work. He also wrote occasional notices of the work, both for the *Family Treasury* and also for an American paper, *The Illustrated Christian Weekly*, to which he was, from the time of his last visit to America, a frequent contributor.

In the autumn of 1874 he once more spent a month on the Continent, and during the winter of the same year he lectured in Exeter Hall to the Young Men's Christian Association. His subject was, "The Foe and the Fight; or, The Trinity of Evil,"—Belial (vice), Infidel (unbelief), Idols (superstition), 2 Cor. vi. 15, 16.

Throughout the winter his strength declined steadily, but so gradually that it was only on looking back over a considerable period that the difference could be observed. A formal application was made in the November of this year to the Assembly, in his name, for a colleague and successor. At the monthly meeting of the Presbytery, in January 1875, the proposal was brought forward, and the necessary steps taken for bringing it before the General Assembly in May. "Little did he then think that by the time it reached the highest court of the Church the need of such an application would be only too apparent. He lived only two days after it was sanctioned by the Assembly."

For two or three months before the end his strength began to fail, and to his friends he would let fall some touching hints that the end was drawing near. To one he said, "I do not know whether it is the *spring* season, or whether it is the *autumn* of my life; but I have never felt before as I do this spring." To another he wrote, "The strength has leaked out of me this spring more than ever heretofore." And so there followed some months of gradual decline and "calm decay." But still he continued to work as his strength permitted him.

In April he went to Stirling, to attend a religious convention; and the same day left for Glasgow, to be present at the funeral of a near relative.

In May he went to London as a deputy from the Free Church to the Synod of the English Presbyterian Church; and during the week he spent there he spoke twice at the Synod, twice at Moody's meetings in the Opera House, and preached on Sunday, in the forenoon, at Hampstead, and in the evening at Regent Square. On the 16th, the last Sunday that he preached, his text in the morning was, "We all, with open face beholding as in a glass the glory of the Lord, are changed into the same image from glory to glory, even as by the Spirit of the Lord." Against the wishes of his family, who feared for his strength, he spoke in the afternoon, shortly and simply, on the wise men from the east being guided by the star to Bethlehem. On Monday he finished the preparation of the June number of the *Family Treasury*. On Tuesday he attended the noon prayer-meeting in the Assembly Hall, when he opened his mouth in public for the last time. "Taking his text, as he so often did, from Nature, he told how that morning, on going into his vinery, he observed a branch drooping. On examining it, to discover the cause, he found that it was a tie which he had himself bound round it, some time before, to give it support. The branch had grown since then, and the tie was now so tight that it impeded the flow of the sap. He took out his knife and severed it at once. He then spoke of *ties* around our souls hindering us from full fruitfulness, and of the means by which the great Husbandman loosens them. 'Sometimes he takes the knife and cuts them through; sometimes he sends such a rush of life through the soul that it bursts every bond.' The friend who after his death reported the substance of what he said, added : 'It seemed to me as if his own soul was being visited with such a blessed rush of life.'"

A few days of weariness followed, during which he was bright and cheerful as ever. The last glimpses which his children got of him, weak though he was and much confined to his room, were very pleasant. Oftentimes he would sit in his easy-chair in his garden, looking at his shrubs and flowers, and gladdened by their beauty. "Never had earth seemed so fair to him in the fresh green of early summer ; and expressions of admiration often burst forth from his happy heart." He knew that he was drawing near the goal ; but the good fight had been fought out and his course finished. " Mark the perfect man, and behold the upright : for the end of that man is peace."

The last day of his life he remained in bed most of the day,— taking pains, however, to say that it was not because he felt worse, but because he felt so useless when he was up. In the evening he rose and went to another room, where he sat for several hours. Some letters arrived by the late post ; they were read to him after he had lain down again. One was from a daughter at school, and he laughed heartily at some girlish fun described in it. Another was from the Convener of the Continental Committee, asking him to go to Rome for the winter. His wife and daughters were delighted with this proposal, knowing his desire to see Rome, and thinking that the rest and change would recruit his strength. When he was asked his opinion, he smiled, and said, " I feel like the laddie who was offered jelly when he was too sick to take it, and said, 'You never give me good things but when I canna tak' them.'" About three in the morning he awoke in profuse perspiration. Noticing the sweet warbling of the birds, he said, "These sweet birds ! they are singing for me." A little after- wards his wife, hearing him speak, asked if he wished anything. "No, dear," he answered ; "I was not *speaking to you.*" In less than two hours she was awakened by the sound of coughing, and running to his side, saw the blood flowing from his mouth. The silver cord was being loosed, and the golden bowl was being broken at the fountain. " He sank back on his pillow as if in a swoon, and without a sigh, without a quiver, the spirit escaped away from its tabernacle of clay."

He was buried in the Grange Cemetery, beside his eldest sister and his infant child. On his monument are inscribed the appropriate words : "He walked with God : and he was not ; for God took him."

This sketch of a good man cannot be better closed than with an extract from the sermon preached by Professor Blaikie on the Sunday following his death : "And now along the golden path, and through the golden gate, he himself has passed to his Father's house. And to you his death just deepens the lessons and exhortations of his life—' Choose the path to glory ; see how it stretches from your very feet upward to the heavenly Jerusalem ; let your citizenship be in heaven ; and while you are on earth walk worthy of the vocation wherewith ye are called.' "

LESSER PARABLES OF OUR LORD

Harvest Field and Harvest Laborers
(Matthew 9:37-38)

" The harvest truly is plenteous, but the labourers are few ; pray ye therefore
the Lord of the harvest, that he will send forth labourers into his harvest."

Part 1 — The Harvest Field

SEVERAL distinct aspects of Christ's kingdom are
represented in the gospel under the figure of
grain, in its growing, ripening, and ingathering.
One view is set forth in the parable of the
sower, another in the parable of the tares, and another in the
separation of the chaff from the wheat ; but the conception
here is essentially different from all these. The harvest in
this similitude springs not from the seed of the word,
but from the root of human nature. The field is the
world, and mankind the crop that covers all its breadth.
The portions that are safely gathered represent the redeemed of the Lord ; and the portions that drop over-ripe
and rot on the ground represent those who perish in their
sins. This field is—

1. *Precious*, in the very fact that it is a harvest-field.
Men, created at first in God's image, and capable yet, when
redeemed, of living in his presence for ever, are the fruit
which this world bears—the fruit for the sake of which

this world was made. If you ask a farmer what has been the produce of a certain field, he will not in reply enumerate roots, stalks, husks, and grain; he will answer, in one word, wheat; the other portions of the plant are valuable, not for their own sake, but for the sake of the grain which they bear. Thus the various vegetable and animal products of the earth are the stalks that support humanity; and humanity is the true fruit, for the sake of which our Father, the husbandman, cultivates his field. The conclusion of philosophy, reached through an examination of Nature, without reference to Revelation, is that all creation, from its earliest embryo, pointed to man. All that lies beneath and that came before him was a preparation for his coming. Creation contains abundant evidence that the conception of humanity was in the Maker's mind from the first, and that the purpose of calling man into being ruled all the successive stages of the stupendous work.

An American citizen from the sunny South, travelling once in New England, and holding its rugged hills in contempt, demanded of a native what his country produced. " My country produces men," said the descendant of the Puritans. He was right. Man, made in God's image to be his servant and his son, is the true, heavy, precious head; plantations of cotton, sugar, rice, are merely the stalks which support it. Silk, wool, flax; wheat, barley, oats, are precious only as food and clothing for the Father's family. These articles are not separately reckoned in the inventory of the great Proprietor's goods. After all these things were made, and the world stored with them, its Maker counted his work only begun; it was then that God said, " Let us make man in our image." All other products served only to make the earth ready for the recep-

tion of man. This is the fruit that God values. With this
he intends to fill his stores. When ransomed men are
gathered into heaven, the cotton crop, the silk crop, the grain
crop, and all the crops, will be left behind like stubble,
rotting in the field when its work is done.

Human beings are the head of God's creation. For these
he formed the green earth, and spread over it that bright
sky; for these he hung the sun in heaven by day, and
sprinkled the stars like gold dust upon the canopy of night:
for these, when they fell, he gave his Son a ransom, and
prepared an eternal home on high; over these, when they
are forgiven and purified, he rejoices with a joy unspeakable and full of glory. O man, reverence thyself! In
God's sight thou art precious; be not vile in thine own!

2. It is *plenteous*. So said he who sees it all and knows
its worth. We soon become bewildered when we try to
realize the numbers of human beings that live or have lived
on the earth; but numbers do not burden God. It would
not weary him to enlighten every human heart, any more
than to send a beam of sunlight into the bosom of every
flower. More than ten hundred million live and breathe
at one time; and many such generations have passed over
the stage in succession since time began; yet the hairs of
every head are numbered, and omniscience is not baffled by
the account. There may be as many blades of grass in one
field as there are persons in Great Britain and Ireland; and
yet every one of these gets its own drop of dew, and its
portion of colouring from the sun's rays. It is not more
difficult for God to care for us than to care for them. One
day is with the Lord as a thousand years, and a thousand
years as one day. In like manner, one man is with the
Lord as a worldful, and a worldful as one man. If the

existing population of the globe were multiplied by a million, none would receive less of God's care; and if there were only one man in creation, he would not get more. We are a great family who have been born into this world, but not too many for the Creator's upholding hand; and if we were all born again, we would find room enough in the mansions of our Father's house. When God's Israel have got through the fire and water, it is "a large place" into which they are ushered as their eternal home.

God has made all these of one blood. He has compassion on the ignorant and them that are out of the way. He will people heaven from every kindred and every tongue. He so loved the world that he gave his only begotten Son. The godly should be like God both in the wideness of their view and the warmth of their love. If love be true, the extent of its range will not diminish its intensity. It is characteristic of God's laws and works that while they grasp the greatest they do not neglect the least. The power that balances the worlds in space, sharpens the down on a nettle stalk. If we, the children of the kingdom, be in spirit like our Father in heaven, no extension of range will dilute the strength of our sympathy. He who has learned from Christ to take the whole world within his embrace, loves his own house more intensely than the man who loves his own house alone.

The world, as distinguished from the people of God sojourning in it, may be roughly divided into the three parts— Pagan, Mohammedan, and Papist. Under the term Pagan may be included all who do not know and worship the one living and true God; under the term Mohammedan, all who, worshipping one God, do not approach him by the one Mediator Jesus Christ; and under the term Papist, all who, worshipping God and acknowledging Jesus, have added a multitude of other mediators.

> Pagans have not God.
> Mohammedans have not Christ.
> Papists have not Christ only.

(1.) Pagans. We should never forget, in this land of light, that the larger portion of the human race is sitting in darkness. We are not near Christ and not like him if we do not take the burden of this fact upon our spirits. More especially, the many millions of India and of Southern Africa have been thrown upon the compassion of British Christians. In respect to those feeble myriads who are subject to our sway, we are like a rich family at whose door a foundling has been laid. That vast multitude, nearly equal to the population of Europe, has been thrown on our hands. When they were sinking in anarchy we came to the rescue. Pushing aside others who offered to undertake the task, we drew the child out of the water. In our hands it is helpless as a child. If she who drew the child out of the water be a daughter of the king, she will bring up the child, not in the bondage to which it was born, but as a prince in her father's house. Alas! we have done little to bring the child up for our Father King. The Chinese, though not directly subject to our sway, have a stronger claim on our compassion. The nation has in time past done them wrong, and Christians in the nation should endeavour to make compensation. We introduced or winked at the introduction of a destroying flood; we should prepare a channel in which the water of life may flow.

(2.) Mohammedans. The region of the false prophet's rule is a study of intense interest to Christians in respect of its geographical position. It constitutes a broad and continuous belt, running across the world from the Atlantic on the west to the deserts of Siberia on the north-east, separating Christianity from Paganism. Observe the skilful strategy of the god of this world. The gross idolatry of the heathen was not allowed to come into contact with the Christianity of the West. To meet the strongest enemy a more ethereal system was pushed forward, and accordingly Christianity and Paganism, previous to the date of modern missions, were nowhere geographically conterminous. The foolish idols were withdrawn into the dark bosom of the East, and a line of stronger lies drawn up to cover them from the onset of Christian truth.

When the power of Mohammed swept over Western Asia and Eastern Europe like a lava flood, some Christian communities were embedded in it, like Herculaneum and Pompeii;-and these fossil Churches have been found of late by some American missionary explorers. If the breath of the Spirit bring life into the petrified skeletons, it will be a grand sight to see a resurrection of dead Churches, after the silence of many centuries, in the very lands where the disciples of Jesus were first called Christians.

(3.) Papists. The greater part of the nations called Christian have remained under the Roman Antichrist, or are bound by the similar superstitions of the Greek Church. I shall mention here only one feature of the many-sided system,—the discovery lately made and proclaimed by the Pope of the immaculate conception of the Virgin. On first hearing the fact we are surprised that the Papacy should thus expose its own weakness. One would think, if they were wise in their generation, they would hold by antiquity, and not confess that there are saving truths in religion which Popes for many generations did not know. But when we examine the state of the case, we find they could not help themselves. They are in the power of a law as mighty and as inexorable as gravitation. "Evil men and seducers shall wax worse and worse." They cannot fix their doctrine at the present point, although they would. On—on they must go, like the fall of a stone or the flow of a river. The Popish system, by the mere weight of its wickedness, sinks necessarily deeper and deeper, until it fall like a mill-stone into a sea of wrath. Priests and people have for many generations been gravitating deeper and deeper into the worship of Mary. In this direction the mighty mass was moving, and it could not be recalled. Any attempt to arrest the movement would have rent the huge bulk of the Papacy asunder. The heads of the great apostasy found themselves in this dilemma : the people with one consent were worshippers of Mary as much as the people of Ephesus were worshippers of the great goddess Diana. They must either forbid the worship or declare its object divine ; they must either go backward or forward. Backward they were not able to go, and therefore, making a virtue of necessity, they went forward. They separated their idol from humanity ; they declared her a sinless being. Happy Mary ! she got safe to heaven before these lies were invented. She rejoiced in God her Saviour, while these her worshippers, if they had been living then, would have told her she was mistaken—that she had no sin, original or actual, to be saved from.

Be of good courage, then ; the apostasy of Rome cannot help itself. Further and faster it must fall by an inexorable law, until the jubilant cry be raised by emancipated nations, " Babylon is fallen, is fallen, and shall be found no more at all."

But in a general survey of the field, we must not overlook the portion that lies nearest ourselves. Multitudes of our own flesh and blood, speaking our own language, and dwelling on our own soil, are living without God and dying without hope. As the Lord intimated to his disciples in Samaria, we have only to lift up our eyes where we stand, and we shall see fields large enough to occupy all our energies. The need of home missions has been fully recognized by the Church, and the work of home missions has been fairly begun. The features of this work, however, with its difficulties and its hopes, may be more appropriately noticed in connection with the latter portion of the parable— the prayer for an increase of harvest-labourers. In the meantime, looking generally to the world as the field to which the reapers must be sent, we gather from manifold symptoms that—

3. It is *ripe*. In the days of our Lord there was a divinely arranged readiness in the world for receiving his truth. It ran like the breaking out of waters over the empty aching breast of Greece and Rome. The Master saw that readiness, and pointed it out to his disciples in a tone of reproof. They were inclined to delay; he was eager to send them forth upon their work. Accordingly (John iv. 35) he said, " Say not ye, There are yet four months, and then cometh harvest?...Lift up your eyes, and look on the fields; for they are white already to harvest." Whatever interval might be needed to ripen the natural grain, the spiritual field was ready for the reaper. There was a panting expectation both in Jew and Gentile then, and the

Master commanded his servants to strike in while the opportunity was good.

I believe at no period since Jesus spoke these words to the twelve in Samaria were the fields so generally and so manifestly ready for the reapers as they are in our day.

The idols of the heathen are losing hold and tottering to their fall. The Euphrates is drying up from its springs, —the doctrines of the prophet are effete, and his followers do not find their hands. The Papacy is rent from within, and its empty and disappointed multitudes, discontented with the teachers who have cheated them, are opener, therefore, to the advent of the truth. Even the Jews are weary with waiting, and the godless multitudes of our great cities are heaving like the sea in a ground-swell, some with dumb, indefinite desires, not knowing what ails them, but some with the grand old question of a quickened soul, "What must I do to be saved?" No worker needs to wait four months or four days for the harvest. The fields are already white. There is a tide in human things which should be taken at the flood. When the grain is ripe it comes easy to the gatherer's hand. But—

4. It is *perishing*. When vast breadths of land have been sown in spring, and few hands can be found in harvest to gather it, the sight is one of the saddest. So much come to the birth, and not strength to bring forth! The heavy ripened fields are bending and growing black, and falling to the ground. Whatever may have caused the scarcity of reapers; whether war or pestilence or oppression may have cut them down or cast them away, or whether it be mere indolence that clogs exertion, the sight of food left to perish is equally a melancholy sight.

Seldom does such a sight present itself, for men value the fruit of the earth. They cannot want it, and therefore they make adequate exertions to secure it. We know what hunger is, and therefore we do not waste food. When our spiritual appetites become as keen as our natural, God will get his work done. When it becomes our meat to do the Father's will and to finish his work, we shall be like Christ; and soon thereafter, I suppose, we shall be with him, and see him as he is.

Harvest Field and Harvest Laborers
(Matthew 9:37-38)

"Then saith he unto his disciples, The harvest truly is plenteous, but the labourers are few; pray ye therefore the Lord of the harvest, that he will send forth labourers into his harvest."

Part 2 — The Harvest Laborers

A HEAVY burden lies on the husbandman's heart when he sees his cornfields fully ripe, and knows not where to find a sufficient band of reapers. The thought that the last year's labour and the coming winter's hope may both be lost together occupies and oppresses him. For the fruit he planned and toiled and spent his means; and shall it slip, now that it is so near his lip?

This heaviness of heart the Man of sorrows employed to express his care at the sight of human generations perishing for lack of knowledge. When he lifted up his eyes and saw the people of Sychar coming out in companies to the well, his soul yearned for their salvation as for the reaping of ripened fruit, lest it should drop and be lost for ever. "Lift up your eyes," he said to the twelve, "and look on the fields; for they are white already to harvest" (John iv. 35). If the mind that was in Christ were in his people now, there is much in the aspect of the world fitted to stir both fear and hope in their breasts.

I. As the world's population, living and dying without God, appears in the Redeemer's eye a great harvest-field, ripe and ready to perish, those who in any sphere strive to win souls are, in his eye, as reapers gathering the wheat into the garner. A labourer need not expect to lead an easy, idle life. To eat his bread with the sweat of his brow is a necessity of his condition. Our Father is our Master; and he says, Son, go work to-day in my vineyard. For a reconciled man who possesses the spirit of adoption work is worship. The labour of his hand, as well as the song of his lips, is praise to the Lord that bought him. Christ the Son made himself a servant, and it was his meat to do the Father's will. Christians are admitted to be Christ's fellow-servants; and the more they resemble the Lord, the more they rejoice in their work.

Labourers are not a high class of functionaries. They need not expect to get all their own will as to the times and places of their toil. It is their business not to select the field that pleases themselves, but to labour diligently at the task which the Master may have assigned them. What thy hand findeth to do, do it with thy might. The Husbandman may send some of the reapers into a thin and comparatively barren field, where they must bend very low and toil very long ere they get their bosoms filled with corn; and he may send others to a more favoured spot, where with less exertion and in a shorter time they may gather many sheaves. Sometimes, in the natural sphere, a jealousy springs up, and a murmuring breaks out among the reapers on this ground; but in the spiritual harvest there is no cause for complaint: there is no respect of persons with God—" Be thou faithful unto death, and I will give thee a crown of life." The Judge of all the earth when he distributes the eternal reward lays the emphasis, not on the number of the talents that may have been intrusted to the servant, but on the faithfulness of the servant in the execution of his trust.

II. In the judgment of the Lord Jesus the labourers were few. They were few then; they are few still. We are not at liberty to set aside the force of the word by pointing out that the circumstances are different in our day. Such a prophecy of Scripture is not of any private interpretation. Jesus spake as never man spake. He spoke to his own generation with his eye on all generations. Although, in point of fact, a much greater number of labourers are employed in the harvest-field to-day, the Lord himself would not retract his word if he were now amongst us. He would still say, " The labourers are few." After a multitude whom no man could number had entered by the narrow gate into the kingdom, he cried, " Few there be that find it." A great multitude have pressed in since that day, and yet he would certainly repeat the same cry were he on earth again. His heart is so enlarged toward a lost world that he will complain, Few are coming, until the last man is safe within the gate. In like manner here he would not retract his plaintive word about the paucity of the labourers because one Church has sent fifty missionaries to the heathen, and another a hundred. All flesh is grass; but the word of the Lord abideth for ever: it is true for us to-day. The labourers are few,—few in proportion to the world's need; few in proportion to the compassion of the Lord. As that same Jesus from his throne to-day looks down upon the world, and counts the numbers that attempt to reap the vast fields of India, and China, and

Africa—the vast fields of our overgrown cities in so-called Christian lands—we may rest assured he will not retract or modify his word, " The labourers are few."

A very remarkable contrast is presented in the multitudes that may sometimes be seen pressing forward to the natural harvest. The pressure has slackened of late ; but a few years ago you might have seen, any day about the beginning of autumn, dense crowds of Irish labourers clustering like bees about the wharves of Liverpool and Glasgow. On one occasion the master of a Londonderry steamer, on arriving at Glasgow, was prosecuted for admitting a much greater number of passengers than his ship was legally entitled to carry. His defence was that the men rushed on board in spite of his efforts to prevent them, and took forcible possession of the deck. Such were the numbers that poured into the Scottish harvest-fields at that time, and such the eagerness of each man to get a share of the work and the reward.

It is even so : natural wants press heavily, and their pressure is keenly felt. The motive is sufficient to throw an abundance of labourers into the harvest. But a spiritual taste and a divine power are needed to fill with reapers that vast ripe field over which the compassionate Saviour looked and longed.

III. When additional labourers enter the field, they are sent into it by the Lord of the harvest. The expression " send forth " in the English version is feebler than the corresponding term in the original. The word which the Lord employs conveys the idea of force. It is literally " throw out," as missiles are thrown in war into a besieged city. The labourers are grasped by the providential hand of God, and thrown upon the field where their services are needed, not indeed against their will, but by means of their will. They are made willing in a day of power. A secret force, like the force of fire, is generated within the man,— as it were behind and beneath his will. While the man is musing alternately on the Redeemer's mercy to himself, and the need of a perishing world, this fire burns and disturbs his rest. To such a height of pressure the force at length attains that he can no longer resist : he is torn from the fastenings where he had said, Soul, eat and drink and take thine ease, and thrown with a great impetus forth from himself and into the field of labour. It is after this manner that missionaries are made. He works best on this field who cannot help working : " Woe is unto me if I preach not the gospel." The power that throws the missionary into the field is the love of Christ to his own soul : it is divine mercy tasted in secret that swells about his heart, until all barriers burst, and the volunteer comes forth with the old offer founded on the old reason, " O Lord, I am thy servant......thou hast loosed my bonds."

The distinction between a missionary properly so called, who abandons his secular calling and devotes himself wholly to the ministry of the word, and a disciple who abides in his calling and commends the gospel to his neighbours, although important, is a distinction of detail and not of principle. The Lord has need of both sorts ; and the world has need of both. Some portions of the work cannot be reached except by men set apart for the purpose ; and other parts cannot be reached except by the silent every-day influence of Christians upon the consciences of those with whom they come into closest contact from day to day and from hour to hour. The Master will send some reapers forth into great and distant fields, and some down into minute openings, where only those can work who are every day and all day upon the spot.

" The poor always ye have with you," not only indicates a fact of history, but reveals a plan and purpose of the Lord. Exercise is provided for the spiritual life. None shall be able to say that the field was too distant, and that he consequently had not an opportunity of rendering service as a reaper. A man cannot sit at meals in his own family, walk·along the streets, or pursue his daily toil on the farm or in the workshop, without passing along this laden harvest-field. Everywhere precious fruit, ready to perish, offers itself to the reaper's hand. Nowhere in the world at the present day can a sadder sight be seen than in the great cities of so-called Christian lands. Great, needy, promising fields have been placed within reach of every disciple of Christ ; none should stand idle. If any stand all the day idle, they will not at last be permitted to urge either that the field was distant or that the hirer made no proposal. Work is offered to every one, and the reward is sure. To win souls is both work and wages.

To illustrate the manner in which it pleases the Lord of the harvest sometimes to throw a reaper into the field, I shall mention one example which came under my own personal knowledge.

In a remote rural district of Scotland, a boy passed through a spiritual struggle of several stages, resisting the Spirit with varying measures of determination, in order to keep himself free for the expected pleasures of the world, but never able wholly to silence the still small voice. At length the love of Christ gained the mastery, and the youth surrendered ; not unwillingly, but because now his will had been won, and it became both a reasonable and a pleasant service to own the Redeemer as his King. Few, perhaps none, were aware of the conflict while it lasted, for he kept it secret as if it were a crime.

Having occasion one day, after he had chosen conclusively his side, to cross a range of hills on his way to the market town of the district, he must needs pass a lonely thatched cottage where he knew a poor and very old man lay dying. He must go in ; he dare not pass by ; the groans of the old man would have followed and haunted him. Nor was he unwilling to go in ; the conflict now lay with a certain conventional and constitutional bashfulness. Grown now, but inexperienced and shame-faced, he stepped in and stood by the old man's bed, repeated some texts, and uttered some timid words to commend Christ to a sinner. He was about to take leave, when the old man's daughter, herself far advanced in life, and of rough, ungainly appearance, came forward, tamed at least for the time by a sense of loneliness, and with a beseeching look from filling eyes, underneath long shaggy eyebrows, and gray dishevelled hair that hung over a weather-beaten, wrinkled brow, said, " Ye'll pray wi' my faither ? " The youth was enclosed ; the net was round him ; his retreat was cut off; backward he cannot, forward he must go. He prayed for the first time in the hearing of strangers. Such was the instrument that the Lord of the harvest employed that day to come behind one reaper who was hesitating and holding back on the border, and to throw him, ere he was well aware, over that dreaded fence into the harvest-field. It is a long, long time ago ; and, God helping him, he is in the field, a reaper still to-day.

IV. The Lord of the harvest presses labourers into the field in answer to the prayers of his people. The request of Jesus possesses a tender interest for us. He who bids us address this prayer to the Father knows the Father's mind, and always does what pleases Him. Let it be settled firmly in a disciple's mind that Christ would not persuade us to say anything to the Father that the Father would not like to hear ; and it is certain that the Father loves to grant the requests that he loves to hear. Indeed, it is because he longs to grant the requests that he delights to hear them. There is an encouragement of peculiar power to induce us to prefer the request in the fact that the Mediator between God and man urges us to prefer it at the throne.

But some who hear, and hear with reverence, the word of Jesus, so far from being themselves ready to be sent forth as reapers, may be in sadness reckoning themselves the wheat that is not yet gathered and ready to perish. Yet even in these circumstances he who hears the word of Christ should obey it,—should pray the Lord of the harvest to send forth labourers. Let the first groans of an anxious soul be shaped into this prayer, and the Lord may send out a reaper to gather thee. We know that the Spirit of God sent out Philip from his mission work in the city to a desert place near Gaza, to meet the Ethiopian treasurer there,—a reaper to gather a precious head of wheat into the garner ; but I think that silent sable African, with his weeping eye bent on Isaiah's gospel, had sent a petition up to the Lord of the harvest for a reaper ; and in answer to his own prayer a labourer was sent out to the field to gather him in.

Fields White Already to Harvest
(John 4:35)

" Say not ye, There are yet four months, and then cometh harvest? behold, I say unto you, Lift up your eyes, and look on the fields; for they are white already to harvest."

T HE conception here is closely allied to the subject of our last paper. The two parables are recip- rocally complements of each other; together they constitute one whole. The second fills up the spaces that were left open in the first; consequently it is convenient and useful to examine them in immediate succession.

Never man spake like this man, because never man was like this man; his lessons, both in substance and in form, sprang naturally and necessarily from his life. The two- fold nature of the Mediator was continually revealing itself in his words and his ways. The life of Jesus, as it lies in the evangelic histories, is a riddle which men cannot read until they find the key in his name, Emmanuel, and his nature, God with us. It is a life within a life; at every turn in his history the divinity glances from human words and acts, as a burning light shines through a trans- parent covering.

In many instances the language which the Lord em- ployed partook of his own twofold nature; and this peculiarity served to deposit his doctrines in the memory of his disciples, without revealing their full meaning until his work was finished. In these cases, while the body of the words represented temporal things, their soul within was occupied with things unseen and eternal. The passage in John ii. 19–21 affords an example of the peculiar duality of meaning which often attached to the words of the Lord: " Jesus answered and said unto them, Destroy this temple, and in three days I will raise it up. Then said the Jews, Forty and six years was this temple in building, and wilt thou rear it up in three days ? But he spake of the temple of his body."

It was his manner, while conversing about common things, to be occupied in secret with his own saving work, and to employ the terms as a channel to convey some law of the kingdom or some purpose of the King. Several examples occur in the narrative where this parable is found embedded. While he continued to speak to the Samaritan woman about the natural water which she had drawn from Jacob's well, he employed the words as a vessel wherewith to pour the good news from a far country into a thirsty soul. While at a subsequent stage the subject in hand between himself and the disciples was the food which nature greatly needed, he was speaking of his own redemption work as the savoury meat which his soul loveth. And yet once more, while the senses of the disciples are occupied with the sown field and the expected harvest, the Master's meaning is, Souls are perishing ; haste to the rescue.

It was seed-time in Samaria when these events occurred and these words were spoken. The period is determined, directly by the terms of the text, and indirectly by the circumstances of the context. It is obviously implied that any one who should look simply to the course of nature would have said at that time and place, Four months hence it will be harvest. Further: from the abundant reference to sowing in relation to reaping which occurs in the succeeding verses, we may gather that on the journey northward that morning they had seen the husbandmen on either side of the path busily employed in the process of committing the seed to the ploughed ground.

Every reader of the evangelic history is aware that the Lord Jesus, looking on creation and redemption from the centre of the eternal purpose in which both were planned, was wont to think and speak of them in parallel lines. None could so well cause the two worlds to throw light reciprocally on each other as the Author and Finisher of both. The Lord saw and acknowledged a many-sided and various analogy between nature and grace. At another time and place the operations of seed-time, as seen on the shores of the Lake of Galilee, suggested to him the parable of the sower; while on this occasion the same scene brings up a completely different lesson. There the sowing suggested the many obstacles which might interfere to prevent the growth and ripening of the grain; here it suggests the vastness of the harvest, the rapidity with which it ripens, and the consequent necessity of having many reapers ready to pour into the field. In the ministry of Jesus, two or more distinct and separate spiritual lessons spring from the same natural fact, as two or more wheat stalks spring from one grain of seed.

It is a remarkable and most instructive feature of this brief parable that it points out both a *likeness* and an *unlikeness* between the natural and the spiritual husbandry.

In general, the sowing of the seed in spring and the reaping of the grain in harvest are like the preaching of the word and the gathering of saved souls; but in one particular feature they are decisively and conspicuously unlike. The points of similarity are many and obvious; the one point of dissimilarity, singled out in the instructions of the Lord, is, that whereas in the natural husbandry four months must intervene between the sowing and the reaping, in the spiritual husbandry, on the contrary, no such fixed and uniform period of time elapses after the gospel has been preached ere its ripened fruits are gathered in the conversion of sinners. In this department the ripe fruit may appear the same day—the same hour in which the seed of the word has been cast into a contrite heart; or it may lie dormant, not only four months, but forty years, and come in great abundance at last.

On this distinction let the form and order of our exposition turn. Notice first the Likeness and then the Unlikeness which the Lord here acknowledges and employs between the natural and the spiritual husbandry, especially in the relation between sowing and reaping.

I. The natural sowing and reaping suggest, represent, and illustrate the sowing and the reaping in the kingdom of grace. The beginning of a process suggests the end. In the spring-time, as you walk along the highway, you may observe either the actual operation of sowing, or careful preparation for it, on almost every field.

The first coming of Christ was the seed-time, and his second coming will be the harvest. From the seed which was then dropped into the ground will spring ripened fruit, like the stars of heaven or the sand of the sea-shore for multitude. The ten thousand times ten thousand that stand round the throne in white clothing constitute the harvest, waving like Lebanon,—a manifold increase from the handful of seed sown on the mountains of Israel, when the Son of God took our nature and gave himself for sin.

Generally, the seed is the word, and the sowers are the ministers of the gospel. Wherever and whenever Christ is preached, there is a sowing of the precious seed.

But in all cases the sowing is only a means to an end. It is the hope of harvest that induces the husbandman to cast his seed into the ground, and sustains him through the heavy labour of the spring. If he did not desire to reap, he would not sow; and if he did not expect to reap, he could not. No man ever yet cast the material seed into the ground for the sake of the sowing. He would be counted mad who should go forth ostentatiously and laboriously to sow seed in the field, performing the operation with a knowing and elegant air, counting his work done when the grain was lost to view under the clods, and never coming back to look for a profitable return. Every man that sows, sows in order to have an increase in harvest. Those who have their bosom filled with the incorruptible seed of the word should do likewise. When we have preached, even when we have preached well, our work is not done, our end is not attained. He is wise that winneth souls. It is enough to console a man for all the pain of spring, when he went forth weeping, bearing precious seed, to tell him that he will return rejoicing, bringing his sheaves with him.

This is the only aim that will animate a ministry as a living soul, and sustain a minister as a commanding motive,—to save a soul from death and hide a multitude of sins.

When many anxious inquirers come to a minister, and many under his advice close with Christ as their righteousness, the joy is like the joy of harvest. Though in harvest the work is heaviest, it is then that the workers are most cheerful. There is a providential arrangement here; and the rule holds good in both husbandries.

II. Consider now the single feature in which there is a marked dissimilarity between the natural and the spiritual husbandry. Whereas in nature a known and uniform period, in each country and climate, intervenes between the sowing and the reaping, in grace the fruits may be gathered at any season of the year, and at any length of time, from the least to the greatest, after the seed of the word has been sown.

In this respect the word of the Lord intimates that there is a specific contrast between the two departments. He put the question to the disciples as an emphatic method of affirming that they were accustomed to say, We shall have harvest in four months. It would have been an inversion of the order of nature if the fields had been ripe on the day that they were sown or the day after. Yet he announces emphatically that the fields were already white to harvest. Lift up your eyes and see. Alas! they were not adept in the art of lifting up their eyes or their souls. It was downward and earthward that they ordinarily looked. It needed an elevation of position and an enlightenment of eye to enable them to understand that in the labour to which they had been called they might reap as soon as they had sowed.

Two lessons, distinct but cognate, emerge here, one on either side. The interval between the sowing and the reaping is not the same in the kingdom of grace as it is in the kingdom of nature :—

        1. It may be shorter.
        2. It may be longer.

On the one hand it is not necessary for sowers of the word to wait four months ere they begin to look for a return ; and, on the other hand, although they have waited four months, or as many years, without seeing a single ripened stalk, they should not despair of success or abandon the enterprise.

1. Do not wait four months, for the harvest may come at an earlier period. The seed that is sown to-day may be ripe to-night. An example of such a rapid progress to maturity was set before the disciples that day beside Jacob's well. Jesus has dropped the seed into that poor woman's heart. See the great, plump fragrant seeds as they drop from the Sower's hand : " Whosoever drinketh of the water that I shall give him shall never thirst ; but the water that I shall give him shall be in him a well of water springing up into everlasting life " (ver. 14). She had gone away into the town and invited her neighbours. In the interval of her absence the conversation took place between the Lord and his disciples in which he told them that though the cultivators in the neighbourhood must wait four months after having deposited the seed in the ground ere they could expect to reap their harvest, it was not so in the kingdom of God. They might sow to-day and to-morrow reap abundantly. Peter, when at Pentecost he saw the heads of the surrounding multitude drooping

on their breasts under his preaching, like ripe ears of grain under an autumn sun, would doubtless remember the words of the Lord Jesus, how he said, on the very day of the sowing, The fields are white already to the harvest.

"Lift up your eyes," he said, perhaps not an hour after the sowing, "and look on the fields...they are white already." At this point he glides from the natural to the spiritual. Those who were on the spot would observe the transition easily; for in point of fact the agricultural fields in view were not white. They were black, as being newly ploughed and sown. But I think it probable that a stream of people from Sychar, stirred by the tidings which the woman bore, were by this time pouring along the road towards the well where the Messiah stood, and that these were the whitened fields on which the Master would send his servants to work. To the left, when they lifted up their eyes, they would see an enclosure of dull black earth, for which, although the seed was already in its bosom, the owner must wait four months ere he could get any ripe return; but to the right, although the seed was only sown that day at noon, already the harvest of anxious souls was waving like Lebanon, inviting the reaper to enter and fill his bosom with the sheaves.

Those who minister the word of Christ, whether more publicly or more privately, are at once sowers and reapers. Like the cultivators in the natural sphere, the same persons must sow the seed and gather in the harvest; but unlike the cultivators of the ground, those who care for souls may and should expect to reap immediately after they have cast away the seed. Here then is the lesson for the reapers whom this Master sends into his field. Never fold your hands and say we must wait—the fruit cannot appear till such and such an interval. Go out to gather, expecting to get your bosom full; lest while you are waiting the harvest whiten suddenly, and soon waste for want of reapers.

The Master gives sometimes to the sowers a glad reaping in the spring, but not uniformly, not always.

2. The second branch of the lesson is,—Do not despond and count your labour lost, although four months, although four—forty years pass and the seed which you have been all the time sowing should lie still hidden in the ground. If the cultivator of the grain field do not see his harvest whitening in about four months, he abandons hope: he knows that if he do not get a harvest from the spring's sowing now, he will get it never. In the spiritual husbandry, where ministers are fellow-workers with God in the saving of the lost, this rule does not hold good. As the seed of the word may ripen earlier, so also it may ripen later, than other seed.

It is well worthy of remark here that although these peculiarities are contrary to each other, the Lord of the harvest makes them both alike work for good to his servants in their toil. To know that some of the seed ripens early, keeps their hopes active from the first; and to know that some of the seed ripens late, prevents their hopes from sinking even to the last.

One most precious aspect of the law that the spiritual seed may bring forth fruit after it has long lain dormant, is specially singled out by the Lord in a subsequent part of the same conversation, where he intimates to the disciples that "one soweth and another reapeth." How broad and deep is the counsel of God in this feature of his covenant! It is fitted to multiply the labourers and intensify their toil. To draw forth the reapers, and give them an impulse in their work, it is proclaimed that seed sown long ago by some who have entered into rest may be now growing white for the sickle ; and that consequently those who now enter the service may enjoy the delight and the reward of reaping where they have not sown. On the other hand, where there is faith in God, a patient sower is greatly comforted by learning that the living seed is not lost, although his own eyes should not behold the golden sheen of harvest. Even when these eyes are closing in death, the servant of the Lord who has been faithful in his day may depart in the joyful hope that many sons shall be brought into glory as the fruit of his saving work.

Both are best, and God has shown his goodness in giving both. We could not hold on, unless some of the seed should ripen in our own sight and be gathered by our own hands ; and we should abandon the work in despair, unless we were held up, on the other side, by the knowledge that after many days the seed sown now may send up a plentiful harvest. In times of special spiritual quickening, beautiful mixtures of both methods occur. Some of the seed sown long before by other labourers ripens suddenly then, and is gathered on the same day with fruit that springs from the sowing of yesterday.

Men are the reapers in this harvest : there is no limit as to the capacity that each shall possess or the numbers that may be employed. As to numbers, the rule is, " Let him that heareth, say, Come." Every one who knows that Christ is precious should make his secret known to his neighbour ; and as to capacity, the Master has need of men —little ones who have one talent, as well as of the great who have ten. These are the reapers in this harvest; but another harvest follows that will be gathered by another class of labourers. Time is the spring season, death is the sowing, resurrection is the harvest, and the reapers are the angels. When the earth and the sea give up their dead, the fields will be white to harvest, and a mighty band of reapers will have their hands full of work.

Some rocky islets are so covered at certain times by white sea-birds, that they seem from a distance islands of snow. When an alarm is sounded the whole multitude rise into the air, like a cloud that hides the sunlight from the landscape. This black earth sailing through space, protruding like a rugged islet from the waters of infinitude, will, methinks, appear one day white like a hill of snow. When the trumpet shall sound, and the dead shall rise, oh, what a harvest! These angel reapers will quickly fill their bosoms with the sheaves. Christ died and rose again, the first-fruits; then shall all that are his arise to meet him, the full harvest of the ransomed that shall at last fully satisfy his soul.

Liberty
(John 8:36)

"If the Son therefore shall make you free, ye shall be free indeed."

FREE indeed! Really free! There must, therefore, be a freedom which is imaginary, unreal, delusive. I know not a feature of our fallen world that is more frequently displayed, or more melancholy to look upon, than this. A whole family or a whole nation in bondage is a sad sight; but the measure of its sadness is multiplied tenfold if the cruel conqueror has put out the eyes of the captives, so that they do not see their prison walls, and fondly dream themselves free. Examples of persons who, being enslaved, foolishly imagine themselves free, instead of needing to be discovered and picked out, are strewn on the surface of the world as green grass in summer or as withered leaves in autumn.

Ask the visitor of a mad-house what was the saddest sight he saw; he will immediately describe to you the patient who had contrived to plait a crown out of rags and tinsel, and strutted about with the toy on his head giving orders right and left, as a king, to imaginary fleets and armies; casting all the while stolen and startled glances toward the iron bars of the window, and trembling when the stern look of the keeper met his eye.   This man is an object of pity even among his fellow-captives, who rave some degrees less wildly than himself.

You have lain down to sleep, perhaps more wearied than your wont, and have dreamt that, free from the law of gravity, you soared at will in all the upper air.   But when you awoke your limbs were stiffer and heavier than heretofore; you could scarcely trail them along the ground. Flying was a dream; the cold reality scarcely amounted to a walk on the earth; it was only a painful dragging of benumbed limbs.

In literary and political circles liberty is plentiful as a profession but scanty as a power.   In those departments, freedom and independence are frequently employed as terms of sarcasm when men desire to make sport of the bondage.

But the cases which are at once most characteristic and most numerous are those in which a man loudly boasts of his liberty, while vice, like a possessing spirit, rules in his heart and lashes him to diligence in his degrading task. I need not describe in detail the miserable drudgery of the slaves.   The description, like the public exhibition of a cripple's sores, would be both repulsive and unnecessary. When a drunkard has been tormented, body and soul, by the demon that possesses him—tormented as cruelly as the martyrs in ancient persecutions—the poor victim's resolution under the compulsion of his keeper is, When I awake I will seek it yet again.   Apart from the redemption by Christ and the renewing by the Spirit, the struggles of a sinful race to shake off their bonds are like those of Samson when his locks were shorn and his eyes out, with the Philistines making sport of the giant's pain.

The Jews of that day took it ill that Jesus should propose to *make* them free. The offer of liberty implied the imputation that they were slaves : this they rejected with disdain. " We are Abraham's seed, and were never in bondage to any man;" and this at a time when the Romans held the province with their legions and made their own will the law. We can see through the flimsy pretexts under which they attempted to cover their pride and poverty ; and other onlookers may perhaps as easily see through ours. Slaves, in very deed, we all are, held helpless in a tyrant's grasp, unless and until the Son of God make us free.

Our inherited and actual bondage has two sides, and there are two corresponding sides in the liberty wherewith Christ makes us free. The two sides of the spiritual slavery may be designated, Guilt on the conscience, and Rebellion in the will. These are distinct and yet united. They are wedded into one spirit, and become helpmeets to one another in offending God and destroying man. Guilt unforgiven on the conscience makes impossible a holy obedience in the life. While God's wrath lies on your soul, your life is not obedience to God's law. The greater the weight that lies on any object, the more difficult it is to move that object along the surface of the earth. If it is weighed heavily down, it will not move easily forward ; if you lift off its load, you draw it easily after you. Like the relation between the perpendicular pressure of a weight and the difficulty of horizontal motion is the relation between guilt and rebellion. Sin, and the wrath which it deserves, constitute the dead weight which presses the spirit down ; and the spirit so pressed cannot go forward in duty.

As in the material department it is the weight pressing

sheer down that causes the difficulty of moving forward, so in the spiritual department it is the conscious want of God's favour that hinders a human being from obeying God. When his anger is removed from me, I will yield myself a willing instrument of his righteousness. When the Son, by redeeming me from the guilt and the power of sin, has made me free, I am free indeed!

Look to these two sides of the primary bondage and subsequent liberty,—look to them separately and successively, as well as in their actual union.

I. The main element of the bondage consists in guilt and the consequent apprehension of judgment. The book in which the debt is registered lies far above, out of our sight. Although a man's account in that book were hopelessly heavy, he might not in point of fact be greatly troubled by it, if there were no counterpart or duplicate of the liabilities transferred to a ledger nearer at hand. The charge against a man is led, by an electric wire, from God's secret book right into the man's own bosom; and fiery throbs from the distant judgment-seat are ever and anon generated in his conscience, disturbing his rest and blighting all his joys.

What we call conscience is a mysterious, tenderly susceptible instrument in the midst of a man's being, bringing the man and keeping him in close and conscious relation to the great white throne and the living God. Here on earth, at one extremity of the connected system, the needle quivers and beats quickly, significantly, terrifically. The still, small tick of that needle, moved by a touch in the unseen heaven, is more appalling to the man than the thunder over his head or the earthquake under his feet.

The pain is in practice deadened more or less by a hardening of the instrument, so that it loses a measure of its susceptibility ; but mysterious beatings sometimes thrill through all the searings, and compel the prodigal to realize the presence of the living God. We sometimes speak of distance being destroyed by the telegraph. A sovereign and his ambassador in a distant capital may whisper to each other across seas and continents, as if they were separated only by a curtain drawn across the room. By the communication which is kept up between God's law and man's conscience, the distance between heaven and earth is practically done away ; and the criminal must rise up and lie down in the presence of his Judge. A man is compelled to eat, and drink, and speak under the eye of the King Eternal.

It is natural that the slave, weary of such complete and constant inspection, should cast about for the means of becoming free. To quench this burning in the unclean conscience, all the bloody sacrifices of the heathen were offered. To the same object all the efforts of self-righteousness are directed ; they are so many blows dealt in order to sever the connecting rod, so that the anger of the Judge may not be felt even now burning like fire in a sinner's breast. But these efforts do not avail : " There is no peace, saith my God, to the wicked."

But a real liberty is possible : God in his infinite mercy has opened a way by which it may be reached. If the Son make you free, you shall be free indeed. He is able to open the seven-sealed book and to blot out the reckoning that stands against us there. We have an advocate with the Father : the blood of Jesus Christ, God's Son, cleanseth us from all sin.

The Mediator—the Daysman who lays his hand upon both—has placed himself in the line of communication between the Judge and the culprit. When I am in Christ, all the throbbing messages that rise from me to God, or descend from God to me, pass through the heart of Jesus. The frown of justice due to sin is changed into love as it passes through the Mediator, and from him descends on me, no longer a consuming fire, but the light of life. On the other side, my sins, rising up to stir the wrath of the righteous God, are absorbed in the suffering Saviour as they pass, and his righteousness ascends as mine and for me.

It is this that explains the agony in the garden and the cry on the cross. Man's sin passing up demanding judgment, and God's answering anger coming down, met in the well-beloved of the Father, and rent him : " My God, my God, why hast thou forsaken me ?"

Am I free from condemnation ? Then with a great price obtained I this freedom. I was not free-born, but redeemed from bondage by the precious blood of Christ.

II. In the department of life and conduct also there is a false freedom wherewith men delude themselves, and there is a real freedom which Christ bestows upon his own.

The essence of slavery, in as far as work is concerned, lies in the terror of the master, that sits like a heavy, cold, hard stone on the worker's heart. After the slave has spurred himself on to duty, and accomplished his task, something still occurs to his memory that he ought to have done ; he trembles lest he should be punished for the defect. " What lack I yet ?" is the dreadful question to the worker who is striving with the load of unpardoned sin on his conscience—striving without love and reconciliation to fulfil all the law of God. There may be a good deal of work without reconciliation, but there is no liberty in it, and no love. The man is hunted forward in his toil by the lash of a master. Even to prayer the slave runs trembling, driven by the fear lest he be punished for not praying.

It is the heavy weight of sin not forgiven lying on the spirit and pressing it into the dust in dull despair—it is this burden that prevents the man from bounding forward fleetly, gladly on the errands of his Lord. When that load is lifted, the spirit, free to rise, is free also to move onward. It is when condemnation is taken away that obedience begins.

Take your stance on the margin of the ocean, on the western coast of this island, where the shore is a bold rugged rock, and when a long blue ground-swell is rolling towards the land. I know not any aspect of merely inanimate nature that tends so strongly to make one's heart sad. I have stood and gazed upon it until I was beguiled into a painfully tender sympathy with a mute struggling captive. Slowly, meekly, but withal mightily, the sea-wave comes on in long, regular array, and striking with its extended front at all points simultaneously against the pitiless rock, is broken into white fragments and thrown on its back all thrilling and hissing with expiring agony. Sullen and sore the broken remnants of the first rank steal away to the rear, and hide themselves in the capacious bosom of the mother sea. Anon, you perceive another long blue wave gathering its strength at a distance; with gloomy, unhopeful brow, as if warned by the fate of its predecessor, and hurried onward to its own, it rushes forward and delivers another assault against the rocky shore. It shares the fortune of the last. Again, and yet again, the water wearily gathers up its huge bulk, and again strongly but despairingly launches itself upon its prison walls, to be again broken and thrown back in utter discomfiture. You weep for the great helpless prisoner, who cannot weep for himself. Year after year, century after century, era after era, that prisoner toils and strikes upon the walls of his prison, but never once succeeds in clearing the barrier and flowing across the continent free. That mighty creature, with its sublime strength, and dumb, patient, unceasing labour, never succeeds in breaking its bonds—never leaps into liberty. Here you find a picture, such as no artist could ever make, of a sinner, or a worldful of sinners in the aggregate, as they lie in their prison, ceaselessly striving for enlargement, but never attaining it. "The wicked are like the troubled sea, when it cannot rest." And can this water never get freedom? Is it doomed to lie weltering for ever in its prison? Cannot the prisoner by any means be ever set free?

The captive may be set at liberty; the captive is set at liberty day by day. Above the firmament are waters, as well as in the hollow which constitutes the ocean's bed. They are higher up—nearer heaven—as you see, these aerial waters; but being high in heaven, they are therefore free to move across the earth. Nothing conveys a more lively idea of quick, soft, unimpeded motion, than a flying cloud. Here is none of the effort visible even in the flight of birds. Absolutely free they are; and sweetly swiftly do the free run on the errands of their Lord. In this respect there is a sublime contrast between these waters that have been made free and those that are still enslaved —held down by their own dead weight within their prison walls.

It is thus that human spirits advance in fleet, gladsome obedience, when the weight is lifted off, and they are permitted to rise. It is when you are raised up into favour that you can go onward to serve. " O Lord, truly I am thy servant." That is a great attainment, David ; how did you reach it ? Hear him give the reason: " Thou hast loosed my bonds " (Ps. cxvi. 16).

Those who are strangers to the liberty of dear children, often fall into great mistakes in regard to the obedience which true disciples render to their Lord. Here is a man who lives for present pleasure, and lives without God. He is good-hearted, in the ordinary acceptation of that word. He lays himself out for happiness, and he would like to see all his neighbours happy as well as himself. If he would not suffer much to promote the happiness of others, neither would he spontaneously do anything to injure them. As soon as one source of pleasure is exhausted, he puts his wit on the stretch to invent another. He denies himself nothing that is pleasant to his taste. Be it eating and drinking ; be it luxury in things more elevated ; be it the midnight dance or play—whatever pleases his palate he tastes in turn. He knows another man, a neighbour in residence or business, who denies himself all these indulgences, and prosecutes some difficult and disagreeable line of benevolence. The free liver looks on that neighbour and studies him, but cannot understand him. If the Christian were a morose and gloomy natured man, he thinks he could explain the reason of his conduct ; but his character is precisely the reverse. He is diligent in business, cheerful in company, affectionate and sprightly at home, literary, it may be, or patriotic. With all this he lives strictly as a Christian. He never turns night into day in any species of revelry; he neither reads newspapers nor attends to business on the Lord's day. He refuses to associate with any who dishonour the name and day and word of God, however profitable the association might seem. The man of the world—called and counted free and easy, although he is neither free nor easy—wonders how his neighbour, being not a morose and gloomy but a cheerful man, can consent to lie under such grievous restraint; how he can deny himself so many liberties, and bind himself so steadily to a round of dull duties.

It is a mistake. This man is not capable of understanding his believing neighbour. His standpoint is low, and his range of vision limited. He counts that liberty which the Christian counts bondage, and that bondage which the Christian counts liberty. The Christian before he was converted entertained the same views; but his world has been turned upside down by the gospel. The disciple of Christ has changed—he has become a new creature; but his neighbour, who is not changed, cannot understand him now. He applies carnal measurement to a spiritual nature, and is out of his reckoning at every point.

It is as if he were told that a certain vast quantity of water has been in a very short space of time removed a distance of a thousand miles over mountains and valleys, from one continent of the earth to another. Forthwith the thought arises of the heavy, sluggish, gurgling mass enclosed within vessels innumerable of vast capacity and strength, and of these being dragged by mechanical power up steep mountain sides and precipitated into the valleys beyond. It is all a mistake. If the water could only have been transported in this manner, it would never have been transported at all. The water in inconceivable quantity was lightened——was set free : being free, it rose into the heavens, and softly sailed away to its destiny.

Thus one who has not entered into peace through the blood of Christ, having no experience of liberty, cannot understand liberty as enjoyed by another. He counts that it must be a dreadful dragging to follow the Christian life. It would be uphill work for himself, if he should attempt it ; and he thinks it must be uphill work for his neighbour too. In reasoning from the capacities and habits of his own physical frame to those of his neighbour's, he reaches a just conclusion ; for in bodily constitution, notwithstanding minor differences, both are essentially the same. But in reasoning by analogy from his own spiritual state to that of his believing neighbour, he errs fatally ; for the one is the old man, while the other is the new : the one soul is in bondage ; the other has been made free by the Son of God. The Christian obedience is not the dragging of a heavy weight over the rugged ground by the sheer force of fear ; it is the easy, fleet movement of the cloud, after its constituent waters have been set free from earth and raised to heaven. " Thy people shall be willing in the day of thy power."

A ship outward bound has struck on a sunken rock ere she has well cleared out of the harbour. There she lies in the water, a mile from land, with the ocean all clear before her from that spot to her journey's end ; but she moves not. What will make her move ? The mechanical resources of our time could bring an enormous accumulation of force to bear upon her, but under all its pressure she will remain stationary. If you increase the dragging power beyond a certain point, you will wrench her asunder limb from limb, but you will not win her forward on her voyage.

No ; not this way—not by any such method can the ship be set free to prosecute her voyage. How then ? Let the tide rise, and the ship with it : now you may heave off your hawsers and send home your steamers. Hoist the sail, and the ship will herself move away like a bird on the wing.

It is thus that a soul may be set free to bound forward on the path of obedience. Dragging will not do it. A soul cleaving to the dust is like a ship aground,—it cannot go forward until it be lifted up ; but when it is lifted up, it will go forward without any violent drawing. Further : the soul cleaving to the dust is lifted, as the ship was, by a secret but mighty attraction in the far-off heaven. Elevated by a winning from above, it courses over life with freedom. " I will run in the way of thy commandments, when thou hast enlarged my heart."

But there is no time to be lost. If that ship be not lifted up by the tide to-day, she may be broken to pieces by the waves to-morrow. Yield to the mighty but gentle upward drawing which God's mercy now exerts upon the world, like the sun-heat winning water from the sea, lest you should be obliged to yield to the tempest in which the wicked are driven away in their wickedness.

True Yet Tender, Tender Yet True
(Mark 9:50)

" Have salt in yourselves, and have peace one with another."

IN this place the Lord is instructing his own disciples. We learn here not how one may become a Christian, but how one who is a Christian should demean himself in the world. The lesson directly concerns not the roots but the fruits of the new life. Every step of progress that a believer makes in practical conformity to his Master's example and precept, is a substantial gain. If we gain in godliness, we shall grow rich; and this species of wealth never flies away.

When a mercantile telegram arrives from a distant land, and is exhibited in the exchange, men eagerly crowd around it. You may see them clustering like bees about the spot, and hanging one on the' other's shoulders, all eyes strained to learn the news. Even when the message relates immediately to battles fought and cities captured—to the slaughter of thousands and the capture of myriads—the interest of the onlookers is absorbed not in the facts that meet the eye, but in the possibilities that lie beneath them. The news of the crushing defeat or the glorious victory is regarded chiefly as an index of the probable

price of cotton or the premium on gold. Such is the pre-
ponderating attraction of gain in the mercantile community.

Now here is a transaction which promises a profit.
Here is a message, short and pithy like the telegrams. It
is a message from a far country, and it points to a good
investment; it opens a prospect of great gain. Let us
press near the intimation that has been flashed down upon
us from a better country, and go in for a fortune on the
field which it lays open. Remember the words of the
Lord Jesus, how he said: "Have salt in yourselves, and
have peace one with another."

The two principal terms are Salt and Peace. Examine
first their *meaning*, and next their *relations*.

I. The meaning of each.

1. *Salt*. As its natural effect is different in different circumstances, so also its meaning differs when metaphorically
applied to moral character. It is not necessary, however,
for our present purpose, to investigate the different shades
of meaning which the metaphor bears, either in Scripture
or in common language; for as used by the Lord and his
apostles, its signification is obvious and sure. "Ye are the
salt of the earth...if the salt have lost his savour"—"Have
salt in yourselves"—"Let your speech be alway with
grace, seasoned with salt." Keeping in view the reference
to salt in the sacrifices, and the solemnizing announcements
conveyed by its means in the immediate context, we gather
easily, from a comparison of these passages, that salt, as a
metaphor applied to human character in the New Testament, signifies in general the grace of God sanctifying the
whole nature, and in particular the sterner virtues,—Faithfulness, boldness, righteousness, truth, purity. The term

indicates holiness on its harder side ; and holiness has a hard side, for it must needs be strong.

In this use of the analogy the preserving power of salt is the predominating idea. Salt appears here as the stern, sharp antagonist of all corruption. Christians baptized into the Spirit of Christ act as salt in a tainted world.

In union with the virtue that preserves, there is a pungency that pains. You may observe, however, that salt does not irritate whole skin. Apply it to an open sore, and the patient winces ; but a healthy member of a living body does not shrink from its touch. A similar distinction obtains in the moral region. Stringent faithfulness in the conduct of his neighbour will not offend a just man : but those who do not give justice do not like to get it.

Purity in contact with impurity makes the impure miserable. Peter's charge against the Jews after the resurrection was : " Ye denied the Holy One and the Just." It was precisely because he was holy and just that they denied him. The member that was covered with wounds violently shook off the salt that touched and by touching tormented it. Like draws to like, and unlike shrinks from unlike.

Salt in yourselves, then, means grace on its sterner side ; an unbending truth and faithfulness, that preserves while it pains, but pains while it preserves.

2. *Peace.* Surely it is not necessary to explain what this word means. You may comprehend it without the aid of critical analysis. It is like the shining sun or the sweet breath of early summer ; it is its own expositor. Wherever it is, it makes its presence and its nature known.

As the traveller who has missed his way thinks more of the light, and understands it better, while he is groping and stumbling in the dark than he did in the blaze of noon; so those best understand and value peace who suffer the horrors of war. You know the worth of it when you know the want of it. In communities, in churches, in families, those who groan under the rendings of strife can best tell you what peace is and how much it is worth. Blessed is peace — blessed are the peacemakers. The greatest peace is, peace with the Greatest; the greatest peace is, peace with God. The Mediator, who makes this peace, is the greatest Peacemaker. Thou shalt love the Lord thy God: this is the first and great commandment; the second, which is like unto it, is, Thou shalt love thy neighbour as thyself. After the privilege of peace with God comes that of peace with your neighbour—peace with all the human brotherhood.

Peace—including all the characteristics of a Christian which make for peace—is holiness on its softer side; and holiness has a soft side, that it may win the world.

As the disciples of Christ should combine the wisdom of the serpent with the harmlessness of the dove, so they should possess and display, in balanced union, the bold, biting strength of the preserving salt and the gentleness of the little child whom Jesus set as a pattern in the midst.

" I withstood him to the face, because he was to be blamed "—behold the salt! " All things to all men, that I might gain some "—behold the peacefulness!

II. The reciprocal relation between salt in ourselves and peace with one another.

In a certain sense, and to a certain extent, these two are true opposites. In some measure salt in you is antagonist to peace with your neighbour; and peace maintained with your neighbour is antagonist to the vigour of salt in yourselves. Accordingly, error appears alternately in two opposite directions. One man has so much salt in himself that he cannot maintain peace with his neighbours; another man is so soft and peaceable towards all that he manifests scarcely any of the faithfulness which is indicated by the salt.

It is interesting and instructive to examine the extent and the limits of this antagonism. In point of fact, and among men, faithfulness does sometimes disturb peace; and peace is sometimes obtained at the expense of faithfulness. At one time you are in a strait, because, if you show faithfulness, you will break the peace; and at another you are in a strait, because, if you keep the peace, you must hold truth in abeyance. The difficulty really exists, and frequently crosses our path in life; but we need not be surprised, and need not be despondent. It is not inherent in the nature, but introduced by the sin of man. When Christ has made an end of sin, the contradiction will disappear from the new world. Those white-robed multitudes that surround the throne are very peaceful, and yet very pure; are very pure, and yet very peaceful. There the salt does not disturb, because there is no corruption to be irritated by contact with holiness; there the peace does not degenerate into indifference, for there is no vile appetite to be indulged. That will be joyful, joyful! when all shall have salt in themselves, and all peace with each other. Nothing shall hurt or destroy in all that holy mountain.

In the meantime—like the necessity for labour—that

which comes as a curse is, under the arrangements of Providence, converted into a blessing. As toil to keep down thorns and thistles is a useful exercise for physical health, so effort to maintain faithfulness without breaking peace keeps the spirit healthful and fits it for heaven. All the more fully grown and perfect will the heirs of the kingdom be when they reach their rest, that they were compelled to exert themselves during their course in the world. No effort is lost; every expenditure of energy in God's work tells on the education of God's child. Every exertion made by a disciple of Christ to soften his own faithfulness and invigorate his own tenderness goes to increase the treasures which he shall enjoy at God's right hand. It is thus that the saved *work out* their own salvation.

Similar antagonisms in the system of nature constitute at once the exercise and the evidence of the Creator's skill. Results are frequently obtained through the union of antagonist forces neutralizing each other. A familiar example is supplied by the centripetal and centrifugal forces, which insure the stability of the solar system.

Take another case, equally instructive, though not so obvious. In the structure of a bird, with a view to the discharge of its functions, two qualities, in a great measure reciprocally antagonistic, must be united; these are *strength* and *lightness*. As a general rule, strength is incompatible with lightness, and lightness incompatible with strength. You cannot increase the one without proportionally diminishing the other. The body of the bird must float in the air, therefore it must be proportionally lighter than quadrupeds or fishes; but the creature must sustain itself for long periods in the atmosphere, and perform journeys of vast length, therefore its members must be strong. The structure of a bird, accordingly, exhibits a marvellous contrivance for the combination of the utmost possible strength with the utmost possible lightness. Every one is familiar with the structure of the feathers that compose the wing. The quill barrel gives you an example of a minimum of material so disposed as to produce a maximum of strength. The bones of birds are formed on the same plan. They are greater in circumference than the corresponding bones of other animals, but they are hollower in the heart. In iron castings we repeat the process which we have learned from nature.

This union of antagonists for the production of a common beneficent result is like the labour of a Christian life. Be gentle to all without sacrificing any truth; be faithful to truth without giving needless offence to any brother. There should be meekness of spirit, speech, and conduct in a Christian, that he may have peace with his neighbours; but there should be a stern, unyielding righteousness in a Christian, that, wherever his lot may be cast, he may act as a salt to counteract all corruption.

The task set before us is difficult, but not impossible. Much watchfulness, prayerfulness, perseverance, and self-sacrifice are required in order that you may do it; but it may be done. The disciple who would accomplish this task must labour hard; but hard labour applied to this task will not be labour lost. In this business the hand of the slothful remaineth empty; but the hand of the diligent maketh rich.

We are ignorant of many things; but the object in creation which most successfully escapes our scrutiny is precisely that which lies nearest us—ourselves. The heart is deceitful above all things. We do not pronounce righteous judgment when our own thoughts and ways are under trial. Self-love, like a huge lump of iron concealed under the deck right below the ship's compass, draws the magnet aside; thus the life takes a wrong direction, and the soul is shipwrecked. Self-love draws the life now to the right and now to the left; the errors lie not all on one side. One man, soft from selfishness, basely sacrifices truth and duty for ease; another, hard from selfishness, bristles all over with sharp points, like thorns that tear the flesh of the passenger, and when he has kindled discord among brethren, calls his own bad temper faithfulness to truth. There is no limit to the aberration of a human judgment under the bias of self-interest. It will not scruple to dispute the distinction between black and white, if it can thereby hope to gain its selfish end. Oh, how precious are these words of our Lord, " Watch and pray, that ye enter not into temptation." It is easier to explore the sources of the Nile, than to discover the true motives whence our own actions spring; and easier to turn the Nile from his track, than to turn the volume of thoughts and purposes which issue from a human heart and constitute the body of a human life. We cheat ourselves and our neighbours as to the character of our motives and the meaning of our acts. Nothing that defileth shall enter heaven; purged we must be ere we go in. It is time to begin and get the work forward a stage or two. " Put off the old man with his deeds." Watch on the right side, and watch on the left.

1. On the side of peace. It is true there cannot be too much peace in a community; and there cannot be too much of the gentle and peace-making in the character and conduct of a man. But if the folds of our peace are so

large, and thick, and warm, as to overlay and smother our faithfulness, the peacemakers are not blessed by God, and are not blessings to the world. This soft carcass that has no salt in it soon runs into decay. To have peace one with another is only half of the commandment; and half of a commandment, like half of an animal body, cannot live alone; it goes into corruption.

One who is constitutionally soft and indolent may not only sinfully fail in faithfulness; he may even take credit for his fault, and blame a brother for want of love who tempers his love with the due proportion of righteous firmness. Let the timid and retiring nature stir up his soul to a greater measure of truthful courage, without letting any of his gentleness go. Let the vine of his tenderness cling to an oak of stern faithfulness; it will thus bear more fruit than if it were allowed to trail on the ground.

2. On the side of truth and faithfulness. There cannot be too much of faithfulness in the character of a Christian; but even faithfulness to truth may become hurtful, if it is dissociated from the gentleness of Christ. The arms that impart strength to the chair may only hurt the occupant, if they lack the cushion that ought to cover them. For strength, there should be an iron hand in the velvet glove; but for softness, a velvet glove should be on the iron hand when it grasps the flesh of a brother.

Some people mistake acid for salt; their own passions for godly zeal. Jehu drives furiously forward to purify the administration of the kingdom; but it is a cruel, selfish ambition that spurs him on. When such a man scatters a shower of acid from his tongue, and sees that his neighbours are hurt by the biting drops, he points to their contortions, and exclaims, See how pungent my salt is! The true savour is in my salt; for see how these people smart under its sting! Ah, the acid, in common with salt, makes a tender place smart in a brother; but it possesses not, in common with salt, the faculty of warding off corruption. Itself corrupts and undermines; it corrodes and destroys all that it drops upon. " Get thee behind me, Satan : for thou savourest not the things that be of God."

Let every one suspect himself. Watch especially the side in which the weakness lies. But, alas! how shall we know that side ? The deceitfulness of a human heart often consists in this, that it persuades the dupe that what is really his weakness is his strength. Blind humanity makes a merit of its besetting sin. How shall we find out our ailment ? " Search me, O God......see if there be any wicked way in me, and lead me in the way everlasting." Carry the war into the enemy's country, and strike home there. But where is the enemy's country ? Alas! it is mainly here ; down in the secret chambers of the heart. Those enemies that are within the fortress have the greatest power to hurt. Strike them first, and strike them with all your might.

If a deadly viper should alight upon your flesh, you would strike a sudden sharp blow with the first weapon that might come to hand. You would not bring the stroke down gently and waveringly, in order to save your skin. You would smite quick and strong, although you should thereby wound your own body, in order that you might destroy the viper ere it had time to sting. " All that a man hath will he give for his life." Would that the children of light were as wise in their generation ; would that ourselves were as wise in counsel, and as prompt in action, when the soul's life and health are concerned, as we are when we are called to preserve the health and life of the body.

But we have apostolic example to sustain us in administering sharp reproof. " Enemies of the cross of Christ," said Paul, in addressing his well-beloved Ephesians. He runs the sword boldly through, and spares not for their crying. But let ignorant and rash physicians beware how they imitate that great master. He did, indeed, administer to his patients a biting reproof; but there were two ingredients in the prescription. One alone would kill and not cure. Such remedies are too potent for being safely intrusted to inexperienced hands. Paul told the Philippians to their face that they were enemies of the cross of Christ, but he told it *weeping*. Ah, those tears, thrown into the potion along with the scalding reproof, took all the burning out, and made the word mighty to save.

Alas! in this form the truth is often turned into a lie. Even the terrors of the Lord rattled forth hard and dry from an unmoved human heart, lose their divinity when they lose their tenderness, and degenerate into a scold. God is love while he sends out his threatenings; man should be loving when he ventures to gather these bolts from the Bible and point them to a brother's breast.

Let us press with all our might, and press always on both sides,—as far towards tenderness as truth will permit us to go, and as far towards faithfulness as the line of love will allow. Between these two divinely balanced opposites —between the salt and the peace—between steadfast truth and a gentle, winsome brotherliness, let the Christian life swing round the circumference of time, as those heavenly orbs revolve in beauty and safety, balanced between the force that drives them off and the force that keeps them near.

Do you ask what mainly hinders the union of Christians in these days ? I answer, it is the practical divorce of this paradise pair, whom God has commanded us to bind in a perpetual wedlock. The softness that suffers sin upon a brother, and the hardness that proudly tears a brother because of his sin—these two are the dividers, the disturbers of Israel. If we could pour enough of love into our faithfulness, and enough of faithfulness into our love, an amalgam would come forth from the crucible fitted to weld into one all the dislocated members of Christ's body, the Church.

Food Jesus Loved and Lived On
(John 4:34)

" Jesus saith unto them, My meát is to do the will of him that sent me, and to finish his work."

A CERTAIN woman who lived in the Samaritan town of Sychar went out one day at noon to the well for water. Although the path between the town and the well was trodden by multitudes every day, the woman on this occasion had it all to herself. She seems to have had nobody in her company, and to have met nobody by the way. All the well-ordered households had laid in their supply of water early in the morning, or late in the evening of the previous day ; for none who can otherwise arrange their plans will bear a burden through an unsheltered plain when the Syrian sun is high. Matters were not well arranged in this woman's house : she led an irregular life in a disreputable home. On this account, probably, she came to the well at noon. Had she been ready when her neighbours came, she would have missed the living water. How deep are God's purposes both in creation and providence, and how exactly wheel fits into wheel as the vast machinery moves majestically round ! It is intimated at the beginning of the chapter that Jesus must needs go through Samaria. The necessity for taking this route lay deeper than the geography of Palestine. In the counsels of Eternal Mercy he must needs go through Samaria, that he might meet a sinner there; and she must needs go out to the well at noon. because only at that hour could she find on the well's brink the Saviour of her soul.

As she approaches the well-known spot, alike venerated for its hallowed associations and valued for its continued usefulness, she espies a way-worn stranger resting on the stones at the well's mouth. Either suspecting him to be a Jew, and therefore avoiding intercourse, or bent only on her own errand without regarding his presence, she proceeded in the usual way to let down her bucket and to draw it up full from the cool depths. Ere she had time to transfer her treasure to her shoulder, in order to bear it to her home, the weary stranger accosted her with a simple request for a drink of water. Now that the ice was broken, and the intercourse begun, she enters freely into conversation; and, as the subject that came easiest to hand, plunged into the feud between Jews and Samaritans. So far from replying to her argument, the Lord instantly glided from the water with which he was refreshing his own parched lips, to the water which would be the life of her soul.

He has requested the woman to give him drink. He has applied his parched lips to the vessel which she presents, and, perhaps in the pauses of his panting draughts, looking into her careworn, uneasy countenance, he mysteriously says, " I will give thee living water." At a later stage of this episode the disciples, having brought some food from a shop in the town and offered it to their master, knowing that he must by this time be hungry, are surprised when he declines their offer. To account for his unexpected abstinence, they suggest the thought that some person during their absence might have given him food. Gliding off that common theme, What shall I eat?—rising and lifting them with himself up from earth to heaven, he replied, " My meat is to do the will of him that sent me, and to finish his work."

Consider Messiah's ministry of salvation, first, simply as a work which he performed; and next, as the food in which he delighted.

I. *His work* :—" To do the will of him that sent me, and to finish his work."

He speaks here in his capacity of Son and servant. He has been sent to execute the Father's will. In his essential nature he is one with the Father, and the purpose of redeeming lost men is his own as well as the Father's; but here the Son speaks in accordance with his place as Mediator. From Father, Son, and Spirit, the one purpose issued; and to Father, Son, and Spirit, will the glory return, when many sons are brought into glory ; but in the actual execution of the divine purpose, and during the currency of redemption, the Son of God, the Saviour, stands in a low place, and speaks as a servant charged with a specific mission, and engaged in performing a specific work.

He is doing the will of the Father that sent him. What is the will—the desire of the Sender ? You may learn it best by looking to the Sent. Look unto Jesus, if you would know the mind of God. He meant not evil to a fallen world when he sent his Son to dwell amongst us, clothed in our nature. The Gift reveals the Giver's heart. Well may we take up the bright, blessed argument of Manoah's wife, as we meditate on the incarnation, ministry.

death, and resurrection of our Lord—well may we adopt faith's strong argument, " If the Lord had meant to kill us, he would not have shown us such things as these." Jesus himself has said, " No man can come unto me, except the Father which hath sent me draw him." The Christ sent into the world is fitted to draw men to God, not to drive them away.

The will of the Father toward the world corresponds with the Messenger who has been sent to accomplish it. God is love ; and Christ came to embody divine love in the actual redemption of the lost. Oh, when will the thought spring up in the heart of a prodigal race, " I will arise, and go to my Father" ? By the gift of the Son the Father has revealed his own heart ; and they are without excuse who still count him hard, and keep at a distance.

" To do the will of him that sent me :" the desire of God could not be carried into effect without Christ sent, the Saviour. As God made the world by his Word, he makes the world anew by the Word made flesh, and dwelling amongst us. The incarnation and dying of the Lord Jesus became the accomplishment of the Father's merciful design. Intention was turned into fact. How precious are God's thoughts towards us ! But his thoughts found body in Christ crucified. Here lies the power to carry into effect the love that lay in the eternal covenant.

" And to finish his work." The work is not left half done. His work is perfect. Creation was completed ere God gave over his work and rested. It was all very good ere it left his hands. His next and more glorious work will be finished too. There will be no patches added after the children assemble in the Father's house.

This earth was complete as a habitation for humanity,

ere the children were brought to it as their home. The mountains were all raised up, and the rivers all flowing in the valleys, and the sea confined within its capacious basin, and the air mixed and made up, suitable as breath for living creatures, clasping the globe round all its circumference. Then, and not sooner, did God make man in his own image. The home of the holy will be perfect when its inmates enter. All things are ready ere the message is sent round to bid the guests assemble. God's works are all finished works.

At the time that Jesus talked with the woman and with his disciples at Jacob's well, the work which he had undertaken was not finished. The agony in the garden lay before him, and lay full in view ; the hiding of the Father's face, the cup of wrath ; all the bearing for his people's sin, and the Father's righteousness, lay before him. This baptism he must yet be baptized with, and he was straitened till it should be accomplished. He hastened to the end. For the joy that was set before him, he endured the cross, despising the shame.

II. *His food :*—To do the Father's will and finish his work, he counted his *bread.*

It is not enough to learn from the evangelic histories what Jesus did and suffered. It is not enough to examine his acts ; we must look, as far as the Scriptures present an opening, into the secret motives that wrought in his heart. At Jacob's well he was carrying forward his great mission as the Saviour of lost men : the twelve looked on, but they looked on as little children look on their father while he is preparing to accomplish some great work of skill. They saw each separate movement, but they could not comprehend the design. Not understanding the whole, they were baffled by the sight of the separate parts. " They marvelled that he talked with the woman."

Knowing full well all that the redemption of his people would bring upon himself, he longed for the work as for his daily bread. It is my meat to do his will, and finish his work. This word we can in some measure understand; for we know what the pain of hunger is, and what the delight of satisfying hunger with convenient food. I can in some measure comprehend the desire that burned in the breast of Jesus that day at Jacob's well; for I have been hungry, and when hungry have been satisfied with bread. In this glass I can see reflected the nature and intensity of the Saviour's eagerness to save.

On one occasion Jeremiah was commanded to go down to the potter's house, that he might there receive a message from the Lord ; and the prophet soon learned the reason why the message was not communicated to him in his own house. It regarded the sovereignty of God in appointing the lot of his creatures, and Jeremiah could more easily understand the lesson while he stood by the potter's wheel, and saw him making from one piece of clay a vessel unto honour and a vessel unto dishonour. Some lessons which God gives us can be more fully taken up in one position than in another. Some texts of Scripture may be most profitably read in a dark night, some beside a stormy sea, and some at the brink of an open grave. You can enter into the spirit of some texts more easily when you are young, and of others when you are old,—of some while you are joyful, and of others when you weep. Methinks this word of the Lord should be thought of when we are hungry, and anticipating the pleasure of enjoying our food.

Like hunger was Christ's appetite for saving work—like the satisfying of hunger is his joy when he is winning souls.

What an agony is unappeased hunger! What contrivances will you adopt, what efforts will you make, what pain endure, in order to obtain bread! "Skin for skin, yea, all that a man hath will he give for his life;" and food is life—the want of it death.

A traveller lost his way in an Eastern desert. His provisions were exhausted, and he had already wandered about for several days without food, when he descried under a palm-tree on his track the marks of a recent encampment. He approached the spot tremulous with hope. He found a bag which the travellers had left behind, filled with something that appeared to be dates. He opened it eagerly, expecting to satisfy his hunger, when lo, it contained only pearls! He sat down and wept. What are pearls to a man who is dying for want of bread?

Jesus is Lord of all. Those glorious stars that stud the heavens are all his. They are the jewels which belong to his crown. He values them; but they do not satisfy his soul. To Christ, these shining orbs are like the pearls to the fainting traveller in the desert. They are precious and pure, but he cannot live on them. Christ does not need to redeem those bright worlds and those unfallen angels, and they cannot therefore satisfy his appetite. To seek the strayed; to redeem the lost; to renew the fallen; to lay down his life for them,—this is his meat: and for this food he must pass those shining worlds. He must leave them, like the ninety-nine unstrayed sheep upon the mountain pastures, and go after the lost one, that when he gets it on his shoulders he may rejoice, with a joy unspeakable and full of glory.

" Blessed are they that hunger ; for they shall be filled." This he said : this he felt. He experiences the truth of this saying to-day in the midst of the throne, while ten thousand times ten thousand of the saved are ministering before him. That fainting, hungry traveller by Jacob's well, obtained a foretaste of his joy when the Samaritan woman received life from his hands ; and his joy will be full when all the ransomed shall rise and reign with him upon his throne.

Behold the man, fainting, hungry, under a midday sun at Jacob's well ! Behold the man, crowned with thorns and mocked at Jerusalem ! Behold the man, as he bows his head upon the cross,—what has brought him to this ? His appetite : it is that hunger for the doing of his Father's loving will, and the finishing of his Father's mighty work. It was his unquenchable appetite for saving, as for the bread of his life, that brought him to a fallen world, and left him under the curse that was due to sin. This appetite burned in his breast like fire. With this appetite unsatisfied, he would have counted heaven unhappy. Under the control of his own divine love, he left his throne, took upon himself the form of a servant, and suffered unto death, that he might feast upon the work of winning souls.

The same feature of his character appeared when he stood on the Mount of Olives, and wept over Jerusalem. Son of God, why weepest thou ? He weeps for hunger. He is like a hungry man in sight of food, but not within reach of it. It is in such a case that hunger gnaws like a worm in the breast. Oh, how he loves !

How deeply and how persistently do the guilty misinterpret and misrepresent the heart of Christ ! Men take the devils' opinion of him, " Art thou come to torment us ?" instead of the view which the true One gives of himself.

It is difficult for us to take in the conception of Christ's passionate desire to save, and yet retain a due sense of his omnipotence as God. We are apt to think that in such a case his power might have been put forth, as the immediate instrument of accomplishing all his desire. Might not the Almighty Deliverer have made short work with the saving of Jerusalem that day ? Might he not have seized a whole cityful, as the angels seized Lot by the hand, and hurried them up to heaven ?

But this would not satisfy his soul ; this is not food convenient for him. It is not pure. It was a gross and carnal conception that the prosperous man entertained, when he tried to feed his soul with the goods that he had laid up in a barn. Material acquisitions cannot satisfy and sustain spirit. Though the Lord Jesus has all power committed to him in heaven and in earth, he will not command stones to be made bread by a miracle to satisfy his hunger ; neither will he lift a multitude to heaven by mere omnipotence. They who are drawn up to him for the satisfying of his soul, rise as the clouds rise from the sea, spontaneous and pure. Nothing shall enter that defileth. He hungers, and saving work is his food ; but as with his servant Peter so with the Master himself,—nothing common or unclean hath at any time entered his lips.

He must needs go through Samaria, not only because that province lay in his way, but because he was hungry, and in poor half-heathen Samaria lay the savoury meat which his soul loved. In the same manner he must needs pass through our nature and our world, as he goes from the glory of the eternity past to the glory of the eternity to come. It was not any physical necessity; for the Maker of all worlds might have found another path from glory to glory without visiting this shooting star. But he must needs pass through the abode of fallen humanity on his way to the throne of the kingdom, because he longed to save the lost with a longing like hunger, and here only could be found the food that would satisfy his soul. His own sovereign love laid the necessity upon himself. The sun, his creature, is under an inherent necessity of giving out light; so Christ, the light of the world, must needs give out the light of life, and therefore he casts himself in the way of a dark world, as the hungry seeks food and the thirsty makes his way towards water-springs.

The Ethiopian found Christ in the desert, and went on his way rejoicing; but also Christ found the Ethiopian in the desert, and went on his way rejoicing that he had tasted his sweetest food.

Within the limits prescribed by our capacity and our condition, the appetite of the Master may be experienced by the servants too, and they after their own way may be satisfied with the food that he loved so well. Our spiritual hunger is first a desire to get and then a desire to give salvation. It is in the second part of the process that the disciple enters in some measure into the joy of his Lord. Out of his own fulness the Lord gives. At first we are empty; but when we have obtained mercy, we shall experience a desire like an appetite to publish it. Oh that we were inoculated with that appetite for doing good that burned in the breast of the man Christ Jesus! We try to do some good, and then we slacken and leave off. When some providential call awakens us, we start into activity again for a season. This is not the way to work deliverance in the earth. The work is not effectually done unless we do it as the Master did it. When saving work is our meat, and idleness gnaws like the pain of hunger, we shall be sent unto our task and kept at it. An appetite is the unslumbering, faithful, effective task-master appointed by our Creator, in the material department, to see that we take our necessary food. When a task-master of the same order keeps our spirits on the stretch for saving work, the work will be vigorously prosecuted, and we shall never be long out of employment.

Food Jesus Gave to His Own
(John 6:51-53)

" I am the living bread which came down from heaven : if any man eat of this bread, he shall live for ever : and the bread that I will give is my flesh, which I will give for the life of the world. The Jews therefore strove among themselves, saying, How can this man give us his flesh to eat ? Then Jesus said unto them, Verily, verily, I say unto you, Except ye eat the flesh of the Son of man, and drink his blood, ye have no life in you."

T O finish his work was bread to himself : his work finished is bread to his people. His food was the subject of the last exposition ; theirs invites our attention now.

As never man spake like this man, so never hitherto has even this man spoken as he speaks here. After intimating generally, " I am the bread of life," he proceeds to declare specifically, " The bread that I will give is my flesh, which I will give for the life of the world." Here he glides from a deep into a deeper revelation. In answer to the perplexed questioning of his auditors, he declares with great clearness that, in order to their spiritual life, they must " eat the flesh and drink the blood of the Son of man." He was well aware, when he uttered these extraordinary words, of the offence that they must give. The conception of eating his flesh, in as far as they took it in a bodily sense, was fitted to shock them as men ; and the conception of drinking his blood was additionally distasteful to them

as Jews, who were forbidden in any circumstances to eat
the blood. He foresaw that many would take offence at
these words and desert his ministry; but he would not on
that account refrain from uttering them. The truth which
these words convey is necessary to the life of men, and
therefore the merciful Redeemer will not withhold them.
He must finish his work. This rock must be laid down
although many of the superficial disciples may stumble
over it, for it is necessary as the foundation of a true disciple's faith and hope. The cross must be held aloft,
although the offence of the cross may drive many of the
unstable away. Already the Lord saw meet to proclaim
his own sacrifice as the atonement for sin.

Let it be distinctly understood at the outset that the
Communion of the Lord's Supper is not the subject of discourse here. The doctrine which the Lord here teaches,
and the ordinance which he afterwards instituted in the
upper room at Jerusalem, are distinct things, although they
are related to each other.

If the instituted supper is like a lofty tower, the doctrine
taught in this passage is like the solid ground on which
the tower rests. This broad world is a greater thing than
any tower or mountain that it bears. There might have
been a world the same substantially as that which is,
although no tower or mountain should have ever raised its
head into the sky; but no tower or mountain could have
lifted its head towards the heavens if there had not been a
deep steady world to bear it.

Not the words of this passage, but the truth which they
teach, is the ground on which the Lord's Supper rests.
The Communion is a lofty monumental tower from whose
summit the spectator can look eastward into the morning

of time, till he meet Abraham's straining faith looking down the ages; and westward, farther and farther toward the end, till he go round the circumference of time and meet another morning—the second coming of the Lord in the clouds of heaven. But that ordinance depends absolutely for all its value on the foundation-truth that is revealed here: that Christ crucified—his flesh and his blood—constitutes the sustaining food and refreshing drink of all who enjoy spiritual life and are heirs of the life eternal.

The evangelist John omits from his history both the ordinances. He mentions neither as an instituted ordinance; but he records from the lips of the Lord the fundamental doctrines on which those ordinances severally depend. In the conversation with Nicodemus you find the ground which sustains Baptism; and in this discourse the ground which sustains the Supper.

The Supper, although it is Christ's own institute, is an outward thing, deriving all its meaning and power from this precious truth. This is the soul which animates the body of the ordinance. If Christ had not made himself the meat and drink of his people, the Supper would never have been set up as a monument of the fact; and if Christ's disciples do not really thus live upon him in secret, their participation of bread and wine at the Table will be to them a stone instead of bread.

Wanting Christ's sacrifice for sin, the ordinance of the Supper would have contained nothing for us; and wanting individual personal faith in Christ crucified, we can get nothing from the ordinance.

For the beginning of this doctrine regarding the spiritual appetite and its supply, we must go back to the conversation with the Samaritan woman (iv. 10). " He would have given thee living water." Living water ! what may that be ? It is not a springing well; it is not a running stream. The water that Christ gives is not only living, it gives life. He who drinks of it is satisfied, and that for ever. The woman failed to comprehend his meaning, as one who had enjoyed a better education had failed before her to comprehend the new birth; but both the woman and Nicodemus, like new-born babes, received the nourishment which they could neither explain nor understand. It is a mistake to suppose that spiritual profit is always in proportion to the intellectual comprehension. A little child may thrive upon the food of whose name and nature he is ignorant, while a physician who knows the constituents and properties of every morsel he swallows may be dying by inches, not for want of food, but for want of hunger. The woman soon got beyond her depth in doctrine ; but she thirsted, and drank the living water. Forthwith she became an apostle, and called the men of her city out to the Lord.

In this portion the same doctrine appears at a further advanced stage. There, it was water for the thirsty ; here, it is meat and drink. Then the Lord gave water ; now his flesh is meat and his blood is drink.

Hunger and thirst inhere naturally in human souls. There is a craving in humanity for more. We are in this respect completely distinct from other orders of living creatures. The craving for something not yet possessed, and not yet visible, is a universal characteristic of our kind. The pressure of that appetite makes the whole machinery of the world go round. It sends armies into the field, and ships across the ocean ; it mines the solid earth, and washes gold from Australian sands. The cry of human nature, blind and unintelligent, but eager and constant, is the cry of the horse-leech—Give, give.

This soul-hunger in humanity human beings attempt to satisfy with body-food. " Soul, thou hast much goods laid up for many years," etc. But when all these have been flung to it, the poor soul is more hungry than before. It is as when the shipwrecked seaman on his raft drinks salt water to appease his thirst, and so makes his thirst burn more fiercely.

This strong but blind appetite is cheated, moreover, by all the idolatries and all the self-righteousnesses that men have invented in name of religion.

To meet and satisfy this craving Christ came into the world, and gave himself a sacrifice. Neither is there salvation in any other. " My flesh is meat indeed, and my blood is drink indeed."

" Except ye eat the flesh and drink the blood of the Son of man, ye have no life in you." Here we have, on the part of Christ, his *incarnation* and *sacrifice;* on the part of Christians, their *faith in exercise,* and their *life thereby.*

I. On the part of Christ, *Incarnation* and *Sacrifice.*

1. *His incarnation:* the Son of man. A deep mine of meaning lies in this form of expression. Not man, not a man, not a son of man ; but *the Son of man.* There is only one to whom this title is due. It points not to the millions who are sons of man, and nothing more ; it points to him who, being Son of God from eternity, became the Son of man in the fulness of time. Neither a son of man nor the Son of God could be our substitute and saviour. The one is near enough to us, but has no power to save ;

the other has power to save, but is not near enough to us. A son of man is linked to us in the sympathy of a common nature ; but this only secures that he sinks with us when we fall : the Son of God is far above, out of our sight, and we cannot rise with him when he rises. Thus, if mere man had been our help, we should have perished, for there would have been no strength to lay hold of ; and if only God had been our help, we should have perished, for we could never have laid hold of his strength.

The incarnation—that is, when he who is God blessed for ever took our nature, and became a man—is the greatest fact in the course of time. It is the knot that binds a fallen world to a stable heaven, that interlaces divine power with human weakness, and imparts divine righteousness to the fallen as their covering and their plea.

2. *His sacrifice.* Beyond question the Lord points already to his own atoning death when he speaks of his flesh and his blood as the meat and the drink of his people. Even the incarnation, if it stood alone, could not save us. Although the Son of God had taken our nature, we must have been left to perish, if he had not in that nature given himself a sacrifice. Without shedding of blood there is no remission of sins. This is the great central lesson of the Scriptures. This cardinal doctrine was imprinted into the being of the Church during the period of its infancy. From Abel's sacrifice to the Passover which Jesus kept in the upper room with the twelve on the eve of his suffering, the blood of sacrifices flowed on the altar like a continual stream. Daily sacrifice ; morning and evening sacrifice ; sacrifice when the sun went down, and sacrifice again to greet his rising : blood, blood ; all things under the law were

sprinkled with blood. Expiation by the victim's blood
was the very mould in which the people's minds were cast
from youth to age, from generation to generation. If that
were only the invention of men, what a waste! but if that
be the appointment of God, what a meaning! When Christ
came he recognized his place and his mission. He placed
himself in the focus of all those converging fires, and owned
himself the Lamb of God, slain from the foundation of the
world. "It is finished," he said at length, and gave up the
ghost.

II. On the part of Christians, *They believe and live.*

"Eat the flesh and drink the blood of the Son of man."
He employs plain, powerful language. Nor does he take
any pains to give warning that it is not the bodily eating
of his material body that he means. He knows what is in
man, and what man needs. He knows that if any would
not perceive his meaning without such a warning, neither
would they accept his meaning with it. Those who entertain the conception of a corporal and carnal receiving of
Christ's flesh and blood would have run into that idolatry
over the back of all the warnings that could have been
written. All through, the Lord speaks not of the hunger
and food of the body, but of the hunger and food of the
soul. If any one misses or rejects this, he would not have
been corrected and instructed by any other form of words
possible in human speech.

But mark well, although it is a spiritual and not a
material food, it is yet a real supply of a real hunger.
The soul's hunger is a greater thing than the hunger of the
body. A Roman poet has called avarice a spiritual thirst
for gold. And this spiritual appetite works greater effects

on earth than any bodily appetite. Correspondingly, a pure and divinely inspired spiritual appetite is a more imperious and far-reaching power than the natural appetites of the body. From the Psalmist downward, it has been common for souls to be so eager for the spiritual food that they have forgotten to eat their daily bread. The soul's appetite has overruled and overridden the appetite of the body. And as hunger is often quickened into sharper activity by the sight or the scent of food, so longing eager souls become more eager when, after long striving in vain for that which will satisfy, they come near their true satisfaction—the Christ of God, incarnate in our nature and sacrificed for our sin. Never did the Ethiopian treasurer more keenly hunger for this flesh to eat and this blood to drink than when, on his journey homewards, he continued seeking, and was blindly groping over the very place where his satisfaction lay—the Lamb of God led to the slaughter —the sacrifice of Christ for the world's sin.

To eat his flesh and drink his blood is to secure and live upon Christ—God with us, and sacrificed for us. As truly a believing soul receives this food as the living body receives its appropriate nourishment ; and as truly does the new life of the soul prosper on this sustenance, as does the healthy body prosper on its convenient food.

" Except ye eat the flesh and drink the blood of the Son of man ye have no life in you." Even intelligent assent to the truth of the gospel does not give life. Even devout admiration of the incarnation, the ministry, and sufferings of Immanuel will not give and sustain the life of a soul. It is the personal individual acceptance and relish of the divine and crucified Redeemer, as your own Redeemer, and this acceptance as real as your acceptance of food for the body's life—it is this that contributes, that sustains, that constitutes the new life of a Christian.

Drink his blood is a striking, and must have been to the Jews who heard it, a startling addition to the more familiar conception of eating the flesh of the sacrifice. He must have intended to startle them, and to shake them out of their lethargy. They were strictly forbidden to eat the blood ; and yet they were taught that the blood was the life. It was like the prohibition laid on the primeval pair against eating of the tree. Yet the tree is a tree of life ; and the Lord means that they shall eat of it yet, and eat abundantly. Not in an unlawful way or at an unripe time, but in time and manner divinely appointed, Israel shall yet drink the blood in which is the life. The time had now come. The way was open ; the barrier was removed. There was now access into the holiest. That which was veiled off before is laid open now, and whosoever will may come and take of this water—may drink of this blood, which is the life, freely.

These words of Jesus have a direct and obvious bearing on the question whether participation in the communion of the Lord's Supper, the external ordinance, is necessary to salvation. The doctrine taught here manifestly settles that question. The words were spoken by Jesus, and recorded by John, in order that they might settle that question. Here the circumstance that John, writing after the other three Gospels were before his eye, gives fully this discourse, and gives not the institution of the Supper at all, is broadly significant. By eating the flesh and drinking the blood of the Son of man believers then had life, at a time when the Supper was not appointed, and none but the Lord himself knew that it ever would be appointed. This is given in full by John, and the ordinance not given at all, to prevent a corrupt priesthood, in a subsequent age, from laying a yoke of bondage on the necks of believers. There were men who then and there did eat the flesh and drink the blood of the Son of man before the external ordinance was appointed; and a multitude which no man can number would have so eaten and so drunk for their own eternal life, in succeeding ages, although it had pleased the Lord not to have instituted the Supper at all.

But although the discourse of Jesus vindicates for all time and all places the possibility of living in Christ here and with him on high, without actually partaking of bread and wine with the Church on earth, it does not make the ordinance which Christ subsequently instituted of no effect, and does not liberate any disciple from the duty of observing it. The fact that he lives a new life, by secretly eating the flesh and drinking the blood of Christ, so far from making a believer careless of the ordinance, is the very thing that impels him with desire and joyfulness to take the cup of salvation in his hand, and so call upon the name of the Lord. It is the consciousness that he has already been redeemed from all evil through the shedding of the Saviour's blood, that induces him to serve the Lord that bought him by a glad obedience to all his commandments. The supposition of a believer living in Christ, and eating his flesh and blood, yet refusing to partake of the Lord's Supper, is vain and useless. For if the refusal spring from some mist that has come over a true disciple's mind, preventing him from seeing the way that the Lord has pointed out, it is like the case of a man who wants a limb—he lives, but his progress is impeded by the calamity. And if it be the case of one consciously, with his eyes open, refusing to obey that dying command of Christ, that despiser is none of his. No man who really trusts in the risen Saviour for redemption and eternal life, will persist with understanding in refusing to obey what he knows to be the Saviour's command.

When one has tasted that the Lord is gracious, you may be well assured he will cast up wherever and whenever new tastes of the same grace are going. As even the dumb brute which draws your carriage will turn aside with a strong determination when he approaches the spot where formerly he has obtained food when hungry or drink when thirsty, so a Christian who has already lived upon the Lord will be found pressing in to whatever places, by the Lord's own appointment, new experiences of his love are given,—in the Closet, in the Church, at the Table.

Pause a moment yet over the word, " Except ye eat the flesh of the Son of man, and drink his blood, ye have no life in you." The Lord seems to ignore the life that we now live in the body. He will not count or call it life at all ; at least, when in his view this life is laid for comparison alongside of eternal life in himself, he deliberately refuses to count it life. He reckons it only a process of dying. We are aware of the general law that one's view depends upon his view-point. Christ, though he is Son of man and our Brother, yet stands within the veil while he speaks to us. He stands on his own footing as the eternal Son of God, with all eternity exposed beneath his eye : in this position he stands while he speaks to us, and he cannot call this fitful struggle to keep death at bay for a few years, a life. In his view, unless we are found in him and so partake of life spiritual and eternal, we have not life at all.

If it were possible for us, by a certain process of union or engrafting, to admit an insect whose life is but a day into a participation of the human life, with its intellect and its span of seventy years ; and if the creature could become aware of the fact, and capable of receiving instruction regarding it, you might, in such an imagined case, approach it while its one-day life was drawing towards sunset, and say, Haste and take such and such measures for engrafting yourself into me ; for except ye be inserted into my flesh and blood, ere that sun go down you have no life in you. From man's view-point, and with his measures, the life of that ephemera is not a life at all.

The figure, though feeble, helps, as far as it goes, to explain the meaning of the Lord when he says, " Except ye eat my flesh and drink my blood, ye have no life in you." With his experience and with his prospect, he counts this fitful life in the body as not a life. In comparison with the life of which we are capable, and which he both has at his disposal and loves to bestow, this is not life. But as in this lower life, if we do not eat and drink it cannot be sustained ; so in that higher life, unless we receive its sustenance we cannot enjoy it. The Hebrew fathers, although they tasted the manna that fell from heaven, died. No material plenty, no spiritual privilege, will secure for you the life of the soul. The body and blood of Christ are the appropriate and necessary sustenance of that only real and perfect life. You must, not after a corporal and carnal manner, but by faith, discern the Lord's body and feed upon it.

A soul can live as well as a body. A spirit can hunger and thirst as well as a body. The hunger and thirst of a spirit are as real as the hunger and thirst of a body. The food that satisfies a spirit is as real as, and inconceivably more substantial than, the food that satisfies a body.

Nor is it true that body-hunger and body-food are substance, and the spiritual need and spiritual supply a kind of shadowy figurative thing. No ; the opposite is the truth. The real, the substantial, the original—the food that is first and shall be last—is the body and blood of Christ, on which Christians live ; and the hunger and the food that bulk so largely in the business of earth are a shadow that endures for a moment and then vanishes away.

THE TWO FAMILIES
The Natural and the Spiritual
(Luke 8:19-21)

"Then came to him his mother and his brethren, and could not come at him for the press. And it was told him by certain which said, Thy mother and thy brethren stand without, desiring to see thee. And he answered and said unto them, My mother and my brethren are these which hear the word of God, and do it."

WHILE Jesus was in the act of preaching in the centre of a crowd, Mary his mother approached the spot, accompanied by some members of her family. Unable to penetrate the throng, they remained on its outskirts, and sent in a message, from lip to lip, that they desired to speak with him. Not permitting his public ministry to be authoritatively interrupted even by his mother's word, he set the demand aside by the memorable answer, "My mother and my brethren are these which hear the word of God, and do it."

From these words of the Lord Jesus I learn—

THAT, WITHOUT REPUDIATING THE FAMILY RELATIONS OF EARTH, HE INSTITUTES AND PROCLAIMS THE FAMILY RELATIONS OF HEAVEN.

The prophecy is not limited to any single or private interpretation; it has a meaning for all kindreds and all times. As a faithful minister of the gospel said once to a despotic sovereign—"There are two kings and two kingdoms in Scotland," explaining how Church and State may live and thrive on the same spot at the same time, giving and receiving help reciprocally, if each will consent to confine itself to its own sphere and exercise only its own functions ; so the Scriptures intimate that two families pervade society, both having to a great extent the same persons as members, yet without jealousy or collision, getting and giving reciprocal support. Both families are of God. He has planned and constituted them. To him they owe their origin, and from him they receive their laws. A place has been assigned to the one in creation ; to the other in redemption. The one has been in full operation since the birth of our race ; the other was long a secret hidden institute, nor was it completely formed and openly manifested till Christ came into the world. The members of the first family enter its circle by birth ; the members of the second by the new birth. The one is the grand Institute of Nature ; the other the grand Institute of Grace. Both are good, each as far as it goes ; but the second is deeper, longer, broader, higher than the first. The first is the family for time ; the second is the family for eternity.

In this text, and in others of similar import, the Lord Jesus, without pulling up the first family, plants another among its roots. The first, being an institute existing from the beginning hitherto and manifest to all, he simply leaves as it is ; the second, being in a great measure new and unknown, he proclaims, defines, and approves. The first, being strong in nature, he leaves to its own resources ; the second, being feeble, he protects against the possible oppression of its robuster neighbour. The rights of the one family are secured in the decalogue ; the privileges of the other are pronounced by the lips of Christ.

In short, as the Redeemer and Head of his ransomed Church, the Lord does not condemn and annul relations of blood ; but he refuses to permit them to burst in and dominate relations by the Spirit. By silence he permits the natural affections to rule in their own sphere ; but by express intimation he forbids them to usurp authority in another. At the proper time and place, Jesus the son owned the law of Mary his mother ; but Jesus the Saviour will not, at this woman's word, interrupt his work, and scatter an assembly of disciples.

Let us therefore endeavour to explain and apply in their order and relations these two lessons :—

I. Christ in the Gospel permits the natural family, in all its integrity, to remain undisturbed.

II. Christ in the Gospel establishes, on the same sphere, a new spiritual family.

I. Christ in the Gospel permits the natural family, in all its integrity, to remain undisturbed.

Jesus was himself the member of a family. He received the benefits of that position, and fulfilled its duties. In his ministry he recognized the institute, and in his conduct he obeyed its laws. Nor is it enough to say that he knew and acknowledged those affections that bind family-groups together : himself had planted them in the human constitution at the first. He is the contriver and creator of humanity, with all its original capacities. Wisdom, as in the Proverbs, was with the Maker " when he set a compass upon the face of the deep," and his peculiar " delights were with the children of men." He who stands in the heart of that crowd, and receives a message from a mother, shared in the mysterious counsel, " Let us make man in our own image." It is essential to the depth and stability of our faith to bear in mind that our Redeemer is the Eternal and Almighty God. He who is now redeeming man from sin made man in the beginning sinless. He imprinted instincts, such as he saw meet, on the core of his creature ; and these, as they came from his hand, were all very good : these are all very good still, in as far as they have been set in his own work by his own hand.

While the incarnation is to us the grand evidence of God's condescending kindness, it is fitted also to exalt to the utmost the dignity of man. Therein we get a glimpse, which the fallen could not have otherwise obtained, of the place which unfallen humanity held, and which the redeemed will enjoy for ever. " The Word became flesh, and dwelt among us." " He took not on him the nature of angels," but ours; and he bears that nature still. We learn here that God is not ashamed of his own conception embodied in the constitution of the human race. He did not repent of his plan, and has not withdrawn it to substitute another. He did not fling his work away, even when it fell. He abides by all that is his own in us ; and will abide by his redeemed, not ashamed to call them brethren when they are at last completely restored. Before the mystery of the incarnation we ought first to adore the condescension of God, and next to reverence ourselves. Honour all the pure affections of human nature, for they thrill in the Saviour's breast ; loathe all the sins that stain it, for they crucified the Son of God.

If you examine the natural affections and instincts of living creatures, you will find that one principle lies like a measuring rod along the whole—utility. These affections are inserted, and inserted such as they are, in the constitution of the creature, because of their usefulness. They are the instruments whereby the Maker works out his own design. " God is good," will explain all. " The eyes of the Lord are in every place." " The hairs of your head are all numbered." The instincts go as far as is necessary for the good of the creature, and no farther. There is no waste in the mechanism of creation and providence. Sufficient power is provided to produce the desired result ; and by a self-acting apparatus the power ceases to operate as soon as the result has been attained. Some living creatures, as fishes and certain species of birds, have no perceptible filial or parental affections at all. In their case the instinct is not needed, and therefore is not found. In others, including all the higher grades of the brute creation, the parental affection is developed in great intensity for a short period, and then altogether ceases. A mother that would have shed her blood for her offspring a month ago, when it was feeble, does not know it to-day, at least does not acknowledge it in the herd. The instinct, having served its purpose, is not left dangling after its work is done. It has been cut off short and clean; remnants would only encumber, and therefore none are left.

Relative affections in human kind expatiate on a wider field, and are more enduring. Here we enter a region in which these affections find room to range ; they become, accordingly, manifold and strong. The roots go deeper down in the deeper, richer soil. A short-lived maternal love would not serve the purpose here ; and therefore a mother's love in this region is not short-lived. In this sphere a moral end is proposed, penetrating through time into eternity ; and in the economy of Providence adequate means have been provided. The relations of the family, like

the flowers, are fair even on the surface and to the casual observer; but beauties unnumbered and unmeasured lie beneath
the leaves to reward more earnest and careful inspection.

Christ was a perfect man. He was not only perfectly
holy, but completely human. He took all our nature,
without its defects and defilements. He experienced filial
and fraternal love. He loved his mother and his brethren
with the true affection of a son and a brother. The bosom
on which he slept when he was an infant, he never tore
when he became a youth and a man. The woman who
cherished him from his birth was dear to his heart till
death. How the filial regard, a merely human emotion,
was affected by the love divine wherewith he, the same
person, regarded Mary as a sinner saved, we can neither
comprehend nor explain. We are treading here on the lip
of the unrevealed and the unrevealable ; if we turn one
step aside, or go forward one step too far, we are in an
instant helplessly beyond our depth. One thing we know
surely—that the man Christ Jesus fulfilled a son's and a
brother's part to the woman Mary and those men of her
family who are called his brethren.

No disciple of Christ is permitted to break the bonds of
kindred, and abjure the affections of consanguinity, on the
plea of his Master's example or command. Superstition
has always shown a tendency to exalt the spiritual relations
by crushing the natural ; it would build up, according to
its own false conception, the family of God on the ruins of
the family of man. It even represents, that to extinguish
by violence every spark of specific filial regard to an
earthly parent, is the way to become a first-class favourite
among the children of our Father in heaven. This is a
mistake—a mischievous will-worship. God has not re-

quired—will not accept this service at our hands; he is not pleased—he is displeased with those who, on any pretence, rudely break the bonds which his own hands have so skilfully constructed.

God did not build up the family in order to pull it down again. By permitting the bonds by which it is united to twine around his own heart, the Lord our Redeemer has intimated that in themselves they are pure, and in the Church shall be permanent; these laws he came not to destroy, but to fulfil.

As the ordinances of the earlier dispensation were a shadow, and so a prediction, of better things to come in Christ, the natural family is a type, and so a promise, of the spiritual and heavenly. That which is earthly is first, and will be superseded when that which is spiritual shall have fully come. It occupies its place and serves its purpose; for its time and its purpose, behold it is very good. Christ came to plant another family beside it—a family which is now growing among its roots and under its shade, and will at last cast it out and assume its place; but in the meantime, and while the world lasts, he leaves all the relationships and instincts of human families untouched, except to hallow them by his own example and approval. He will not permit the affections of the present time to grow too rank, draining off all the heart's riches, and starving the affections that are unseen and spiritual within his own; but even in the act of checking the family instincts and forbidding them to travel beyond their sphere, he leaves them honoured and approved in all their integrity to expatiate within their own sphere. He will not permit the family to exalt itself above its own place; but neither will he depress it beneath its own place: he will neither banish it from earth, nor permit it to intrude into heaven.

On this, and on one or two other occasions, the Lord Jesus maintains towards Mary his mother a measure of reserve which at first sight attracts notice, and perhaps even excites surprise. We know from the record of his life that equally in his childhood and at his dying hour a fervent filial love glowed in his breast ; but some incidents also recorded in the Gospels, although not contrary, distinctly point in another direction. Two lines in regard to this matter, not hostile or inconsistent, but articulately distinct, seem to run through the Lord's life on earth. Here emerges a true, deep, human, filial love ; there appears a subdued and measured, but meditated intentional reserve. These facts, I believe, were prophecy ; and upon them, as upon the spoken prophecies, subsequent events have thrown light. He saw the end from the beginning, and so acted from the first ; we now see the beginning from the end, and perceive the reason why he acted thus.

The Mariolatry of modern Rome, lying, like all other events, open before the mind of the Lord during the period of his personal ministry, must have sensibly affected those of his words and actions whose relation to it he, in his omniscience, foresaw. In short—for I desire to throw out this thought frankly and without ambiguity—I believe that the Lord Jesus, deliberately and presciently, adopted towards Mary, the mother of his humanity, precisely that line of conduct by which he might on the one hand sanction by his own example all the relations and affections of the family, and yet, on the other hand, withhold from a great but grossly superstitious community, in these latter days, every semblance of pretext for citing his authority in support of a loathsome idolatry on which he foresaw they should absolutely go mad. Why should we hesitate to accept this solution ? Wist ye not that he must be about the Father's business ? Even in smaller matters we enjoy to-day the benefit of ancient prophecy, not spoken in figurative language, but deeply relieved in historic fact. For what purpose has the Holy Spirit permitted and directed the record to be inserted, in two distinct and far distant portions of Scripture,* that the Apostle Peter was, and continued to be, a married man ? If Rome had chosen any other one of the twelve than Peter as the head of her celibate priesthood, I am not aware that direct proof could have been found in the Scriptures that, in the matter of marriage, the practice of the chief condemned the precepts of his followers. Why, when the family relations of the rest have been permitted to pass into oblivion, as unimportant to the Church, have two witnesses separately testified in Scripture that Peter was a married man ? If you ascribe this to chance, you may ascribe all to chance, and refuse to recognize in the world the traces of an intelligent government. For my part, I see God's finger in the fact; and I read it as a prescient, prophetic condemnation of the Romish celibate—a system that brands a divine ordinance with a stigma of reproach and elevates at its expense a mischievous invention of man.

In presence of the idolatrous worship addressed to Mary, which has been swelling like a tide for ages, and has reached its culmination only in our own day, practically superseding Christ in the devotions of the multitude, I reverence and love with peculiar interest that chastened reserve wherewith Jesus saw meet to modify his filial tenderness throughout

---

* Matthew 8:14, 1 Corinthians 9:5

his intercourse with Mary his mother. Ah, there was no sorrow like unto his sorrow, because there was no knowledge like unto his knowledge of the desperate wickedness which from generation to generation broods in human hearts. In that distance and coolness, approaching almost to coldness, with which he treated Mary, I see the Man of sorrows covering his human filial love, and limiting to the utmost the visible expression of its fervour, that misguided men might not in later ages wrest his words to justify apostasy—might not be able on any pretence to plead his authority for turning aside to trust in another Saviour.

II. Christ in the Gospel establishes, on the same sphere, a new spiritual family.

The Redeemer's mission was to re-establish the relations which sin had broken between God and man, on the one hand, and between man and man on the other. The redeemed on earth are united to their Head and to one another by affections which are completely different from, but not in any sense contrary to, the natural instincts. If any man be in Christ he is a new creature : in the new creature a multitude of new affections spring and flow, but being on a higher level, they never run foul of the affections that expatiate on the lower sphere of temporal things. Mind, conscience, immortality, have been imparted to man, and these faculties have free scope for action ; but those operations of the higher nature do not in any measure impede the inhalation of air, the circulation of the blood, or any of the other processes which belong to us in common with inferior creatures. Now, as mind, acting in another sphere, comes not into collision with the functions of the body, so the new spiritual affections, which belong to us as Christians, do not interfere with the original affections which belong to us as men.

It is a great thing to be in the regeneration a child of God ; it is a great thing to be a brother or a sister in that family, which is already like the stars of heaven in number, and will yet be like them in purity and glory. The new relation is formed, and through the earlier stages of its growth consolidated, while the old relation remains in vigour. The germ of the new sonship and brotherhood is rooted in the heart unseen, without disturbing the sonships and brotherhoods of the present world, which grow thick and fresh all around.

There is a process in agriculture which presents an interesting parallel to the simultaneous and commingling growth of relations for time and relations for eternity in human hearts. A field is closely occupied all over with a growing crop which will soon reach maturity, and will be reaped in this season's harvest. The owner intends that another crop, totally different in kind, shall possess the ground in the following year ; but he does not wait till the grain now growing has been reaped—he goes into the field and sows the seed of the new while the old is still growing and green. In some cases a method is adopted which is, from our present point of view, still more suggestive : the seed which shall complete its functions within the present season, and the seed which, springing this year, shall bear its fruit upwards, are mixed together in the same vessel and scattered together on the same ground. Nor does the one lie dormant for a season while the other monopolizes the soil ; both spring up at the same, or nearly the same time. The plant for the future germinates at once, but it does not reach maturity till the following year ; the plant intended for the present season—the wheat or the barley— grows rapidly and ripens ere the winter come. Lowly, meekly at the roots of the waving grain springs the plant of the future ; it passes through its earlier stages while the tall stalks of the wheat are towering over its head. It springs although the grain is growing on the same spot, and springs better because the grain is growing there. The vigorous growth of another species all around it shelters its feeble infancy ; and after the winter has passed, in another season, it starts afresh and comes forth in its own matured strength.

Thus the affections and relations that belong to the future spring and grow under the shadow of the affections and relations that belong to the present. The Sower who came forth into time to sow a seed that ripens in eternity, did not first cut down and cast away as cumberers of the ground all the natural affections which he found covering its surface with a luxuriant growth ; he sowed the seeds of the future among the growing crop of the present, and these seeds grow better there than in a soil bared of human loves and joys. The seed of the word for eternal life, other things being equal, thrives better in a heart where all the natural emotions of the family circle swell, than in a heart that has been prematurely shorn of human affections, and caged in a cloister for protection from the world. The two seeds are of different kinds, and for different seasons ; there is not a collision of interests when both grow on the same spot and at the same time.

The question whether or how far the ties of nature, as we know them here on earth, will survive or revive in the resurrection, has been often raised, but from the nature of the case cannot be fully answered. The family relations, as they are exercised here, do not go into heaven in the lump,—to this extent the Scriptures definitely inform us ; but how many and how much of them may be permitted to pass through the narrow gate we cannot tell. I would not venture to pronounce that the bonds which so sweetly bind heart to heart on earth, leave no mark of their existence in the world to come. I think it is not probable that those lines which have graven themselves so deeply into our being here will be all blotted out in the middle passage.

One thing strongly favours the supposition that the affections of nature will in some form survive,—the longings of believing hearts certainly do go out with great intensity after their own who die in the Lord. It would seem contrary to the analogy of his ways in other departments, that our Father should plant that desire, or permit it to flourish in his children, if he had provided no satisfaction for it at his own right hand. In this matter I would venture to apply and appropriate the promise of the Lord, " Blessed are they that hunger and thirst : for they shall be filled."

But while we are straining to see where there is hardly any light, a thought, containing all the force of an axiomatic truth, rises up to cheer us,—if those best earthly bonds survive not—if, in heaven, all be the same to all, the absence of individual affections will not constitute any diminution of happiness. If such a levelling of distinctions shall take place in the better land, it will be because love to all the saved brotherhood has risen to such a height that particular affections have been overwhelmed in the flood. If those particular preferences which stand out, to our view, like mountains on the horizon of time, are in eternity altogether lost, they are lost because love to the Lord and all his redeemed has covered them as the ocean covers the vegetation in its bed. If those deep traces of affinity and consanguinity shall be blotted out, they will be blotted out by a river of blessedness that will leave them unregretted, as the childish things which in manhood we forget. Most certainly if, in the place of rest, mother be nothing more to son, and son nothing more to mother, than any of all the redeemed, the love of all to each, and of each to all, in eternity, will be immeasurably greater and sweeter than the most loving heart has ever been able to conceive in this place of pilgrimage. If mothers and brothers melt into the mass, it is not because mothers and brothers become less dear in heaven than they were on earth, but because Christ and all the saved become more dear.

Those stars that studded the dark blue canopy of the sky were lovely : often through the weary night did the lone watcher lift his eyes and look upon them. They seemed to him a sort of company, and, while he gazed on the bright glancing throng, he felt himself for the moment somewhat less lonely. Yet you hear no complaint from that watcher's lips when those stars disappear ; for the cause of their disappearance is the break of day. Either the many fond individual companionships which cheer disciples in the night of their pilgrimage will remain with them, as bright particular stars in the day of eternity, or they will fade away before its dawning : if they remain, their company in holiness will be a thousand-fold more sweet ; if they disappear, it will not be that those joys have grown more dim, but that we do not observe them in the light of a more glorious day.

Two practical lessons, one in the form of a warning, and

the other in the form of an encouragement, depend from the subject visibly, and claim a notice at the close.

1. Reverting again, for a moment, to the analogy of seed for the future sown and springing under the shade of a crop that is growing for the present season, we may gather from nature a caution which is needful and profitable in the department of grace. When this season's crop, amidst which next season's seed was sown in spring, has been cut in harvest and carried home, I have seen the field in whole or in part destitute of the young plants which ought at that time to have covered its surface, the hope of future years. Sometimes after this season's harvest is reaped, no living plant remains in the ground. As you walk over it at the approach of winter, you see rotting stubble, the decaying remnants of one harvest, but no young plants, the promise of another year. Why? Because the first crop has grown too rank in its robust maturity, and overlaid the second in its tender youth. It is somewhat like the heavy slumber of a drunken mother, that quenches the life of her child by night. Ah, it is not safe to feed and fatten too much either the corn of our farm or the natural affections of our hearts : when either grows too gross, it both injures itself and oppresses a more precious plant that is seeking shelter underneath.

The principle of this lesson applies to the business of life as well as the reciprocal affections of kindred. Beware! Open your hearts and take the warning in. Have you hope for pardon and eternal life in the Son of God, the Saviour? Then bear in mind that, under the shade of your city-traffic and your home-joys, a tender plant is growing, native of a softer clime—a plant whose growth is your life, whose decay your ruin, in the great day ; a plant that needs indeed the shelter of honest industry and pure family affections, but dies outright under the choking weight of their over-growth ; and see to it that the profits and pleasures of time do not, by their excess, kill the hope for eternity. What is a man profited although he gain the whole world, if he lose his own soul ?

2. It is ever true, according to the symbolic prophecy of the Apocalypse, that the earth helps the woman—that the occupations and affinities and friendships of this life may and do cherish the growth of grace in the soul. In many ways the loves and cares that appertain to the family institute, growing normally, healthfully vigorous, and not morbidly, feebly rank, do in point of fact shield and stimulate the seed of eternal life that has been sown, and is springing, in the heart. Many a son can tell, and will tell in heaven, that the good seed of the word would have been scorched and blasted, if it had not lain for a time under the kindly shade of home. Many may say with truth, If I had not been born at first in such a family on earth, I probably would not have been born again into the family of God.

Let us be content with our lot ; especially let us beware of fretting against family responsibilities, and the demands of lawful business, as if these were necessarily impediments to the growth of the spiritual life. If these affections and occupations were taken away, the spiritual life, deprived of its shelter, would be burnt by the heat or blasted by the wind. Beware of that intemperate rankness in the growth of temporal affairs which would kill in its infancy the planting of the Lord in your heart ; but fear not when the lawful cares and affections of time spring thick and grow vigorous : God has sown these seeds with his own hand in creation, and he will employ them to cherish and protect that " Christ in you " which is his own special delight. For the safety and the increase of the life of faith, the best place to be in is the place in which God has put you. He that believeth shall not make haste : it is not change of place, or change of occupation, that will make you safe or holy. Shake off sins, as Paul shook the viper from his hand into the fire ; but as to the affections and cares that spring in nature, and accord with the divine law, fear them not when you feel them penetrating your being and warping round all your faculties. All things work together for good to the people of God. His children may thrive equally in circumstances the most diverse ; but if it were his will to give me my choice, I would, even with a view to the prosperity of my soul, request him to plunge me into the tide of merchandise that flows through London, rather than send me, an unemployed annuitant, to some rural retreat ; or to hang on my shoulders the cares of a large family, rather than leave me with nothing but myself to bear. The affections of nature in time, will help and not hinder the affections of grace for eternity; for, each in its own place, both are equally the planting of the Lord.

Trees of Righteousness
(Matthew 12:33)

Part 1

"Make the tree good, and his fruit good."

THERE are two kinds of religion in the world; and perhaps we would not greatly err, if we should say, there are two only. They stand over against each other, not only different but opposite in their essential characteristics; and the manifold varieties that have sprung up in diverse periods and diverse regions, may be classed under the one or the other of these two great normal types.

These two kinds of religion, so radically distinct that they cannot by any art be amalgamated, and yet so comprehensive that they include all religion under their ample folds, are not Christianity and Paganism,—are not Protestantism and Popery,—are not Presbytery and Episcopacy,—are not the Church spiritually free and the Church submitting to Erastian control. The two great genera, which between them comprehend all subordinate species, have distinct natures, but not distinguishing names. They cannot be designated by single words; they must be described by their essential features.

One kind of religion teaches that men are not so holy as they should be, but that by a little attention they may be improved; the other kind of religion confesses that men are all and only evil, and must be made new creatures ere they can be pleasing to God or fit for his presence. The first starts with the assumption of something good to begin with, and busies itself in making good better; the second starts with the assumption that all is evil, and seeks from God the grace to change the evil into good: the one mends, the other makes.

The one looks up to heaven and says, " I am not as other men; I fast, I pray, I give alms:" the other looks down to the earth and cries, " God be merciful to me a sinner." The one builds his house upon the sand, which, while the weather is fair, seems to his eye firm enough: the other refuses to build at all until he get down to the living rock.

Both confess failing; both seek help; and both seek help from Christ. In outward aspect they are like each other; so closely do they resemble each other, that in some aspects they are distinguished only by one little word. One says, Christ and I: the other says, Christ, not I. The one says, I cannot live alone, but I can live if Christ is near me: the other says, I live; nevertheless not I, but Christ liveth in me. The Lord *and* my righteousness, says this man: the Lord my righteousness, says that.

Of these two that seem so familiar, the one is falsehood, the other truth; the one is darkness, the other light.

The great Teacher himself took pains with his pupils on this point. At one time he allowed a self-righteous man to try his own method, that by the fall which it entailed he might be crushed out of his error. " Good master," said a promising scholar once, " Good master, what shall I do that

I may inherit eternal life ?" " Keep the commandments."
" I have kept them ; what more ?" " Go sell all that thou
hast, and give to the poor, and come follow me." Under
this pressure the good resolution broke down ; he went away
sorrowful. On another occasion the Lord taught the same
lesson in a gentler form to a more gentle inquirer : "Except
a man be born again, he cannot see the kingdom of God."

It behoves us to know well this human error that undermines the spiritual life. It springs within, and circulates
secretly but mightily, like the blood in the veins. By making
light of the disease, it makes light also of the cure provided. By failing to estimate aright the fall, it forms a
false judgment regarding the unspeakable gift of God.

It is not indeed written in the creed that mankind are
holy in nature and in life ; but the habit of the heart's
thoughts, flowing strong and steady like a river, counts the
man in the main good, and seeks in religion not the new
creation of the lost, but the gradual improvement of the
defective.

This system takes the word of Christ and turns it upside
down. Christ says, Make the tree good, and his fruit good ;
but it says, Make the fruit good in the first place, and the
tree will improve of its own accord. Leaving the tree as
it grows, this system directs all its energies to the task of
making the fruit good, or at least seem good. It is the
weary work of dropping buckets into empty wells and
growing old in bringing nothing up. It is the labour of a
life-time to gather grapes off thorns and figs off thistles.

The tree has grown from seed. For a while in its infancy it bears no fruit, and it is not expected to bear any.
Before its nature is developed, it neither does good nor evil,
in a tangible or practical form. Its nature and tendencies

are fixed, but they are not known. People who look on the tender plant putting forth its leaves, expect that when it comes to maturity its fruit will be good. At length, while the tree is yet young, it begins to bear fruit. There is not much at first. The quantity is diminutive, but the quality is well defined. There is no mistake here. The fruit is bitter—is bad. But it is young. What could you expect ? Wait for wisdom. They wait, they fence, they water ; but the fruit is still bitter.

In the case of the tree, as long as you look only on its fruit, you may be deceived in your judgment. The fruit may be thoroughly evil, and yet in colour and shape it may be like good fruit. It is only by tasting it that you can certainly determine its character.

Our Father is the husbandman, and we are his husbandry. When we bear fruit, he is not contented with looking on its external appearance. He comes near and tastes it. A man cannot certainly determine the taste of the fruit that his neighbours bear—cannot certainly determine the taste even of his own. " Ye know not what spirit ye are of." Peter did not discern what was the taste of his own soul's emotions ; but his Master knew and loathed it : " Get thee behind me, Satan."

The outward appearance of a gift, for example, may have all the lineaments of charity ; yet to Him who looketh on the heart, it may be a nauseous outgrowth of selfishness or pride. We must be purged from dead works as well as from bad works ere we can acceptably serve the living God. Dead works, though in form they may be the fulfilment of his law, are not sweet to his taste. That is a dreadful sentence which the risen Saviour pronounced on the fruit of a bitter tree : " I will spue thee out of my mouth."

I shall assume that the reader knows in the main how the common fruit trees of our gardens are made good. Instead of explaining the process of engrafting, I shall take for granted that it is known, and proceed at once to deduce and apply the lessons which the Lord's brief parable suggests. The essence of the art consists in this, that the tree is not mended but made new. The old tree is cut off and cast away, and another is inserted in its stead. It is not amelioration, but regeneration. As in man's husbandry, so in God's. Good fruit is attained by *making the tree good.*

I shall now submit a series of lessons suggested by the analogy. Let us prolong for a little our walk through these avenues of nature, gathering as we go the precious fruits of grace. Among these trees of the garden we may now hear, not for judgment, but for mercy, the voice of the Lord God.

I. Although the tree has been made good by engrafting, and has consequently begun to bear good fruit, the young trees that spring from the seed of that good fruit, when it is sown again, take after the original bitter root of the parent tree, and not after the sweetness subsequently imparted to it. Trees that spring from the seed of an evil tree that has been made good, are not good but evil. Bitter is every one, and bitter the fruit it bears, unless and until it put off itself and put on another.

Such is our condition as fallen; such is the law that lives in our members, whether we find out that law or not. The child of a Christian man is not by birth a Christian. We are born into the condition which our parents had by nature, not into the condition into which they may have been brought by grace. It is true that blessings exceeding

rich and precious accrue, in God's covenant, to the children
of believers, in virtue of their relation to godly parents;
but the benefits do not include or amount to safety and
holiness through the natural birthright. " Born not of
blood, nor of the will of the flesh, nor of the will of man,
but of God " (John i. 13). Children, you may learn from
the trees of the garden, and by the teaching of the Lord,
that although your parents are saints on earth or in heaven,
except ye be born again, ye cannot enter their home or
join their company. So far am I from undervaluing the
privilege of descent from the people of God, that every day
I live I learn to give more fervent thanks to God that I
was in this sense the seed of the righteous. I have no
memory of my mother, for soon after my eyes were opened
hers were closed ; but something clearer, stronger than
memory—something allied to faith, but not to sight—has
for many years kept her by my side, as one that walks
with God in white, and gently beckons me to follow her as
she followed Christ. I do not undervalue the privilege of
being by natural birth the seed of the righteous: I know
it ; I enjoy it ; I have been enriched by it, more than they
whose corn and wine have most increased. But I warn all
who enjoy the privilege, that it will not save them. There
is only one Saviour. You cannot be carried into heaven
by clinging to a parent's skirts. Your place in the family
of God's children will aggravate your condemnation, if you
do not yourselves accept Christ as your own ; as they who
fall from the greatest height are most deeply bruised by
the fall.

II. As the first lesson is one of warning to those who
presume upon their privileges, the second lesson is one of

encouragement to those who have had in youth no privileges to presume upon. This lesson, too, we shall read from
the tree that is made good.

Although a young tree has sprung from the seed of an
evil tree, it may be made good by engrafting as easily and as
effectually as if its parent had been the best in the garden.
These two lessons, both on the natural side and the spiritual,
are precisely the converse of each other. The first is
gathered from the natural fact that the tree which springs
from the seed of one that has been made good needs to be
engrafted ere it can become good like its parent ; the
second is gathered from the natural fact that a tree which
has sprung from a parent not made good may by engrafting attain the goodness which its parent never knew. The
one fact teaches that the privileged should not presume ;
the other fact teaches that the unprivileged need not be
despondent.

In point of fact, the cultivator of fruit trees does not
make much distinction between the trees that have sprung
from renewed and those that have sprung from unrenewed
parents. He looks not to the parentage of the original
root, but to the character of the new branch which is
inserted. This new good branch is necessary to the plant
that came from the seed of the best tree ; and it is sufficient for the plant that came from the seed of the worst.
The rule that the character of the tree follows the branch
that has been grafted on as head, and not the root out of
which it has sprung, points equally in two opposite directions and tells in two different results. Pretensions of
good in the root, and fears of evil, are equally destitute of
validity. Those do not count in favour of the tree, and
these do not count against it.

Most necessary and most precious is the corresponding fact in the spiritual sphere. As we have already seen that the goodness of the parents, although they are new creatures in Christ, cannot pass through the natural birth into the children, so as to save them, so we now, in the second place, assuredly gather, that the badness of parents, although they remain in the gall of bitterness and the bond of iniquity, does not penetrate through the conversion of children so as to condemn them. As certain substances, although in quantity small as a quivering film, act as non-conductors, and, when interposed effectually, bar the passage of electricity, however strong may be the current, or however near may be the congenial receiver, so generation is a non-conductor of grace, and regeneration a non-conductor of corruption. Grace, though pulsing strong in the parent, cannot pass through birth into the child; corruption, though pulsing in the parent, and communicated also to the child, cannot pass the regeneration, and reduce the child who is born again into the spiritual condition of the unconverted parent.

The cultivator of fruit trees can make as good a tree from the progeny of an evil parent as from the progeny of a good parent; so our Father, the husbandman, is wont, in his own inscrutable purposes, to create again in Christ many children whose parents remain in sin.

I have endeavoured to utter a needed warning to those who are descended from godly parents: Beware of a false hope; ye *must* be born again. I now, in turn, address a word of glad encouragement to children who have not known these privileges: Give not way to false fear; ye *may* be born again.

The promise runs not, Him that is born of a godly

parent, but, Him that cometh, I will in nowise cast out. Some of the bitterest reproaches cast against Christ in the days of his flesh became hymns to his praise. The wrath of man praised him when enemies exclaimed, " This man receiveth sinners."

To those who were not in childhood brought up in the nurture and admonition of the Lord—who either had no living father, or, sadder still, a father of whom they had cause to be ashamed—comfort and encouragement spring here. There is no respect of persons with God. The rule of the kingdom is, Whosoever will. His father's light did not bring one child into the kingdom, and his father's darkness did not keep another out. The owner of a garden, when he is about to make his young trees good by engrafting, scarcely inquires which of them sprang from renewed trees, and which from trees that remained in the bitterness of nature. Placing all on a level, and treating all alike, he engrafts them all, and all the engrafted become good : in due time all bring forth good fruit together.

Of these two classes, the church on earth—of these two classes, heaven on high is full ; and, as they mingle in the praises of their Lord, nor man nor angel can distinguish between them. In the general assembly and church of the first-born, it will never be said, This one was the son of a saint, and that one the son of a sinner. These distinctions are lost ; they were written only in the earth, and the earth with its records will be burnt up. The son of a saint cannot be distinguished in the circle ; he wears not a whiter robe, he bears not a fresher palm, he sings not a sweeter song than his neighbour. One baptism has blotted all distinctions out, and one description serves to designate all the throng,—They have washed their robes and made them white in the blood of the Lamb.

Privileged, beware! What will your name to live avail you if you be dead? If you are not "found in Him," nothing in heaven or earth can open the door to let you in.

Destitute, be encouraged! Arise, lo He calleth you. If you come at his call, all the sins that ever defiled man, and all the devils that ever tempted him, cannot shut the door to keep you out.

Trees of Righteousness
(Matthew 12:33)

Part 2

" Make the tree good, and his fruit good."

ALTHOUGH an evil tree ought to be made good by engrafting while it is young, it may be made good by engrafting after it has grown old. Such also is the law of the kingdom in regard to spiritual life. A man may indeed be born into God's family when he is old; but it is in all respects better if he enters the childhood of grace before he has emerged from the childhood of nature.

In fruit-trees fully grown you may sometimes observe a ring round the stem, midway between the ground and the branches, resembling somewhat the mark of a healed wound on a living man. This indicates the place where the natural stem was cut off and a new branch inserted. You perceive at a glance that this tree has been engrafted, and that it was well grown ere it was made good. In the same garden another tree may grow which exhibits no such mark; yet the owner does not value it less on that account. These two trees are equally good and equally prolific. They differ not in their present character but

in the period of life at which they were severally renewed.
This latter tree must have been engrafted when it was
very young : the cut was made close to the ground when
the stem was very slender ; and thus the mark has been
obliterated by the subsequent growth of the tree. The
cicatrice is concealed under the grass, or perhaps under the
ground. The renewing has certainly taken place, but
when or where no man can tell. The date of its new
birth is no longer legible.

Such similarities and such differences obtain also among
converted men. Some who were born when they were
old bear the mark of their regeneration all their days.
When the old nature was matured and developed before
the change, the memory of the fact is more distinctly
retained, and the contrast more vividly displayed. It was
thus in the experience of the Apostle Paul. The spiritual
man did not in his case obtain the sway while the natural
was yet young and tender and easily moulded. Paul was
a man, every inch of him, before he was a Christian. " I
verily thought with myself that I ought to do many
things contrary to the name of Jesus of Nazareth ; which
thing I also did " (Acts xxvi. 9, 10). His principles and
his conduct were strong and consistent, while both were
contrary to God and man. When such a character was
changed, the change was manifest, and the mark of it
permanent. That fall and rising again on the way to
Damascus stood out a well-marked girdle round the mighty
stem of his life, even to its close. He frequently pointed
to that healed wound as evidence both of his enmity
against God and God's marvellous mercy to him. But
Paul's son Timothy was not less surely in the Lord, although no such great landmark towered in the heart of

his history. This tree was made good while it was yet young, and ere its native badness had got full room to reveal itself. The healed wound in this disciple's life lay so near the root that in maturity it could not be seen.

In heaven these two may lovingly contend with each other, either striving to show that himself is the more deeply indebted to sovereign, redeeming love. God showed a peculiar mercy to me, says Timothy, in that he made the tree good while it was young, ere yet it had begun to bear visible fruit. But God showed greater mercy to me, the apostle rejoins, in that he made the tree good, although it had grown old in evil, and spread much bitter fruit over the whole land. Those who, by a great rending, have been converted in mature age, bear the fact in memory, and weave it into their songs of praise; but, on the other hand, let not those who have been earlier and more insensibly won to Christ complain that the mark of their engrafting is not visible as a girdle round the middle of their life. There are diversities of operation, but the same Spirit.

All's well that ends well: God's way is best; all his people will see this truth, and sing it yet. But if you ask me what choice I should make, if choice in the matter were given to me, I would rather be one of the converted who could not tell the time or manner of his conversion, than one of those who were born when they were old, and bear many scars as monuments of the agony. The aged are not shut out from hope, but the earliest time is the best time.

It is a peculiar glory of the gospel that it holds out free pardon and immediate peace to the chief of sinners, whether that chiefdom in evil may have been won by quantity of work or length of service. The blood of Jesus Christ cleanseth us from all sin.

You may see this glory of grace reflected from the field of nature. Perhaps you have looked over the hedge and seen, in a garden by the wayside, a sight that attracted your eye and excited your curiosity. A tree, old, thick, and rusty, has been cut off, not by the ground, but about the height of a man, and the bare stump left standing. On a closer inspection you see one or more small fresh twigs fastened to the bark on the top of the desolate trunk. They are budding and putting out green leaves. It is a tree that had grown old, either barren or bearing bad fruit. Its owner would not longer permit it to occupy uselessly the precious ground. But it is not necessary that he should cut it down and cast it away, in order to make room for another tree. Even this tree, grown old in evil, may be made good. It is not cut down, but cut off, and a new nature engrafted on its stem. Even in old age it will yet be fresh, and flourishing, and fruitful. The owner of the garden counts that he will sooner get a large return by engrafting the old tree than by rooting it out and planting another. The tree was full grown and in vigorous health. The owner will utilize all these powers by sending the sap through a new and better head. It is thus that our Father, the husbandman, takes full-grown vigorous natures, charged with gifts of understanding, and eloquence, and zeal, that have been hitherto occupied with evil, and makes them new creatures by his power. Forthwith they are fit for able-bodied service in the work of the Lord.

It is a very gladsome truth for an evil world—that a man may be born when he is old. Blessed be God, it is possible that he who has long been accustomed to do evil may by union to Christ become a new creature. Certain places, much desired under the government of the country, are open only to the young. If you do not enter before you attain a certain specified age you can never enter. The rule there is not, Him that cometh, but, Him that cometh while he is young. This is not the rule in the kingdom of God. There is no alien on earth too old for being admitted into the family of God.

The truth which I have stated is too precious to be held back or only spoken in a whisper, lest some should abuse it. It is true, self-deceivers will abuse it to encourage themselves in sin; but if this truth were concealed, they would find some other pretext.

Let the warning be distinctly, fully given on the other side. If the tree is permitted to grow up and grow old in evil, there is danger lest, by storm or fire, it should be destroyed, and so never be made good. But even although it were insured against all accidents, there is no reason why another, and yet another year an evil tree should cumber the ground, merely to put off the time of its change. Who would say, Permit it to bear bitter fruit all the time of its youth, and make it good only when it has grown old? If any one should make this proposal, the fact would prove that he was not sincere, that he did not wish the tree made good.

The plea that there is time enough, when advanced by way of deferring the period of decision, is not only delusive and dangerous, it is positively false and dishonest. Men postpone only what they dislike. You will not decisively follow the Lord now, but you will some day. But if you have no desire to be good and do good to-day, you have no desire to be good and do good any day. There is no such thing as putting off for a time : it is simply, We will not have this man to reign over us. You want to waste the broad sunny surface of life in pursuing your own pleasures, and you promise to throw a narrow strip of the outmost edge of life, withered and tasteless, as an offering to the Lord. Be not deceived ; he who is weary of sin wants to be quit of it now. He who hungers wants the bread of life to-day, not to-morrow. Blessed are they that hunger.

IV. A tree that has been made good does not again become evil ; but evil latent in its roots may, if it be not watched and crushed, spring up and bear bad fruit, and mingle with the good, and to a great extent outgrow and choke the good. The same law obtains in the spiritual sphere. The old man is more or less active in every Christian. Thoughts and desires are continually springing up from the old stock—thoughts and desires that do not belong to the new creature. If these are not in good time crucified, they will bear fruit in actual wickedness; and when they are permitted to bear, the fruit of the better nature will disappear for the time, or become very small in quantity.

One clear example of this tendency I knew well in my youth. I think it remains to this day, and I could point to the spot. A grove given over, by the time I knew it, for the purpose of affording shady pleasure-walks, had originally been a fruit-garden. Some of the old fruit-trees had been left standing as ornaments, when the owner no longer looked for a profitable return. These trees were left growing for the sake of their beauty merely, not for the sake of their fruit. They were allowed, accordingly,

to run wild, that their appearance might be more pictur-
esque. An aged pear-tree stood there, with a tall, bare,
straight stem and round bushy head like an Eastern palm.
But while not a single branch grew on the naked trunk,
from where it emerged out of the moss to where its head
began to spread at three times the height of a man, a
number of lively vigorous shoots sprang from its roots, or
rather from its stem where it touched the ground. Thus
the long bare stem had a bushy head of branches on either
extremity. These lower branches had been permitted to
grow freely till they reached maturity on their own account,
and bore fruit of their own kind. I have seen fruit growing on these suckers, and fruit hanging at the same time
high over them on the tree's towering head, with a large
portion of the bare stem between. I have compared them,
and found that which grew from the old root hard and
bitter, while that which grew on the head that had been
made new, although somewhat deteriorated, retained still
the sweet flavour of its best days.

Here were two kinds of fruit growing at the same time
on one tree—evil fruit growing on the original root, and
good fruit growing on that which had been made new. If
the tree had been rightly cultivated for the sake of its
fruit, those suckers would have been without pity torn
off in the bud as soon as they showed themselves, and
never have been permitted to open their blossoms or bring
forth their fruit. You do not ordinarily see these out-
growths from the old stock growing to the size of bearing,
on fruit-trees. This, however, is not because they do not
manifest a tendency to throw out these shoots, but because
the shoots are, in ordinary cases, wrenched off by the husbandman as soon as they appear.

Here is a parable. I saw that tree with its two kinds of fruit, and got it insensibly photographed on my memory as a curiosity, before I learned the lesson which it taught. It remains before my imagination to-day, the same object; but it has now become a glass in which I see reflected myself and my fellows. The lesson contains both reproof and encouragement.

Reproof.—There remains in a Christian something of the old carnal mind. This corruption in the root is continually sending out thoughts and purposes of its own. These, if neglected, will soon ripen into manifold sins. Forewarned, forearmed. Watch and pray. Crucify the flesh with its affections and lusts. Kill those suckers that spring from the carnal root. Kill them day by day as they appear: beware of permitting them to make head.

Encouragement.—When acts appear in a Christian—yourself or your neighbour—acts unlike his place and his name, you should not thereby be driven into despair. An unchristian act done by a man does not prove that the man is not a Christian. Perhaps some may think this is a dangerous doctrine. No; it is a true doctrine, and truth is safe in the long run. The contrary doctrine would extinguish hope; and wanting hope, what would become of holiness? If a sinful act done is held to prove that the doer is not in Christ, the nerve that sustains effort is cut, and the soul sinks soon in absolute despair.

In the man, as in the tree, two natures meet. The old man has been made new; and yet the old man, in a sense, remains. From this remaining original evil the evil thoughts and words spring; while from the new man spring thoughts and words that are good. He cannot sin because he is born of God (1 John iii. 9). Two natures struggle in the man, as two nations in the womb of the Hebrew mother. In his perplexity and amazement, the distracted spirit cries out, Why am I thus ? The true solution is that which brave Paul reached after a sharp conflict, " It is no more I that do it, but sin that dwelleth in me."

That tree, with its two natures, and its two kinds of fruit, which I knew so well in my youth, was the shadow and the symbol of David the king. In his busy working days his fruit was good. The tendencies of the old corrupt nature were kept down. But when he sat upon a luxurious throne, and thought only of his pleasure, the old corruptions sprang up in strength, and vile fruit ripened on the lower, baser part of his being. But even this, vile though it was, did not cast the king out of the covenant. Even this rank outgrowth from a bitter root did not wrench the king's head from its place on high. It wasted his faculties for a time in carnal indulgence, and left his better being shrivelled and barren; but when the Husbandman, displeased yet loving, visited his tree, and by terrible things in righteousness hewed off the low indulgences, the head revived again, and even in old age was fat and full of sap and flourishing.

V. Although the natural head of the tree either in youth or age is cut off, and the new good branch brought near to touch it, unless the new branch take to the old tree, and the old tree at its wound take to the new branch, so that they become one, no change will be effected in the old tree. The wounding—the cutting off with a view to engrafting—will produce no effect if the process is interrupted before it is completed. The cutting of the tree makes it bleed—makes it languish as in pain, but does not make it good. After that wound it will grow again, and its fruit will be evil as before.

In this aspect also the law of the spiritual kingdom follows the law of the natural. The sword of the Spirit cuts deep into the heart and conscience. The terrors of the Law overwhelm the soul like a flood. The countenance that formerly was radiant is now fixed in gloom. The fountains of the great deep are broken up, and the penitent makes his bed to swim with tears. Oh, wretched man that I am, who shall deliver me? What is this? Is it the godly sorrow that leads to peace in believing? We cannot tell; no man can yet tell what is the nature of this sorrow, or what will be its fruit. As far as man can observe, it is such a grief that goes before the living hope. They who are now rejoicing in the Lord have passed through such fire and water ere they reached their wealthy place. But not every one who enters this deep gets through it into safety on the other side.

The wounds of conviction prepare the way for Christ; but if the wounded do not in the end close with Christ, his wounds will not make him safe or holy. If he has been pierced by conviction, and thrown into alarm about his sin, his pain should give the Saviour, the Healer, a welcome into his heart; but if, notwithstanding his fright, he keep the door shut, the fright will not renew the man.

The great outstanding specimen of this process is the experience of Felix. His convictions were terrible, but they did not make his heart new. As the tree, after being cut through, grows up again an evil tree, unless at the wounded place a new branch has been inserted, so a man that has trembled between a sight of his own guilt and the approach of the judgment, grows up as unjust, as unclean, as intemperate as before, unless, while he is in distress, he close in simple faith with Christ the Saviour.

LESSONS OF GRACE

Adam, a Type of Christ
(Romans 5:14)

" Adam......who is the figure [type] of Him that was to come."

T HIS is the earliest of all the types: in time, it comes first; in position, it lies deepest. There are none before it—none beneath it. Bowing down from heaven in love, God the Spirit grasps the first fact of man's history, and therewith prints the lesson of man's redemption. There was no delay, for the King's matter required haste. The Giver was prompt and eager; the receivers have been indolent and slow.

Mark the nature of the relation that subsists between a type and its letter—between a seal and its impression. There are at once likeness and diversity; they are the same, and yet they are opposite. The type, whether it be a single letter or a varied landscape, is of the same size and shape as the object which its impress leaves behind; and every several point or turn in the one has an equal and corresponding point or turn in the other; and yet there is a complete and pervading difference, or rather contrariety, between them. Look first to the engraving on a seal, and then to the image which it has left on wax: the two are in certain aspects the same, and yet they are reciprocally opposite. They agree, and yet they are antagonist. The left of this is the right of that: where this reveals a hollow, that exhibits a height: where this is shaded, that lies in the light. In their whole aspect they are the reverse of each other.

After this manner is Adam a type of Christ. In some aspects there is likeness; and in others, not only diversity, but contrariety. Observe first the *agreement*, and then the *difference*.

I. The agreement or similarity.

1. Adam and Christ were the true sources or heads of their respective families.

There are two conceivable methods of constituting humanity. Whether both were possible, in consistence with all the attributes of God, we cannot tell. One is, to make men such that each should be absolutely independent of all, and the conduct, good or bad, of any one should have no effect, physical or moral, on the condition of any of the rest. The other is, to constitute the race such that the first man should be the head and source of humanity, and that the state and tendencies of all should be determined by the standing or the falling of this one.

This latter method our Maker has adopted, and it is useless to agitate the question whether the other method would, in its own nature, have been honourable to God and salutary for men. When the bird is shut up within an iron cage, it is better for itself that it should not dash itself against the bars. It was in an attempt to be as God that our first parents fell. If we would escape their fault and fate, we should abandon speculations on what might have been and address ourselves to what is. We are men ––creatures with a short lease and a narrow boundary.

Let us leave with God the things that are God's, and evidently require omniscience for their solution, and let us mind our own business.

In point of fact we all come into the world with darkened minds and wayward hearts. As water flows down and sparks fly up, human beings, as they emerge successively into consciousness, turn aside into sin and fall into suffering. The grandest of God's works is most awry and out of joint. The highest creature falls furthest short of fulfilling its destiny. The Scriptures, acknowledging this fact, explain it by the *Fall*.

Some people complain much of the difficulties which they find in the Scriptures regarding this subject. A serious mistake is made, however, in the statement of the question. The difficulty lies, not in the Scriptures, but in the fact : it would have been all there although there had never been a Bible. Creatures manifestly the head of creation, having an intellectual and moral nature in conjunction with an exquisite physical frame, under the government of a Being who is at once omnipotent and beneficent, lie weltering in sin and suffering, like the sea when it cannot rest. This state of things has endured from age to age, without intermission and without mitigation. This is the difficulty ; all the difficulties that you meet in the Bible are small when compared with this. The aim of the Bible is to throw light on the darkness ; but even if some parts of the scene remain obscure, we have no right to lay the blame of the obscurity on that which, to some extent at least, has brought us light.

The first man, according to the actual constitution of humanity, stood as head and representative of the race. His fall brought all down. At the head he stands, and from him the long line stretches away down the course of time. Two hundred generations constitute the links of the chain, and its length extends to six thousand years.

At first the line of march is narrow : on the apex one ; and behind him two or three walk abreast : broader and broader grows the stream as it recedes from the source, until, in our day, the file of march is a million of millions deep. Adam, like the point of the wedge, stands on the summit, a unit alone ; the generations in the ranks immediately beneath him are numbered by tens, and anon by hundreds, until they have in our day reached a number that can indeed be expressed in figures, but cannot be adequately comprehended by finite minds.

On the other side stands the second Adam—he that was to come. Alone he stands at the head ; and his also shall be a numerous offspring. Here and there, in the earliest ages, appears a righteous Abel offering faith's sacrifice, or a righteous Enoch walking in newness of life with God. Yonder a Noah preaches righteousness over a world lying in wickedness ; and here an Abraham is called from his home and his kindred to a better country and a higher life. Broader now is the line of their marching since Christ came in the flesh. Already a multitude, which no man can number, tread the pilgrim's path, and shall in due time enter the joy of their Lord. All the redeemed in heaven and on earth are Christ's,—their life as certainly flowing from and dependent on him as the natural life of humanity flows from the first man.

The chief feature of similarity between the figure and the greater fact which it predicts is that each stands for all his own ; and this principle of God's government, introduced at the beginning, runs through to the end.

The line of march was suddenly changed at the resurrection of Christ. Then the column left the narrow track of Palestine, and overflowed on the wide field of the world. Admitted into the capital of the Gentiles when Jerusalem fell, it speedily found a larger sphere and became a more numerous company. As centuries pass, it grows still greater; and now we look wistfully forward to that time when it shall reach from sea to sea—when the kingdom of Christ shall absorb the kingdoms of the world—when the stream of the second Adam's children shall be co-extensive and coincident with that of the first.

2. These two representatives stood side by side from the first, and redemption began to flow from Christ as soon as sin was brought in by Adam. The promise did not tarry; it sprang at the gate of Eden, an echo of the curse. When the first man fell, and so entailed on all his posterity an inheritance of woe, Christ, within the veil unseen, began to be the head of a new and saved family. In eternity within he dwelt, and there he began to act the head of the redeemed the moment that the first man outside became the head of a fallen race. An impenetrable partition veiled off the unseen from the eyes of men; but the Redeemer within the veil, delighting from the first in his saving work, approached the curtain, and often permitted softened rays of his glory to shine through.

Let a veil be hung up impervious to light and vision; it may yet be such that a magnet within will, when brought near the boundary, attract kindred objects on the outer side. You may observe them to quiver and move, and lift themselves mysteriously off the ground. The magnetic power from within grasps the objects that lie without, and leads them whithersoever it will. Under the Patriarchal and Jewish economies many felt the drawing of Christ's love who never with the bodily eyes beheld Christ. Caught by the deepest affections of their souls, they arose from the dust, and quivered tremulously after him, whom having not seen they had yet learned to love.

Similarly in the days of his personal ministry, although he manifested himself only to the lost sheep of the house of Israel, he had compassion on the surrounding heathen, and hastened forward to the day of their redemption. On one occasion he walked to the boundary of his allotted sphere, and touched the coasts of Tyre and Sidon. In that outer land a Syrophenician woman felt the drawing of his love, and followed him—the first fruit of the Gentiles to Christ.

3. Another point of likeness lies in this, that on both sides equally it is by birth that the members are united to their head and his destiny. It is by birth that we are knit to our inheritance of sin. If we had not descended by birth from a fallen father, we would not have been in this condition of sin and misery.

The thought sometimes presses for admission—What if we had never been born; or if we had descended from the holy?—but the conception is too hard for us. The mind cannot bear its weight; to entertain it long would overwhelm our faculties. Not only is the thing impossible of attainment; the conception of it exceeds our power.

We have been born to this inheritance of sin and suffering; we cannot shake it off. We may weep over the discovery of our sad condition, and cry with an exceeding great and bitter cry, "Oh, wretched man that I am! who shall deliver me?" but to that cry, apart from the gospel revealed, no comforting answer can ever come. The depths saith, " It is not in me :" it is not in earth, it is not in heaven, to cause that to be not which is. By birthright our dark heritage is ours, and the link that binds us to it we cannot break. We are in it, and cannot escape.

But be of good cheer, prisoner of hope : the chain that binds you by birth to the first Adam, it is true, cannot be broken ; but if by a corresponding new birth you are one with the second Adam, you have no cause to weep. Greater is He that is for you than all that be against you. You cannot, indeed, escape from being a man ; but if you are a new creature in Christ Jesus, the second birthright is as irrevocable as the first. If you are once born, nothing can separate you from your heritage, except to be re-born. But if you are born again, nothing can separate you from your new inheritance. Both birth-bonds are indissoluble. Though the weight of a world were fixed to you, and flung into infinite space, it would not avail to wrench you off your stem in Adam, with all the twofold death that it involves ; but though all the weight of a world were fixed to a member of Christ, and flung free into infinitude, it could not separate the living member from the life-giving Head.

It is a fixed principle of natural science that species do not change. In the material department of God's creation there is no way over from one nature to another : once in a nature always in it, without a new creation. But that which is impossible with man is possible with God. He has undertaken in the gospel to make a *new* creature. As the principle operates in the first Adam's posterity, so it operates in the second Adam's posterity. " I am persuaded that neither death, nor life, nor things present, nor things to come, nor height, nor depth, nor any other creature, shall be able to separate us from the love of God, which is in Christ Jesus our Lord" (Rom. viii. 38, 39).

II. The difference.

The chief point of contrast lies in this, that whereas Adam's seed derive from their head sin and death, Christ's seed derive from their Head righteousness and life. This birth is meanness; that is honour: this birth is darkness; that is light: this birth is death; that is life.

One of the strangest facts in human history—a fact which I suppose angels desire to look into, and yet shudder when they see—is that multitudes of the human race are proud of their first birth, and do not give themselves any concern about a second. They count the little great, and the great little; the evil good, and the good evil. Woe to them that so turn upside down the very ground themselves must stand upon!

This contrast between the type and the thing which it represents is over all. The two are in this respect not only unlike each other, but complete and absolute contraries.

Under this, however, there are many specific points of difference.

1. While Adam's seed in this world possess the moral nature of their head complete, Christ's seed possess the moral nature of their Head only in part. We get the evil in full, the good only in part. It comes about in this way: When we derive a sinful nature from the first man, we have previously no other and better nature, that may mingle with it and mitigate its evil; we possess the evil all, and the evil only. The imagination of the thoughts of his heart are only evil, and that continually. In me, that

is in my flesh—in all that I derive from man my father—there dwelleth no good thing.

But on the other hand, the regeneration is not the birth of a being who did not previously exist. It is the getting of a new nature, indeed, and that a holy one, through union in spirit with Christ, the holy Man; but it is gotten by one who previously possessed an evil nature, and that evil nature is not wholly cast away. It is cast down from the throne, but not cast forth from the territory. It no longer reigns, but it continues to disturb. The old mingles with and spoils the new. The two contend against each other; and there is not peace, but a sword. The actual life of a Christian, accordingly, is neither wholly carnal nor wholly spiritual—it is neither a straight line in the direction of goodness, nor a straight line in the direction of badness; it is a sort of diagonal, traced by the opposite pressure of the two forces. (See Rom. vii.)

The union with Christ in the regeneration is likened to the grafting of a fruit-tree. Now the tree at the first, which springs from seed, is wholly evil—root and branch. When it is grafted it is made good; but not so completely as it was originally made evil. Its head is taken away; but its root, and the lower portion of the stem, are left living in the ground. On this old stump a new and good branch is grafted. It is the new branch that grows upward and bears the fruit, but it must lean on and get its life-sap through the old root and stem of the old evil tree. Although the good head ingrafted always brings forth good fruit, the old evil root is continually putting forth shoots and buds and blossoms of its own, that are evil, and that waste the strength which should go to the good.

A similar defect, from a similar cause, adheres to Chris-

tians as long as they are in this life. They are still the
same persons that they were before. The lower parts
remain: the physical frame and the intellectual faculties
remain; it is the higher or spiritual nature that has been
radically changed. The old spirit has been taken away,
and a new spirit inserted. The seed of Christ in the higher
part has been inserted in the seed of Adam in the lower
part; and, alas! the fruit that grows even on a Christian
tastes of the old corrupt root on which it still stands and
grows.

In some way, we know not how, the remnants of the
old will be filtered out in the dissolution of death; and
nothing shall enter heaven that would defile its golden
streets or be a jar in its new song.

2. The two bands are not equally numerous. Adam's
company includes absolutely the whole of the human race;
Christ's company is contained within it, and is therefore
necessarily smaller, as the whole is greater than a
part.

"As in Adam all die, so in Christ shall all be made
alive" (1 Cor. xv.). These words do not intimate that the
two companies are co-extensive and coincident: no man
with his eyes open can read the words in their connection,
and think that this is their meaning. The meaning is, In
Adam, Adam's all die; in Christ, Christ's all live. It tells
that all who are in Adam die, and all who are in Christ
live; but it does not tell how many either company contains. We know certainly from other scriptures that Adam's
company consists of all the born, and Christ's of all the
born-again. To cleave to the letter here, and understand
it to announce that all the human race are actually saved
in Christ, contradicts the whole spirit of the Scriptures,

and makes both their exhortations and their warnings of none effect.

God's creatures of the old and new creation seem to envelop each other, after the manner of a sphere within a sphere, the most precious being embedded in the heart. Humanity, comparatively small in bulk, is surrounded by the mightier mass of the inferior creatures, the beasts that perish. Men, immortal, made in God's image, lie in the heart like the kernel, and all inferior organized beings encompass it like a huge husk.

The husk will in due time rend and rot and return to the dust. But within the mass of humanity that remains is an inner seed, encased around by a harder, rougher shell. In the heart of humanity lie the regenerate—the true, vital seed of the kingdom; and the crust that surrounds them, compact and highly organized though it be, will crumble and be cast away. The Bridegroom and they that were ready went in to the marriage; and the rest were shut out. When the earth and all that it contained have passed away, Christ and Christians will remain, inheritors together and alone of the eternal life.

3. Another point of difference. Although we inherit this corruption from the first man, we personally have no immediate relation to him. We inherit directly from our own immediate forefathers. With Adam we have no personal relation, in the matter of a descending moral taint. Although it came from the first man originally, we received it from the last that stood before us in the line. If we could suppose our first progenitor to be from this time forth annihilated, we should remain in the same state as to inherited corruption. We derived it not immediately from him, but from our nearest father.

It is not thus in the relation between Christ and Christians. It is from him that their life flows as its fountain. But further: each generation of believing men, down to the end of the world, continue to draw their spiritual life and justifying righteousness directly and immediately from the person of Emmanuel. It is not that Christ gave forth a germ of new spiritual life, once for all, and that each new generation of Christians derive their better life from those that went immediately before them. No; the new creature does not propagate its kind. A Christian now gets his life as directly from Christ as those who lay in his bosom or sat at his feet. Death once imparted at the sources of humanity, runs down its stream; but life imparted to one man by the God-man Christ, needs to be equally imparted to every saved sinner, by personal relation with the Saviour. If the first Adam were annihilated, the born of the human race would still be born in sin; but if Christ were no more Christ, there could be no more for any man a new, a holy life.

The difference is somewhat like that which may be found in nature between a tree propagating its kind by seed on the one hand, and a tree sustaining its branches on the other. When once the seed is ripened and cast, the progenitor tree may be burned; from the seed, trees of the same kind will spring. But even when the branch has been put forth by the tree, the branch is every year, and all the year, directly dependent on the tree. If the tree should die, all the branches would die too. The corruption we inherit from Adam, as the seed has come from the tree; the new life we can only have in Christ, as the branch lives in the vine. Adam might say, I was the tree, and ye grew from the seed which I shed; but Christ says, I am the vine, ye are the branches.

And as Christians hold directly of Christ, Christ holds individually by Christians. The Vine bleeds and languishes when the branches are torn away : " Saul, Saul, why persecutest thou me ?" The Head endures pain when the members are injured. How safe is that life which is hid with Christ in God !

4. Yet another point of difference. The gain by the second Adam is greater than the loss by the first. The scripture intimates, indeed, that there is a likeness,—that Adam is a figure of Christ. But having made the intimation of the similarity, it proceeds immediately to intimate that there is also a dissimilarity : " But not as the offence, so also is the free gift. For if through the offence of one many be dead, much more the grace of God, and the gift by grace, which is by one man, Jesus Christ, hath abounded unto many " (v. 15). The gain in Christ is not merely the loss that we sustained made up. He pays our debt, and makes us rich besides. He sets free the slave, and makes him a son. " Where sin abounded, grace did much more abound." A blessed word this " much more" !

There is a mystery here. We may stand on the brink of this great deep, and reverently gaze into its far-receding, limitless light ; but this is a thing which we cannot fully comprehend ; and attempts to be wise in it above what is written may do us serious harm. In Christ we are far better than we would have been as unfallen children of Adam. Had we entered the society of heaven as men that had kept their first estate, we should have been accepted as perfect men ; but when a ransomed sinner is admitted to the joy of the Lord and the company of angels, he enters as one with Him who sits upon the throne. With man unfallen, there would, as far as we can see, have been no incarnation of the Eternal Son. God in Christ would not have been so near to us ; we would not have been so near to him. The unfallen would have been good servants ; but the ransomed, by brotherhood of nature with the Divine Redeemer, have attained the place of beloved children.

Great was the joy set before our Redeemer when he undertook our cause ; great is the joy he is reaping now when his work is finished. He has gotten a multitude, like the stars of heaven, nearer to himself, and higher than the angels. God compels evil to become the instrument of good on a wider sphere than this world. When a portion of the angels fell, that fall, by omniscient forethought and infinite love, was so directed that it set agoing a process which never ceased until it had raised from the dust a countless family of God's children to a higher place than angels ever held.

This hope might be the source of unmeasured joy to believers. This union to the Lord that bought us, and this destined elevation to sit with him upon his throne, should surely cheer us in the house of our pilgrimage. This promised dawn should give us songs in the night. But he who hath *this* hope in HIM should purify himself even as He is pure. No unfair or foul thing should lodge in the bosom of the man who is already in a flutter of expectation, as not knowing what moment he may be called into the presence of the Great King.

Epistles of Christ
(2 Corinthians 3:2-3)

"Ye are our epistle written in our hearts, known and read of all men......
manifestly declared to be the epistle of Christ ministered by us, written not
with ink, but with the Spirit of the living God; not in tables of stone, but in
fleshy tables of the heart."

FROM the example of the Master, Paul had acquired
the habit, in his teaching, of gliding softly and
quickly from a common object of nature to the
deep things of grace. In his conversation with
the woman of Samaria, for example, Jesus led his scholar,
ere she was aware, from the water of Jacob's well to the
water of life. In like manner, the apostle of the Gentiles
was accustomed to make any common topic that arose the
stepping-stone by which he carried his pupils over into the
concerns of the kingdom of God.

In this case, the question concerned the testimonials
which a minister or missionary might present when he
reached a new sphere. The practice of asking and obtaining certificates seems to have been introduced at a very
early period into the Christian Church. Already, in Paul's
time, some abuses had crept in along with it. A minister
of very moderate gifts, or even of doubtful soundness,
might carry in his pocket a voucher signed by some great
names. We may gather from this epistle that some very

well recommended missionaries had been spoiling Paul's work at Corinth.

Virtually challenged to exhibit his own certificates, he boldly appeals to the profession and the life of those who had been converted through his ministry. He does not need to present letters of recommendation to them when he comes to Corinth, or to request letters of recommendation from them when he goes away : " Ye are our epistle." The work which God had done by him is evidence that God has sent him to work. He will not deign to submit any other proof of his call.

But Paul always reckons himself a small subject. Although compelled sometimes to introduce it, he will not dwell on it. The conception of the disciples being an epistle to recommend him is no sooner brought in than it is abandoned. He glides instantly into a greater thing. The Christians are an epistle of Christ. Their lives are a letter in which men may learn the Lord.

Regarding these living epistles of Christ, consider,—

I. The paper, or *material*, on which the marks are made.—Many different substances have been employed in successive ages of the world to receive and retain a written language ; but one feature is common to all,—in their natural state they are not fit to be used as writing materials. They must undergo a process of preparation. Even the primitive material of stone must be polished on the surface ere the engraving begin. All the rough places must be made smooth, otherwise the writing would not be legible. The precious stones containing the names of the twelve tribes, and together constituting the high priest's breastplate, were not capable of taking the engraving on when first the Hebrews found them. Much labour was expended ere all the sharp corners were rubbed off, and a glassy polish imparted to the surface. The reeds, and leaves, and skins, too, which were used as writing materials by the ancients, all needed a process of preparation. Therein they are like the living epistles of Jesus Christ, who must be renewed in the spirit of their minds ere they can show forth the Redeemer's likeness in their lives.

But the preparation of modern materials for writing, although it was not before the apostle's mind when he wrote this text, contains, in fact, more points of likeness to the renewing and sanctifying of believers than any of the ancient arts.

Although Paul does not here directly refer to paper—a substance not invented when he wrote—there is a remarkable likeness between the method employed in its manufacture and that work of the Spirit by which a human life becomes fit to receive and exhibit an epistle of Christ. Filthy rags are the raw material of the manufacture. These are with great care and labour torn into very small pieces and washed very clean. They are then cast into a new form, and brought out pure and beautiful, ready to get a new meaning impressed on their smooth, bright breast. Paper from rags is, in an obvious and important sense, a *new creature*. It has been cleansed from its filthiness. There is now no spot nor wrinkle upon it, nor any such thing.

A similar process takes place every time that a writing material is prepared for receiving an epistle of Christ. You might as well try to write with pen and ink upon the rubbish from which paper is made, as to impress legible evidence for the truth and divinity of the gospel on the life and conversation of one who is still "of the earth, earthy."

The paper manufacturer is not nice in the choice of his materials. He does not reject a torn or a filthy piece as unfit for his purpose. All come alike to him. The clean and glancing cloth from the table of the rich, and filthy rags from a beggar's back, are equally welcome. The clean cannot be serviceable without passing through the manufacturer's process, and the unclean can be made serviceable with it. He throws both into the same machine, puts both through the same process, and brings out both new creatures.

The Pharisees were scandalized on observing that publicans and sinners came in streams to Christ, and were all accepted. "This man receiveth sinners," they complained. Yea, *receiveth* them : sinners are taken in between the wheels at the commencement of this process ; but at the end of it saints in white clothing are thrown out, fit for the kingdom of heaven. Go ye into the highways and hedges, and as many as ye can find bid to the marriage. Christ does not find any pure on earth ; he makes them. Those that stand round the throne in white clothing were gathered from the mire. They were once darkness, though they be now light in the Lord.

Let no man think he can go into heaven because he is good ; but neither let any one fear he will be kept out of it because he is evil. Him that cometh, the Lord will in no wise cast out. Though your sins be as scarlet, they shall be white as wool. The blood of Jesus cleanseth us from all sin.

Not on tables of stone, like those on which the law was graven, but on tables of flesh, must the mind and likeness of Christ be written. Give him your heart. Surrender it to him, that he may blot out its stains and mark it for his own. The Lord hath need of epistles to recommend his grace in this world : Lord, here am I ; use me.

II. *The writing*, or the mind and meaning which is fixed on the prepared page.——It is not Christianity printed in the creed, but Christ written in the heart. When that writing is fixed on the heart, it shines through every opening of the life, and conciliates favour for the Lord.

It is well understood that a person's character may be very well gathered from his letters. These seem to be windows in his breast through which you can read his true character. How eagerly the public read the letters of a great man, if they are printed after his death ! People expect to learn better by these than by any other means what the man really was.

As our Lord left no monument of himself in brass or marble, so he left no letters written by his own hand. He did not write his mind on tables of stone or on sheets of parchment. Even Rome, with all her rage for relics, does not pretend to show a specimen of his hand-writing. Yet he has not left himself without a witness. He has left letters behind him which truly reveal his mind. " Ye are epistles of Christ."

Disciples, when he desires to let the world know what he is, he points to you. Nay, more, and further, when he would have the Father to behold his glory, he refers him to the saved : " Father, I am glorified in them." It is not only that the world, in point of fact, judges of Christianity by what it sees in Christians, but it has authority so to do. The Lord himself consented that it should read him there.

So Jesus sends a letter to the world—sends many letters —sends a letter to every city, and every street, and every house. A merchant who is a disciple of Christ goes to India or China. He sells manufactured goods ; he buys silk and tea. But all the time he is a letter, a living epistle, sent by Christ to the heathen. A boy becomes an apprentice in a warehouse or factory ; but before he was bound to a master on earth he has been redeemed by a Master in heaven. He is now, therefore, a letter from the Lord to all his shopmates. In his truth, and love, and gentleness, and fairness, and generosity, they should learn the mind of Christ.

I confess that this thought is fitted to make us afraid. How shall we fulfil such a function ? The solution is—it is the Lord's own method. He has chosen earthen vessels in order that the glory may be to God.

III. *The writer.*—This letter is written by the Spirit of the living God. Some writings and paintings look well for a while, but are easily rubbed off by rough usage, or grow faint with age. Only fast colours are truly valuable. Human art has found the means of making them lasting. The flowers and figures painted upon porcelain, for example, are burned in, and therefore cannot be blotted out. As long as the vessel lasts the painting remains bright.

How shall we get a writing or a likeness made durable in a human heart ? One thing we know,—many features which people admire are blotted out in the wear and tear of life. Lessons which human hands lay on are not able to stand the rough usage of the world. The education which can be obtained at schools is not sufficient. Its fair characters may soon be stained by evil passions from within, or scratched by cruel treatment from without. We cannot make the writing deep enough on those mysterious tablets. We cannot warrant the colouring.

No writing on a human spirit is certainly durable, except that which the Spirit of God lays on. The process is in one aspect like writing; but in another it seems rather a species of printing. The meaning is in the Scriptures set up like types—once for all. Then the Scriptures are impressed on the heart, as the types are applied to the page. It is when divine truth, taken off the divine Redeemer, is pressed on the human heart by the Spirit of God, that one becomes a new creature. Old things pass away, and all things become new. Henceforth the Christian bears about on his character the likeness of Christ.

And there is also a kind of burning to make the writing durable. In conversion there is a sort of furnace through which the new-born pass. We must take up our cross when we follow Christ. We must part with all that crucifies the Lord, although it were dear as a right arm or a right eye. Through such fire and water the Spirit leads us; but he brings us into a wealthy place. It is gladsome, as well as safe, to pass from death unto life in conversion; but there is something to be stripped off, and something to be put on, in the passage, which you will never forget.

In the wide-spread religious activity of the day some marks are made on the people,—not made by the Spirit of God. A cry; a swoon; a fear of wrath; an imagination of the judgment-seat; a gift of prayer; a profession of faith,—may be shown by the event to have been only marks on the surface made by some passing fear or nervous sympathy. The writing made by the Spirit does not go out again. This baptism is a baptism of fire as well as of water—it not only washes off the old; it also burns in the new.

IV. *The pen.*—In writing the new name and new nature on the tables of the heart, the Holy Spirit employs an instrument. It is expressly said in the text that Paul and the younger evangelists who assisted him had a hand in the work. The terms "ministered by us" point to the presence of man in the work of conversion and sanctifying. It is not a high place that the human ministry occupies; but it is the right place, and it cannot be wanted.

In photography it is the sun that makes the portrait. There is no drawing of the outline by a human hand, and no shading of the figure by the rules of the painter's art. The person stands up in the light; and the light lays his image on the glass. Yet even in this there is room and need for the ministry of man. Without the ministry of man the work could not in any case be accomplished. A human hand prepares the plate and adjusts the lens. Although in the real work of making the picture the artist has no part at all—although he has nothing more to do in the end than stand still, like Israel at the Red Sea, and see the work done by the sun—his place is still important and necessary.

A similar place is assigned to the ministry of men in the work of the Spirit. God does not send angels to preach. We learn the gospel from men of flesh and blood like ourselves. Cornelius and his house will be saved; but for that end Peter must go from Joppa to Cæsarea, and there declare the way of life. The Ethiopian treasurer will find

the Saviour whom he seeks; but not until Philip is sent
from Samaria, a skilful evangelist to guide the earnest but
ignorant African. It is thus that the Lord employs parents,
teachers, pastors, at the present day, as instruments to break
hard hearts and bind up broken ones.

This is the most interesting and honourable employment
in which any human being can be engaged. Whether he
be a ministering child or a ministering man, the agent who
stands between the living and the dead—a channel through
which the light of life may run—occupies the most honourable place and discharges the greatest function competent
to any creature.

Here above me is the depending extremity of the wire
whose upper end is dipped in heaven—dipped there in
everlasting love—dipped in God, who is love; and here
beneath me, within reach, is a brother " dead in trespasses
and sins." I grasp with one hand the conducting rod, and
with the other the cold, stiff hand of my brother; then, not
from me, but through me, the light of life flows from its
eternal fountain into the empty soul. Here is an example
of the first resurrection. The living is now an epistle of
Christ, written indeed by the Spirit, but yet " ministered
by us."

Printing nowadays is done by machines which work
with a strength and regularity and silence that are enough
to strike an onlooker with dismay. Yet even there a
watchful human eye and alert human hand are needed to
introduce the paper into the proper place. Agents are
needed, even under the glorious ministry of the Spirit—
needed to watch for souls.

V. *The readers.*—They are a great number, and of

various kinds. The terms of the text have a wide range—
"known and read of all men." The writing is not sealed,
or locked up in a desk, but exposed daily, and all the day,
to public view. These living epistles walk about upon the
streets, and mingle with the crowds in the market-place.
Every one may read them at will.

Some who look on the letters are enemies, and some are
friends. If an alien see Christ truly and clearly represented in a Christian, he may thereby be turned from
darkness to light; but if he see falsehood, and anger, and
selfishness, and worldliness in one who is called a Christian,
he will probably be more hardened in his unbelief. Those
who already know and love the truth are glad when they
read it clearly written in a neighbour's life; are grieved
when they see a false image of the Lord held up before the
eyes of men.

Here, however, in justice I ought to say that many
readers fail to see the meaning of the plainest letters.
None so blind as those who will not see.

Every one's life is an open letter. Every man, whether
he is a Christian or not, is written and is read. Some are
epistles of Christ; some are epistles of vanity; some are
epistles of covetousness; some are epistles of selfishness;
some are epistles of the wicked one. The main features
of the father of lies are written largely on the life of some
of his followers. The spirit that reigns within is more or
less visible in the outward conduct.

In some countries the master's name is branded in the
flesh of his slave, so that, if the slave should run away,
every one should know to whom he belonged. The captive may, indeed, be bought with a price; and then he
receives the mark of his new master. Thus, whether we

like it or not, people may read in our lives, with a considerable degree of accuracy, whose we are and whom we serve. The surest way to appear a Christian, in all places and at all times, is to be one. The surest way to make people, when you go out, take knowledge that you have been with Jesus, is really to be with Jesus.

Considering how defective most readers are, either in will or skill, or both, the living epistles should be written in characters both large and fair. Some manuscripts, though they contain a profound meaning, are so defectively written that none but experts can decipher them. Skilled and practised men can piece them together, and gather the sense where, to ordinary eyes, only unconnected scrawls appear. Such should not be the writing on a disciple's life. If it be such, most people will fail to understand it. It should be clear and bold throughout, that he may run who reads it.

Benevolent ingenuity, in our day, has produced a kind of writing that even the blind can read. The letters, instead of merely appealing to the eye by their colour, are raised from the surface so as to be sensible to touch. Such, methinks, should be the writing of Christ's mind on a Christian's conversation. It should be raised in characters so large, and sharp, and high, that even the blind, who cannot see, may be compelled, by contact with Christians, to feel that Christ is passing by.

Christians, the Light of the World
(Matthew 5:14-16)

"Ye are the light of the world......Let your light so shine before men, that they may see your good works, and glorify your Father which is in heaven."

THE first section of the Sermon on the Mount (verses 1–10) represents God and his saints; the second (11–16) represents believers and the world. Redeemed men in the body are exhibited first in their relation to God on high, and next in their relation to the world around. In the first picture, you behold believers in contact with their Friend; in the second, you behold them in contact with their foe. In the first, you learn what good they receive; in the second, what evil they suffer. From the Father of lights, every good and perfect gift comes down; from the world, lying in wickedness, every kind of danger springs up.

Between these two opposite poles the Christian life is suspended and balanced. The fountain opened in heaven supplies all a believer's need; and the pressure of temptation in the world sends him the oftener and the closer to his supplies. The Father's love draws, and the world's enmity drives; but though these forces spring on opposite sides, they act in the same direction. Thus all things work together for good to them that love God. A Christian need no more fear to plunge into the current of life than a planet to launch forth on its course. Opposite forces conspire to keep them safe, and urge them on.

In the first section, you learn from the double line of the seven beatitudes what God is to his people, and what his people are to God. He blesses them, and they trust in him. In the second section, you learn what the world is to the disciples of Christ, and what they are to the world. It is to them a persecutor; they are to it a salt and a light.

Omitting in the meantime the first of these analogies, we fix our regards on the second. Let us fairly look in the face this grand function assigned by the Lord to his followers—to be "the light of the world." In verse 14th, the function is defined; and in verse 16th, a particular instruction is given regarding its exercise. The first tells disciples that they are a light in the world; and the second exhorts them to keep it blazing. We shall explain shortly the nature of this office, and then more fully enforce the command to exercise it well.

I. It is the function of a living Church to be a light in a dark world. In order that we may determine in what sense the disciples of Christ are lights, let us read two cognate scriptures, one in the Old Testament, and the other in the New: "Arise, shine; for thy light is come, and the glory of the Lord is risen upon thee. For, behold, the darkness shall cover the earth, and gross darkness the people: but the Lord shall arise upon thee, and his glory shall be seen upon thee" (Isa. lx. 1, 2). "That ye may be blameless and harmless, the sons of God, without rebuke, in the midst of a crooked and perverse nation, among whom ye shine as lights in the world; holding forth the word of life" (Phil. ii. 15, 16).

From these texts we learn clearly that renewed men are first receivers of light; then and therefore givers. They are not the source whence the light springs, but channels through which it is distributed. The Lord alone is the light of the world; but he has been pleased to arrange his covenant so that those who receive his beams also spread them. It is so arranged also in the material world. Not much of the light which guides us in life comes in direct lines from the sun: most of it reaches us at second hand, reflected from surrounding objects. Thus, in the spiritual sphere, the glory of the Lord arises and shines on Israel; then and therefore Israel is expected to arise and reflect the light around to attract the Gentiles. The Philippian converts, walking in the light of God, are expected to shine among the heathen as lights. They are not rays, but reflectors; they give out, with more or less of truth and fulness, the light which they receive from the Sun of Righteousness after he has risen upon them.

The conception of Christians being lights, not as Source, but reflectors, might perhaps be profitably examined somewhat more minutely. Reflectors are ordinarily either metallic or vitreous. In either case, two preparatory processes are necessary: there must be a melting first and a polishing afterwards. Ah! search and see that those Christians who have really been eminently useful as attractive lights—winning many from the world by the beauty of their character—have been in the furnace, and have there had the dross taken away; have been under the pressure of providential trials that have rubbed their inequalities off. There is no royal—that is, no soft and easy—road to eminence in the Christian calling. The good soldier of Jesus Christ has suffered some privations and seen some service. Men who have never seen any other than parade service are not reckoned good soldiers in either army.

If a stranger, ignorant alike of means and end, had been permitted to see Lord Rosse engaged in preparing the speculum of his great telescope, he would have formed a false judgment regarding the usefulness of the work and the wisdom of the operator. This huge, heavy casting, cooled with so much care,—when it is at last removed from its bed, it seems a coarse, black, shapeless, useless mass. What is the use of it? the observer inquires. To reveal the stars that have hitherto lain hid in heaven. That lump of black, irregular metal! How can it reveal the stars? But the operator knows what he is about. This uncouth mass will yet receive on its bosom the light from burning orbs, so many and so distant that hitherto they have seemed to be little white clouds, sailing without a compass in the sea of infinitude.

The Day only will reveal the wisdom and the pains displayed by the omniscient Worker in preparing the hearts and lives of his witnesses for receiving from himself the light of life and spreading it around.

II. Leaving now the fundamental fact—that Christians are lights, to rest on the Word of the Lord—we proceed to examine more particularly the specific exhortation addressed to them in that capacity,—to let their light so shine before men, etc.

In the verse immediately preceding this injunction there is an interesting reference to the elevation of the light as a necessary condition of its usefulness. A lofty position, breadth, and brightness, must be combined in order to produce the greatest effect.

In a trigonometrical survey of our country, it is necessary often to obtain an`exact view of an object placed at a great distance; and some ingenuity is displayed in overcoming the obstacles. Goatfell, a mountain in Arran, is visible from the summit of the Ochils, east of Stirling, a distance of about seventy miles in a straight line. But at such a distance you can scarcely distinguish between a mountain and a cloud; no object can be seen with sufficient exactness for the purpose of measurement. But they bring a looking-glass to the top of Goatfell, scour its surface well, watch for a sun-blink, and turn it then in the required direction. On the summit of the Ochils they observe the flash, as a single point of glory, like a star in the broad blue sky. They measure their angle with security now.

A great elevation does not belong to every Christian. This is a matter that does not lie in his own hands. It is not like the climbing of the mountain by a man; it is like the uplifting of the mountain from the plain, which is the prerogative of the Creator. Some he both elevates and kindles, that their light may stream afar; but he has use for most of his lights on moderate elevations, and close to the benighted world.

The great business of Christians is to keep their light bright, and make it broad, that all who are within reach may be compelled to see it. A mirror besmeared with mud, although it is set in the sunlight on a mountain-top, will not be seen; whereas a bright burnished glass ʻwill reflect the light truly over a greater or a smaller sphere, according to the height which it may have attained. Thus,

Christians should take care that their light should be large and pure, leaving it to God in his providence to determine the height of their elevation and consequent radius of their influence. All who have let their light shine, like all who have used the intrusted talents, will be welcomed with the same words, Well done! whether their position has enabled them to spread the truth among many or only among a few.

Among a crowd of placards, varying much in size and subject, which jostled and overlapped each other on a piece of neglected wall at the entrance of a large city, one particularly arrested me. At the distance at which I stood, it exhibited only these words: "Large Type Christians." Doubtless intermediate lines in smaller letters, invisible where I stood, informed the nearer reader that some publisher had prepared a series of tracts in large type for the special use of aged Christians. From my view-point at the time only the larger letters were visible.

I passed on with what I had got, not desiring to exchange it for the meaning that a closer inspection would have revealed. Large type Christians! That is not the conception which the writer of the handbill intended to convey, but is the conception which in the circumstances it conveyed to me, and I determined to retain it. This shadow, which the publisher's circular projected on the wall, was to me a tenfold greater thing than the circular itself would have been. Large type tracts may be good for the conversion of the careless and the edification of believers; large type tracts may be good, but large type Christians are better. Tracts, large and legible, may win their thousands of captives in the battle of the kingdom; but Christians large and legible, if we had them, would win their tens of thousands.

As young and struggling colonies advertise amid the teeming population of the mother country for able-bodied farm-labourers and skilled artisans, covertly hinting, by their silence, that certain other classes would only be in the way ; so the Church, charged to colonize and cultivate the world for Christ, should distinctly own and loudly proclaim her need of large type Christians.

We have many who are really Christians—more, perhaps, than either a scoffing world or a desponding Church would acknowledge ; but not so many who are clearly, largely, unmistakably Christ-like, whatever they may be doing, and whoever may be looking on. If the graces of the Spirit, though real, are small and stunted, and especially if they are overshadowed by a rank growth of vanity, worldliness, and self-pleasing, they will not be seen by those who most need their evidence. The careless passenger will class you according to the earthliness which is large in your life, and not according to the heavenliness which is small. If conformity to every vain show make up the bulk of your history, while your compliance with Christ's will can only be detected by the microscope, your influence will, in point of fact, tell on the side of the world.

Christians, although the Light of life be within, yet, if it is choked and hidden by an abounding worldliness of spirit and conduct, you are in point of fact hindering the kingdom of Christ. Let your light so shine before men, that they may see your good works, and glorify your Father who is in heaven.

Observe here how closely the lines of a true disciple's life approach at certain points to those of a hypocrite's course. The Pharisees gave their alms and repeated their prayers that they might be seen of men ; and therein they are condemned by the Lord : but when his disciples let their good works be seen by men they are commended. Paul was frequently in a strait betwixt two here. He abhorred the Pharisees' ostentation,—I am less than the least of all saints ; and yet, when he saw that he could promote the kingdom by boldly taking the place which belonged to him, he flashed forth in the face of the world the lofty claim that he was not a whit behind the chiefest of the apostles. The hypocrite performs what are accounted good works in order that he may be seen of men, and get glory to himself ; the true disciple, doing necessarily the things that please God, in conformity with his new nature, endeavours carefully to do them in such a way as will best commend the gospel to his neighbours, and so extend the kingdom of Christ.

The redeemed should consider well the end of the Lord in redemption. To save the perishing is not by itself the aim and the hope which directed and animated the Redeemer in his work. As a husbandman makes an evil tree good by ingrafting, in order that he may enjoy its good fruit, so our Father in heaven saves us from condemnation, that he may delight in the new obedience of his children, and employ them in his work. Man's chief end is to glorify God and to enjoy him for ever.

What is contained in yonder vessel ? I inquire of a stranger who, like myself, is passing by the door of the threshing-floor where it stands. Chaff, he replies, turning a momentary glance towards the object, and so passes on.

His answer is all that I could expect him to give ; and yet it is not true. It was not true, for the vessel was mainly filled with wheat ; but it was what seemed true, for it was chaff mainly that met the traveller's eye. The measure standing on the floor, while the process of threshing proceeded, was gradually filled with what fell from the sheaves—with wheat and chaff commingled; but as it has been shaken somewhat roughly from side to side, the wheat grains have for the most part sunk to the bottom, and the chaff for the most part risen to the top.

In some such way many real but defective disciples are set down as hypocrites in the books of a careless world, because the things of the Spirit gravitate downwards, and lie hidden in the secret parts of their life; while the vanities of time usurp and occupy almost all the visible space on the surface of their history.

I do not know any means by which the gospel of Christ is more effectually hindered. Alas! the Lord knows we have all too little of the true Christian life in the visible Church; but if even that which exists were well employed, it would soon change the face of the world. Christians have in them more of Christianity than they have the wit to employ well in the cause of the kingdom. Oh, if the talents that belong to our Master were as wisely and vigorously laid out as those which we count our own, the kingdoms of this world would be won over!

That which is the fruit of the Spirit in Christians should not be small, but large and full-grown—should not be jostled out of its place by the urgency and impudence of mere worldly fashion. That which is Christ-like in Christians should not be hidden under a thick shade of cares and pleasures. If you would let your light shine before men, you must labour to cut down and kill off the covetousness, the pride, the evil-speaking, the equivocation, the falsehood, the dishonesty—all the bitter roots, whose branches weave themselves together into a thick veil, so as to turn your light into darkness.

You have asked the question, What must we do to be saved? and through the blood of sprinkling you have obtained an answer of peace. Another question demands now all the energy of a saved soul—the question, Lord, what wilt thou have me to do?

There are many wandering in the darkness, and stumbling even to a final fall. To enlighten and win and save them, the Lord hath need of you. Yield yourselves instruments of righteousness unto God. In particular, he calls for lights. In us there is not a light which can give life to any; but from the Lord the light of life is streaming down like the rays of the sun: if we receive it and reflect it, the light of life may through our means reach the perishing.

Occasions turn up daily in every one's experience when he must make a choice between faithfulness to Christ and conformity to the world's ways. Take no hesitating, double-minded course. Be on the Lord's side; and be on his side out and out. Let your Christianity be written in large characters for the sake both of friends and foes. A halting walk is a painful walk: plant your foot firm on the path of righteousness, and a new joy will be infused into your life. A life devoted because it is redeemed is not a wearisome but a joyful thing. It is not like a stagnant pool, but like a sparkling river: bright is its course over time; blessed its issue in eternity.

A Comprehensive Confession
(Isaiah 64:6-7)

"But we are all as an unclean thing, and all our righteousnesses are as filthy rags; and we all do fade as a leaf; and our iniquities, like the wind, have taken us away. And there is none that calleth upon thy name, that stirreth up himself to take hold of thee: for thou hast hid thy face from us, and hast consumed us, because of our iniquities."

I T is not enough to say of this brief prayer that it is figurative in the form of its expressions. It is a combination of many types. Natural analogies are piled upon each other, as the penitent strives to give all his emotions vent in language. It will be our effort to analyze the compact conglomerate, and examine in succession each of its constituent parts.

A quickened and repenting people in those ancient times pour forth their confession through Isaiah's lips. The speech is simple and sweet and tender, like the wailing of a suffering child. The conscience has been reached and melted, and here in our sight the confession flows. Obviously this sinful man "pours out his heart unto God;" he keeps nothing back.

Let us draw near and listen while an exercised human spirit makes full confession of sin to God, that we may make his prayer our own.

The confession consists of six several but consecutive and closely connected parts. We shall enumerate them as they follow each other in the text, and then endeavour to obtain for ourselves the lessons which they teach. There is much meaning in each separate ingredient of this confession considered by itself, and more in the relations and union of the whole :—

1. The taint of sin, that from the springs of humanity has poisoned all its streams—" We are all as an unclean thing."

2. The worthlessness and positive loathsomeness of all the efforts which a sinful man can make to set himself at first right with God—" All our righteousnesses are as filthy rags."

3. The frailty, uncertainty, and shortness of human life —" We all do fade as a leaf."

4. The power and success of internal corruption in hurrying the man away into actual transgressions—" Our iniquities, like the wind, have taken us away."

5. The inability and unwillingness of these helpless sinners, as they are drifting down the stream of sin towards the gulf of perdition, to lift themselves up and lay hold on God—" There is none that calleth upon thy name, that stirreth up himself to take hold of thee."

6. God's method of dealing with such a case—" Thou hast hid thy face from us, and hast consumed us, because of our iniquities."

I. The taint of sin, that from the springs of humanity has poisoned all its streams : " We are all as an unclean thing."

What feature of his dreadful case is first revealed to an awakening soul, we cannot tell ; the beginnings of life are kept secret. Probably, as there are diversities of operation in the process of bringing a man out of death into life, there may also be diversities in the process of revealing to him that he is dead in trespasses and sins. One man, when conviction by the Spirit first begins, may have his eye chiefly fixed on one feature, and another man on a different feature, of the carnal mind. But whether the discovery begin with the root or the branches,—with the deep rebellion of the heart or the manifold transgressions of the life,—it is certain that when a really awakened sinner proceeds to make an articulate confession to God, he is inclined, like Isaiah in this text, to begin at the beginning : "We are all as an unclean thing." When the patriarch had learned at length to know himself and God, and to bring the two together, a short formula best expressed his experience : "Behold, I am vile." This is the confession of faith, on its under or subjective side, which all who are taught of the Spirit are willing to sign.

This confession does not yet proclaim the way of salvation, but it has unveiled the necessities of the lost ; it points not yet to the sun in the heavens, but it owns and laments the darkness which broods over the earth. This darkness does not create the light, but it makes the light welcome when God commands it to shine.

True confession of sin, like its counterpart, true faith in Christ, is not partial, but universal. It belongs to all, and it belongs all to each. There is none that doeth good, and there is no good thing in any one. When one who has been convinced by the Spirit takes words and turns to God, he begins at the heart, as the spring whence the many unclean streams of thoughts and words and deeds flow out in the daily life.

This simplicity is a mark of truth. It is not an inventory of remembered shortcomings that disturbs the conscience in the prospect of the judgment. He has looked in on his own heart, and back over his past life, and forward to the great Day, and upward to the righteous Judge, and has discovered that his character is sin, his condition misery. Around the circle of his life he sees no spot where a troubled conscience can find a resting-place. When he opens his lips to express his state, the complaint is not a superficial gleaning of the bulkiest sins. He does not dally on the surface; he goes right to the root. An unclean thing. He counts himself a defiling spot on God's fair creation, and loathes the self which, notwithstanding, he cannot fling away. "O wretched man that I am! who shall deliver me from the body of this death?"

II. The worthlessness and positive loathsomeness of all the efforts which a sinful man can make to set himself at first right with God: " All our righteousnesses are as filthy rags."

Most naturally this ingredient of the confession comes next in order. He looked first to his sins, and told what he thought of them; he next looks to his righteousness, and we shall learn what his opinion is in regard to it also.

This is the natural history of the process—the process of conviction. By this way the soul went in order to reach true repentance. The path is rugged and painful. It is a voyage of discovery, in which all that lies before you is unknown, and where every increase of knowledge is acquired at the expense of falls and bruises. When a sense of guilt and a fear of wrath force their way into the conscience, nature's instinct prompts to the method of making peace by doing better for the time to come. There is no

instinct more uniform than this recourse to self-righteousness as soon as conviction of sin becomes alarming. After
the discovery of our sin, another discovery, still more terrible, remains to be made—-the discovery that our righteousness will do no more for us in the judgment than our sins.
In the first stages of conviction, although one by one the
pretensions of innocence fail the culprit, he has still hope
in another resource,—a second line of defence,—in which
he may make a stand. If he must own that the sins
deserve wrath, he will betake himself to righteousness, in
the hope that, though it cannot be expected to be complete,
it may yet go far as a protector.

It is when the fugitive soul is driven from this inner
line of defence that the crisis of the case arrives. It is
this feature,—this step of the confession,—that we examine
now.

Perhaps the memory of some painful dream will afford
us more help in the examination of this point than any
phase of our waking experience. You have dreamed that
you were in a strange, unknown place, and that all imaginable difficulties were gathering round you. Among other
misfortunes, by some unexplained and unaccountable neglect,
you were left without clothing far from home and from
friends. In the dreary, shuddering apprehension of the
moment you eagerly clutch at the first thing that lies to
hand, and wrap it round you with convulsive haste. Glad
to have gotten something that feels like a covering, you
proceed on your way somewhat more hopefully for a time.
The dawn, although it may be discerned in the east, does
not yet sensibly diminish the darkness that broods over
you and your path. You step forward with a comfortable
sensation of being at least clothed. Quickly the light in-

creases, and soon bursts into day; the path is leading to
frequented thoroughfares; now you discover that the garment which you hastily snatched is a bundle of unconnected
rags, very poor and very filthy. This garment is a conspicuous badge of shame, and you have none other. A
sinking of the heart, and a choking in the throat, awaken
you from sleep, and you discover that it was but a dream.
Gradually the wildly-pulsing heart sinks down again into
its normal peacefulness, and nothing remains of the terror
but an involuntary sob at intervals, like a ground-swell
after a storm.

Not more naturally do you in such a perplexity snatch
any covering that lies within your reach than does a sinful
man, when convictions first begin to prick his conscience,
betake himself hastily to a self-wrought righteousness.
As uniformly and necessarily as a rebound in the opposite
direction follows the blow, a soul, when first alarmed by a
sense of sin, endeavours to deprecate dreaded wrath by
getting up a painful and forced obedience. How busily
the naked, when he discovers his nakedness, labours to get
a covering, and how long he labours sometimes in vain!

For a time a man may be so busy gathering the rags
and putting them on that he does not perceive their filthiness: more terrible, on that account, is the discovery that
awaits him when the quickening Spirit sheds in a brighter
light, and he learns at length that the King is coming in,
while he is destitute of a wedding garment.

Those who have never experienced the distress which
the dream represents cannot, even in imagination, form a
conception of the dismay and sinking of heart that would
overwhelm them, if they found themselves, the observed of
all observers, entering the presence of royalty clothed in

filthy rags. Your limbs would totter beneath you, and your tongue would cleave to the roof of your mouth. Your heart would seem to be a heavy, hard, cold stone lying within your breast and crushing it.

Such in kind, but inconceivably magnified in degree, is the dismay that seizes a sinner who has been busy preparing a righteousness for the judgment-seat, when in the light of the great white throne, now felt to be very near, he discovers that the righteousness wherewith he has covered his sins is yet more vile in God's sight than the sins which it is employed to cover.

Nor let any one lightly deem that this representation is introduced as the necessary filling up of a well-favoured theological system. The scripture and reason concur in demonstrating that the righteousness which the convicted but unreconciled soul throws over its uncleanness is itself at least equally unclean. Love is the fulfilling of the law; and in these hasty, painful efforts to provide a satisfying obedience there is no love. You make these efforts while you are strangers to pardon and reconciliation in Christ, not because you trust in God's mercy, but because you dread his holiness. These are peace-offerings flung to an enemy, not love lavished on a friend. If you were near a lion and in his power, you would throw him a piece of flesh, in the hope that, soothed and satisfied with the morsel you had given him, he might not be disposed to tear you. Men, stung by apprehended wrath, and not reassured by tasting mercy, treat God thus. Their diligent tread-mill round of duty, and painful penances, and costly offerings, are a stratagem cunningly contrived to occupy the attention of the omniscient Watcher while they turn round a corner and escape.

Wanting pardon and reconciling in the Mediator, there is no love in the good works which men bring to God; and wanting love, there is no life in them; and wanting life, they are dead; and the dead run to corruption; and the more of the dead you heap together, the ranker is the decay. From dead works as well as from acts of sin we must be purged through the blood of the covenant ere our service can be pleasing to God. Such prayers and penances add insult to injury. Hatred of God's holiness is the motive of the deeds. As long as you toil unforgiven, unreconciled, unrenewed, to work a righteousness under which you may be safe from God's displeasure, you are in effect vainly trying to throw dust in the eyes of your enemy. If you could be assured that he did not hate sin and would not punish it, you would instantly cease to strive after righteousness. Ah, these filthy rags! how intensely loathsome they seem to the dear child when Christ has made him free.

III. The frailty, uncertainty, and shortness of human life: " We all do fade as a leaf."

The time is short, and even the short time is uncertain. Any day, any hour, thy soul may be required of thee. This thought, coming on the back of the discovery that your righteousnesses are filthy rags, adds to the agony. Our own righteousness is worthless, and our breath may be taken away before we have time to cast about for another. We have suddenly awakened and found our lamps out and our oil-vessels empty; alas! while we go to buy the Bridegroom may pass and the door be shut.

You are in debt. It has been announced that you must be ready with payment in your hand to meet your creditor face to face whenever he may call. You stand among a crowd of fellow-debtors in the outer court. From time to time the awful voice of the judge resounds from within the veil, calling now one and now another of your neighbours by name into his presence. Every man rises and goes in the moment that he hears the summons; some enter cheerful, and some with terror in their look and trembling in their limbs, but all enter instantly as they are called. You know well that your turn cannot be far distant, but you know not at what hour or moment it will come. Will you, in these circumstances, be at ease or in wretchedness? This depends on another question. Have you enough to pay your debt, or have you nothing? If you have enough, you await your call with composure, and obey it when it comes with a light heart; if you have nothing to pay, your heart beats hurriedly at every movement in the crowd; and when your name is called, you faint and fall to the ground.

It cannot be denied that many who would fain seem free are, through fear of death, all their lifetime subject to bondage. Two classes occupying the two opposite extremes contrive to enjoy life, although its term is short and uncertain: those on the one hand who have never been disturbed by conviction; and those on the other who have, through the Mediator, entered into peace. But to the multitude in the middle, who have been made aware of their own guilt, and not yet got it washed away in the blood of the cross, Death in the distance darkens by his shadow all the joys of life.

The fading of a leaf supplies a correct and affecting emblem of our mortality in both its main features—its certainty and its uncertainty. In one aspect nothing is more sure than the fall of the leaf, and in another nothing more uncertain. Look to this fruit or forest tree: of all the leaves that it bears to-day, glittering in the sunshine and quivering in the breeze, not one will remain in winter —all will be strewn on the ground. But when each leaf will fall is secret and unsearchable as the purposes of God. One, touched by an imperceptible mildew, may drop soon after it has unfolded itself from the bud in spring; a second, bitten by a worm, may wither as soon as it has fully spread out its surface to the sun of summer; a third may be shaken off by a boisterous wind, and a fourth nipped by an early frost. On what day of the season any leaf will drop no man knows; but that all will drop ere the season is over is absolutely sure.

Such is our condition in this life. We fade as a leaf fades. The generation will in a few years be laid in the dust, but the individuals composing it may be led away at any hour into eternity. This is our condition. It is a sad picture, but it is true; and it would be foolish to hide or forget it. We are on our warning, every one of us. We know not what a day may bring forth. Every day we perform a march, and every night lie down to sleep, a day's journey nearer home. These busy hearts are beating the dead march to the grave. But the hope in Christ turns this sad world upside down; to them that are found in him, these pulsations mean a life-march to the rest that remaineth.

IV. The power and success of internal corruption in hurrying the man into actual sin: " Our iniquities, like the wind, have taken us away."

It is a mark of true repentance when the penitent lays

all the blame upon himself. He who tries to shift the burden so as to lay it on his neighbour, has not yet, in faith, gotten his burden laid on Christ ; on the other hand, he who has gotten his sins laid on Christ, is not under the necessity of shifting the guilt upon a fellow-creature. This confession bears the mark of truth. *Our* iniquities have carried us away. There is indeed a spiritual wickedness in high places, as well as evil communications between man and man ; but when a soul is truly convinced of sin by the Spirit, and draws near to the Father in confession, these outward enemies are forgotten, and the sin is felt to be all the sinner's own. Every one is tempted when he is drawn away of his own lusts and enticed.

Like the wind, in the secrecy of its origin and the greatness of its effects, is the spirit of evil as well as the Spirit of grace. As the wind carries chaff away, so the impetuous passions of an evil heart overcome every resolution of amendment, and direct the whole volume of the life. It is strange that this confession follows immediately upon the reflection that we all do fade as a leaf. You might suppose that if men believed themselves immortal they might dare to sin with a high hand ; but that the knowledge of death being certain, coupled with the uncertainty and suddenness of its approach, would compel them to live soberly and righteously and godly in the world. Vain expectation ! The knowledge that death is sure, and the day of it uncertain, does indeed exert a force in the direction of restraining sin. It is a power which, to the extent of its ability, binds the evil spirit ; but it is like a green withe round Samson's limbs. It opposes wickedness, but it has not power to stop its career, or even to diminish its speed.

A great ship is lying in deep water, close to a precipitous beach, with two or three lines made fast to the shore, and all her canvas spread. A breeze off the land springs up, and increases to a gale. Will the ship retain her position ? No; she will be driven out to sea. But is she not bound by these ropes to the shore ? Yes, these lines hold her to the shore with all their might; but when such a blast fills the sails, they snap asunder like threads.

Such and so feeble is the thought of death to keep a man back, when the passions of his own heart carry him away like the wind. Sometimes—and the experience is by no means rare—those whose business it is every day to dig graves and handle the dead neither fear God nor regard man. The scripture is entirely accordant with experience when it intimates that the man who knows that he fades like a leaf permits his own iniquities notwithstanding to carry him away. The fear of death has not power to turn us from sin.

V. The inability and unwillingness of these helpless sinners, as they are drifting down the stream of sin towards the gulf of perdition, to lift themselves up and take hold on God : " There is none that calleth upon thy name, that stirreth up himself to take hold of thee."

Here again we might at first sight suppose, that as there is help at hand, the feeble will grasp it, and be saved. Because there is a God to lay hold of, we would think, those who are carried away to perdition like chaff on the wind will lay hold of God, that they may not perish. His feet have well-nigh slipped into the pit; but surely on that very account he will stay himself upon his God.

Alas ! it is not so. If a man were carried down against his own will by some external force, he would gladly grasp

any friendly hand that might be stretched out for help.
But the state of the case is different,—is opposite. It is
his own iniquities that are carrying him away. To grasp
God's hand as it is in Christ stretched out would indeed
save him—would snatch him out of that impetuous flood,
and hide his life with Christ in God; but this would tear
the man asunder—would separate the man from himself.
He would indeed be saved, so as by fire, leaving a right
eye and a right hand behind him. This kind of safety he
is not yet willing to accept. If he were invited to stir
himself up to lay hold of a safe heaven, he might make a
shift to obey; but he has no inclination to stir himself up
to lay hold of a holy God, and to abide in the light of his
countenance. " Thy people shall be willing in the day of
thy power." " Put off the old man with his deeds."

VI. God's method of dealing with such a case : " Thou
hast hid thy face from us, and hast consumed us, because
of our iniquities."

The Holy One hides his face from his creatures while
they live in sin.

" And hast consumed us, because of our iniquities." I
prefer to take this clause in its most literal sense, as it is
given in the margin—" Thou hast melted us by the hand
of our iniquities." God melts the hardest sinners, and he
employs their own sins to make the flinty hearts flow
down. If this melting take effect in the day of grace, it is
repentance unto life. What a mystery is here! All are
his servants. He can employ a man's own sins as the
burning coals poured on his head to melt him into confession and trust. We have often found souls undergoing
this process. There is great grief and great tenderness :

the fountains of the great deep seem to have been broken up within them, and their eyes have become fountains of tears. Ask what ails them, and from the groans, and cries, and broken words you soon discover that their own sins have in some way been lifted up and poured over them like melted lead.

This is the hand of God. He is melting these high-handed transgressors—melting them down in order to mould them again as new creatures in Christ; and the means whereby he makes the stony hearts yield are their own sins treasured up, and poured in a scalding stream over their own consciences. Ah! when they are softened in that furnace they will be poured into another type, and emerge new creatures. By terrible things in righteousness the Lord is answering their cry.

But if the sinful are not so melted in the day of grace, they will be melted when that day is done. By their own iniquities, too, will the judgment be inflicted. Their own sins on their own heads will be at least a material part of the doom of the lost in the great Day.

Having examined somewhat fully what the text is, we shall now, in a concluding sentence, point out where it lies. Many lessons may be obtained from its contents; at least one, exceeding great and precious, may be drawn from its position. After having looked to the text, we shall look at that which touches it, before and behind. The gem is the chief object of attraction, but its setting may be both beautiful and precious. When a diamond of great size, of historic interest and almost fabulous worth, now the property of the Queen, was some years ago exhibited to the public, it was supported on either side by the representation of a human hand made of gold, and artistically constructed to represent at once firmness and tenderness, as a living human hand would hold fast and hold forth that which is unspeakably precious. In that case, a measure of interested attention was given by the spectators to the setting, second only to that which the gem attracted to itself.

Here, too, when, in the expanse of Scripture, a gem so precious was about to be held up to view, care seems to have been taken to give it a setting, precious in its own nature, and in its form betokening tender care and deep appreciation. A hand of gold protrudes from either side, expressively and impressively holding forth the precious and full-bodied confession of the ancient prophet. The word that touches it on the one side (end of verse 5) is, " We shall be saved ;" the word that touches it on the other side (beginning of verse 8) is, " But now, O Lord, thou art our Father."

It is not by chance that this great deep confession lies between these two words—is held up and held out in these two tender loving hands. " We are saved by hope," not by terror. It is God's mercy that melts. If these arms of love had not been thrown round the stony heart, the stony heart would not thus have flowed down like water. When they propose to melt the rugged ore, and bring the precious metal out, they put a fire below it and a fire above it, and fan both into a sevenfold glow. Between these two fires the rock at length gives way.

It is thus that the melting of repentance and the outflow of confession are produced. Terror alone, even the terror of the Lord, does not avail. The weight of apprehended judgment lying on the guilty will only compress the soul into a harder, intenser atheism, unless redeeming love burst through. Surround a fallen human spirit with the immediate and certain apprehension of divine vengeance due to sin—leave no chink in that wall of brass to admit a ray of hope from the face of Jesus—confront the creature with the Creator's almighty anger—and nothing more, nothing else : you will not thereby melt that human spirit into repentance and faith. That creature, though guilty now and feeble, is, in his origin and nature, great and Godlike. That spirit, despairing, will curse God and die—die hard.

It is another thing than divine anger that really melts and remoulds the man. Isaiah, in this case a representative man—for the word is not of private interpretation—Isaiah, secretly conscious of sin, looks this way, and the signal hung out is, " We shall be saved ;" looks that way, and the signal displayed is, " Thou art our Father." Between these fires the heart is melted, and flows down into the great confession of the text. This, O Isaiah, is " repentance unto life ;" but the goodness of God, compassing thee behind and before—-" the goodness of God leadeth thee to repentance."

Rooted in Love
(Ephesians 3:17)

" Rooted and grounded in love."

O N bended knees and with bursting heart the
Apostle of the Gentiles, from his prison at
Rome, pleads with the God and Father of our
Lord Jesus in behalf of his beloved brethren at
Ephesus, that they may be " rooted and grounded in love."

These two distinct conceptions are very frequently
united in the Scriptures.*   Two cognate conceptions—
one borrowed from the processes of nature, and the other
from human art—are employed to indicate at once the
life, the growth, the strength, and the stability of a Christian's hope.   A tree and a tower are the material objects
which are used here as alphabetic letters to express a
spiritual thought.   More particularly, as a tree depends
for life and growth upon its roots being embedded in a
genial soil, and a tower depends for strength and stability
upon its foundation, the apostle desires, by aid of these
conceptions, to express and illustrate the corresponding
features of the Christian life.   If disciples are compared
to living trees, love is the soil they grow in ; if they are
compared to a building, love is the foundation on which it
stands secure.

---
* For examples of this union, see Psalm 144:12 and 1 Corinthians 3:19.

Dropping from view now the second of these associated conceptions, we shall confine our regard to the first. A believing man, pleading with God in behalf of fellow-believers, prays that they may " be rooted in love."

The picture, thus limited, contains only two objects. These are the ground that sustains the tree, and the tree that grows in the ground. The ground in which the tree grows represents the love that faith feeds on ; the tree that grows on that ground represents the faith that leans and feeds on love.

I. The soil in which the living tree is planted : it is *love*. A question rises here at the outset which must be settled ere we can advance a step with the exposition,— What is the love in which the trees of righteousness are rooted ? Whether is it God's love to man, or man's love to God and to his brother ? The question admits of an answer at once easily intelligible and demonstrably true. The love in which the roots of faith strike down for nourishment is not human but divine. It is not even that grace which is sovereign and divine in its origin, but residing and acting in a renewed human heart : it is the attribute, and even the nature, of Deity, for " God is love." The soil which bears and nourishes the new life of man is the love of God in the gift of his Son.

The analogy introduced absolutely demands that the text should be so understood. To explain it otherwise would destroy the consistency of the analogy, and distort the spiritual lesson which it is employed to teach. It would be, in effect, to turn the parable upside down. When Paul prays that the Ephesian Christians may be rooted, he obviously thinks of them as living plants.

Whatever the soil may be in which the plant grows, it must be something distinct from the plant itself. It introduces an inextricable confusion of ideas to think of believers as trees rooted in their own love—an emotion that has its abode and its exercise within their own hearts. The roots of a man's faith and hope must penetrate, not inward into the love he exercises, but outward into the love which is exercised towards him. The roots of a tree grow, not into the tree itself, but into an independent soil, which at once supports its weight and nourishes its life. In like manner a Christian's faith does not lean and live upon anything within himself; it goes out and draws all its support from God's love to sinners in the gospel of his Son.

The same result may be obtained by looking to the twin analogy of an edifice resting on its foundation. The term "grounded" refers specifically to the foundation on which a building rests. "Foundationed," if there were such a word in our language, would be a more exact and literal translation. The two analogies here united in one clause are obviously parallel throughout their whole length. The foundation on which a house stands is something external to the house itself; and so the soil in which a tree grows is something external to the tree. Love, on the spiritual side of the comparison, corresponds both to the ground which sustains a tree and the rock which sustains a building. That love, in both cases, is demonstrably something completely distinct from the soul that leans on it. The love which satisfies a soul is not emotion that springs within itself. "God is love." Behold the Rock of Ages on which the building stands; behold the generous soil which satisfies these towering trees of righteousness!

But the question may be decided more shortly, if not more surely, by a direct appeal to the written Word. In the Epistle to the Colossians, where the same apostle about the same time is discoursing on the same theme to a sister Church, occurs an expression which, being precisely parallel and yet not completely identical, brings out the significance of our text in the manner of an algebraic equation. "As ye have received Christ Jesus the Lord, so walk ye in him; rooted and built up in him, and stablished in the faith" (Col. ii. 6, 7).

No one can fail to perceive the identity of the two associated conceptions as they occur in the two epistles. In both letters alike, a tree rooted and a building founded are brought together in the same order, for the purpose of setting forth the spiritual life and steadfastness of believers. Obviously the apostle meant to express to the Colossian Christians the self-same idea by the term "rooted" that he had already conveyed thereby to those at Ephesus; but while in the one epistle he writes "rooted in love," in the other he writes "rooted in him,"—that is, in Christ. Here is demonstration that the love in which faith finds its sustenance is God's love in the covenant to his own; for Christ, the unspeakable gift, is the issue and embodiment of that love. In Paul's mind—that is, in the mind of the Spirit—"Christ" and the love which faith lives on are identical. The terms are used alternately and indifferently to signify the same thing. To be rooted in him manifestly means to be rooted in the love wherewith he first loved us.

Having determined the first point,—that the soil in which faith's roots can freely grow is found in God, not in man,—we must now weigh well what attribute or manifestation of God it is that permits and invites the confidence of the fallen.

The justice of God does not afford a soil on which the hope of sinners can thrive. " Our God is a consuming fire ; " and as often as the straining hopes of men stretch forth in the direction of the judgment-seat, they are driven back in dismay. As well might you expect the tender roots of a living plant to strike kindly down into hot ashes, as expect the trust of a guilty soul to go into the righteousness of God for support. No ; there is nothing on this side but a fearful looking for of judgment to devour.

Neither can human hopes grow in a mixture of mercy and justice such as men, in ignorance of the gospel, when conscience is uneasy, may mingle for themselves. You may indeed find some who for a time seem to grow in such a mixture ; but the roots never go deep, and the hold is never secure. In the plant so nourished there is no freshness of life, no blossom of joy, no fruit of righteousness. If the unclean conscience, apart from the blood of sprinkling, qualify the divine justice with a proportion of imaginary tenderness, and qualify the tenderness in turn with a proportion of avenging wrath, the result will be a miserable halting between two.

There is only one place in which righteousness and peace can meet without mutually destroying each other, and that is in the cross of Christ the Substitute. In Christ, but not elsewhere, God is at once just, and the justifier of the sinful who believe.

Disturbed by an accusing conscience, and not perceiving the way of righteous peace through the death of Christ, the sinful strive to make matters right for the judgment-seat ; but, striving unlawfully, never succeed. They throw into their conceptions of God as much unappeased anger as serves to destroy all the pleasure of their religion, and as much softness for sin as serves to extract all its power. Their God is not very kind, and therefore they have no pleasure in his company ; their God is not very just, and therefore they take liberties with his law. Thus " the double-minded man is unstable in all his ways."

It is not in divine justice, nor in a spurious compound of justice and indulgence, that human souls can securely place their hope for eternity. If ever an immortal spirit is rooted at all, it must be in love—in love that is infinite —the love of God in the gift of his Son. " In him dwelleth all the fulness of the Godhead bodily ; and ye are complete in him." Those that are rooted in him live and bring forth fruits of righteousness. These are not plants growing for a few days on rocky ground. They may plunge their roots down as far as their faculties and their lives extend, they will never meet any obstacle to check and repel their confidence. God is love ; and they cannot by their penetrating pass through that and strike a barren rock beyond. " Happy are the people that are in such a case ; yea, happy are they whose God is the Lord."

II. The plant that is rooted in the ground represents a believer getting all his support and all his sustenance from the love of God which is in Christ Jesus our Lord.

Under this head, the first point that occurs is the very obvious one, that before any measure of growth can be obtained there must be life. Of what avail would rich- ness of soil be to rows of dead branches ? A withered branch draws no sap from the most fertile ground. Faith fastens on God's revealed love in the covenant, and satisfies itself from this inexhaustible treasury ; but who and what first creates faith ? The living will, by the instincts of nature, seek convenient food ; but how shall the dead be restored to life ? Let it be granted that faith, appropriating God's love, sustains the living, the question remains, Who quickens the dead ?

In the last resource, an answer to this question must be sought in the sovereignty of God and the ministry of the Spirit ; but we must beware of so regarding God's part in it as to miss or neglect our own. " Live " is the first thing in the Spirit's ministry ; but " Believe" is the first thing in the duty of man. To God's eye, looking downward from his own eternity, the order of events is, Live, that you may believe ; but to our eye, as we stand on earth and look upwards, the order of events is, Believe, that you may live. Our part is not to produce life, but to exercise trust. Honour God by referring the origin of life to his sovereign grace and power ; but obey God by believing in Jesus Christ whom he has sent. Let us neither intrude into his province nor neglect our own. His command is, " Believe on the Lord Jesus Christ, and thou shalt be saved ; " " His commandments are not grievous." If we in simplicity render this service, we shall find to our joy in that day that his work was perfect before we responded to his call. Here we may well appropriate to ourselves the advice which the neighbours gave to the blind man when Jesus was passing by : " Be of good comfort ; rise, he calleth thee." The fact that he calls us should be sufficient warrant for us to come.

O Spirit, breathe upon the dead bones, that they may live,—upon the dead branches, that they may grow !

But even when the plant is living, many obstacles may intervene to prevent it from freely pushing down its roots and drinking up the richness of the soil. Stones of stumbling lie in the way of the living root, and hinder its growth. "An enemy hath done this." Desponding thoughts, of various shape and source, may mar the peace and stunt the growth of a disciple, but they cannot quench his life. The natural history of faith's life on earth will be an interesting study, when the day shall reveal all its windings—all its days of drooping, and all its days of growth.

Sometimes the history of vegetable life, concealed for generations, is afterwards thrown open. When a forest tree, that has outlived several generations of its owners, is at last thrown down by a tempest, and its roots all exposed to the inspection of the passer-by, many secret passages of its early history are at length revealed. Each bend of those gnarled roots has a tale to tell,—of various efforts and disappointments, and conflicts and victories. Here, in the centre of the circular mass, the main stem was pointing perpendicularly downward when the tree was young, perhaps a century ago ; but ere it had gone far in that direction, it had struck against a stone. The fibre, then young and pliable, had sensitively turned as soon as it felt the obstacle, and grew for a little upward, as if retracing its steps. Then it had bent to one side and crept along the surface of the stone, intending, so to speak, to turn its flank and plunge into the deep earth beyond its outmost edge. Once or twice in its horizontal course it came to hollows in the stone, and ever instinctively seeking downward, penetrated to the bottom of each ; but finding no opening, it came always up again, and pursued its course on the horizontal line. But, long ere it reached the margin of the great rock, it found a rent, narrow, indeed, but thorough. Into this minute opening it thrust a needle-like point. It succeeded in pushing that pioneer through. Tasting thereby of the rich soil below, it thence drew new strength for itself. Strong now in that acquired strength, it increased its bulk and rent the rock asunder. You may now see the two halves of the cleaved rock hanging on the mighty root that rent them. Now the victor has overcome its adversaries, and makes a show of them openly. It holds the remnants of its ancient enemy aloft as trophies of its victory.

It is thus that a living soul struggles against all obstructions, and either round them or through them penetrates into the unlimited love of God as it is in Christ. There the life satisfies itself and becomes strong. This man is more than conqueror through Him that loved him.

A soul has been quickened by the Spirit. The new life has begun; the new tastes are felt; the appetites of the new nature are stirring. Why am I thus? This thirsty soul now longs for God, and strikes out for satisfying in the direction of his covenant. But something comes in the way. Through the wiles of the devil a great rock of offence is cast right in between that sinner and the Saviour's love. In one case, the stumbling-block is the doctrine of election: If I am not among the chosen number, I need not try. In another case, it is the sin against the Holy Ghost: If I have committed the unpardonable sin, I need not strive, for God will not hear me. In another case, it is such a view of his own sins as leads him morbidly to think that while there may be pardon for others, there can be none for him. Ah! this quickened soul, in the beginnings of life, while the intelligence is yet feeble like an infant's mind, when feeling for the love of God in Christ to live upon, often strikes upon a stone. This is not God; this is not love. Thus the root finds so many stones, and these so close together, that it cannot reach the rich ground underneath for nourishment; but the root, true to its nature, never gives up. It strives without ceasing to reach its object. Worming its way along the surface of the obstruction, to find a passage round it—fretted and frightened, and thrown back often, but never despairing, never slackening—it holds on, until at length between these opposing rocks it reaches and tastes the sap of the unlimited soil beneath. Then it becomes strong enough to throw the obstruction aside, and expatiate at will in its element.

When the saved are drawn at length from the ground in which the new life secretly grew, and all the history of their redemption revealed in the better land, themselves and others will read with interest the record of the struggle, and the final victory. It will then be seen that every hindrance which the tempter threw in faith's way only exercised and so strengthened faith. They who have had the hardest conflict in throwing obstacles aside that they might freely draw from redeeming love in Christ, draw most freely from that love when they reach it: as that woman who had pined many years in disease, and spent all her means on other physicians, drew proportionally a larger draught from the fountain when she touched its lip at last. As if surprised and delighted with the suddenness, the eagerness, and the largeness of her demand upon his healing power, the Lord stood and looked round and cried, "Who touched me?" So, I suppose, yet in his glory, Jesus has occasion from time to time to say in glad surprise to surrounding angels, Some one has touched me, when a sinner who has long tried, and been long kept back by stones of stumbling, at last gets the lip of thirsty faith laid upon the fountain of living water.

" Fear not, little flock ; it is your Father's good pleasure to give you the kingdom :" fear not, little roots ; the stones which lie in your way are many and hard, but when you work past them or through them, there is love infinite and eternal, all the fulness of the Godhead bodily, in Christ, that you may live upon and luxuriate in. Have you been brought through fire and water ? Then all the more sweet will the " large place " be when at length you reach it. Seek, and ye shall find.

Many things go to increase the fruit-bearing, but all are subordinate to this,—the free plunging of the living root into the rich, unobstructed ground. Pruning, and watering, and weeding will do nothing for the tree if its roots have struck a rock. In like manner, the main requisite to a productive Christian life is the liberty that the soul enjoys to spread itself to the full extent of its capacity into the love of God in Christ. It is the receiving that produces the doing. The law of grace is not, Give freely, and you shall in return freely receive : the law of grace is the opposite,—" Freely ye have received, freely give."

This analogy suggests many practical lessons ; but it is not necessary even to enumerate them, for they spring spontaneously before the reader's eye as soon as he has apprehended the main features of the similitude. The storm, for example, that shakes the living tree, ordinarily serves but to compel its roots to take a deeper hold, and make it stronger to bear the next onset. So afflictions exercise and strengthen faith.

Again—a needful lesson in an age of many words and little tendency to silence—the roots grow best when they are least meddled with. The child who pulls up his young tree two or three times every day in order to show his companions its roots, will soon have nothing but a dead stem to show. Encourage by all means the meek confession of a convert's hope, but do not lay open all the spiritual experience of a novice to satisfy the curiosity of some passing Talkative.

Once more, we have had fathers of our flesh who did not give us a stone when we asked for bread. The more we counted on their love the better pleased they were. Let us beware of mistaking and distrusting the Father of our spirits. Alas! if our roots were exposed, they would tell a tale of constraint and suspicion. How often even a disciple refuses to plunge openly into offered love, and draws back as if he expected a repulse. It was Jesus who said, " The Father *ran*, and fell on his neck, and kissed him."

Drawn and Dragged
(James 1:14)

" But every man is tempted, when he is drawn away of his own lust, and enticed."

WE are tempted, it seems—" drawn " into sin. Who tempts us—who draws us ? Not God. He is perfectly holy, and by a necessity of nature does good and not evil. God is our friend—in all the ordinations of his providence and in all the revelations of his grace. God is for us; who is against us ?

There is indeed a tempter—an evil spirit unseen, the enemy of man ; but let us beware what use we make of the scriptures which reveal the fact. If any one should be disposed to excuse himself on this ground, James, the Lord's brother, gives him here a clear warning. The evil spirit has no power at all over any of us, except what we concede to him. He " goeth about seeking whom he may devour : " he cannot devour whom he will. Only they who " give place " to the devil—and that place within their own bosoms—can be hurt by his fiery darts. The tempter is elsewhere described as " the prince of the power of the air, the spirit that now worketh in the children of disobedience " (Eph. ii. 2). These two branches of the definition explain and qualify each other. As the prince of the power of the air, he could do a soul no harm : it is when he is admitted and welcomed within a man's own heart that he defiles and ensnares.

So then, in the last resort, as we have it in James, " every man is tempted, when he is drawn away of his own lust, and enticed."

From the striking figures here employed we learn some specific features of the sad process. The two terms are literally, " drawn out, and hooked."

The first expression does not yet mean drawn by the hook ; it means rather drawn to the hook. There are two successive drawings, very diverse in character. In classic Greek, the first term is indifferently applied to both ; but in this case the circumstances confine it to one. The first is a *drawing* towards the hook, and the second is a *dragging* by the hook. The first drawing is an invisible spiritual power, the second is a rude and cruel physical constraint. The first is a secret enticement of the will, and the second is an open and outrageous oppression by a superior force, binding the slave and destroying him.

The first process, as applied to hunting and fishing, is well known and easily understood. This part of the process is carried on with care and skill and secrecy. No noise is made, and no danger permitted to meet the eye of the victim. Everything is artfully and falsely made to assume the appearance of innocence and safety. With quiet stealthy steps the hunter or the fisher moves about. When necessary, he will lie down on the ground, that he may the better conceal himself. His whole art consists in these two things—exposing an enticing bait, and concealing himself and his snare. By smell or by sight, the fish or the wild animal is " drawn " from the safe, deep hiding-place in the bush or in the river. The victim, not perceiving the danger, is by its own " lust "—its own appetite —drawn to its doom.

It is thus that a man is drawn—but mark it well, by his own lust, his own appetite for pleasure—out of safe paths and into danger. Forewarned, forearmed. Oh, " watch and pray, that ye enter not into temptation."

The next part of the process is the act of fixing the barbed hook in the victim's jaws. The word is " baited ; " that is, enticed by the bait to swallow the hook—the hook that is in the first instance unseen and unsuspected. When the hook is fastened, there is another drawing ; but oh, how diverse from the first! The angler does not now hide himself, and tread softly, and speak in a whisper. There is no more any gentleness. He rudely drags his helpless prey to shore, and takes its life.

I have often seen the same process, with the same difference between its commencement and its conclusion, in the tempting and ensnaring of human souls. At first all care is taken not to alarm the conscience. It is a temperate cup, and it contributes to health and friendship. It will refresh and cheer you, and it will bind you in warmer love to your brother. But when the barb goes into the flesh—when the drug has bitten—when the appetite, insatiable as the grave, has been generated, the poor slave is dragged, without disguise and without ceremony, through the mire. His morbid, fiery appetite is now his governor, and he is dragged about, exposed as a spectacle, " whithersoever the governor listeth."

The best, the only real preventive against these baited

hooks, is to be satisfied with a sweetness in which there are no sin and no danger. The creature that is hungry greedily takes the bait and is caught. The human soul that is empty—that is not satisfied with the peace of God —is easily drawn into the pleasures of sin.

In a certain Highland lake, I have been told, sportsmen at one season of the year expect no sport. There are plenty of fishes, but they will not take the bait. Some vegetable growth on the bottom at that period is abundant and suitable as food. Being satisfied at home, they will not go away to follow the offer of a stranger. As long as they have enough in their own element, the fisher dangles his bait in vain over the surface of the water. They cannot be *drawn to* the hook, and so they are not *dragged by* it.

I have observed, in the process of fishing, that on the part of the victim there are two successive struggles, both violent, both short, and both, for the most part, unavailing. When first it feels the hook, it makes a vigorous effort to shake itself free. But that effort soon ceases, and the fish sails gently after the retreating hook, as if it were going towards the shore with its own consent. What is the reason of its apparent docility after the first struggle ? Ah, poor victim ! it soon discovers that to draw against the hook, when the hook is fastened, is very painful ; therefore, for the sake of immediate ease, it yields and follows. Then, when it feels the shore, and knows instinctively that its doom has come, there is another desperate struggle, and all is over.

I think I have observed these two struggles, one at the beginning and one at the end, with the period of silent resignation between them, in the experience of an immortal man, my brother. There is an effort to resist the appetite, after the victim discovers that he is in its grasp. But the effort is painful, and is soon abandoned. " I will seek it yet again," is the silent resolution of despair. The struggle, with all the agonies of remorse, may be once more renewed when the waters of life grow shallow, and the soul is grazing the eternal shore. The result ? Alas! the darkness covers it ; we know it not.

After the first drawing, which is soft and unsuspected, the way of transgressors is hard. The fish with the hook in its jaws is the chosen glass in which the Scripture invites us to see it. The snare of intemperance is the one in which the victim is tormented, and made a show of openly, in sight of the world. There are other snares that are secret in the second stage, as in the first : because they are secret, they cannot be freely named among us ; but, oh ! many strong men are caught and destroyed by these baits.

It is blessed to be free. " If the Son make you free, ye shall be free indeed." Hear ye him : " Take my yoke upon you and learn of me ; for I am meek and lowly in heart : and ye shall find rest unto your souls. For my yoke is easy, and my burden is light."

The Fixed Compass
(Psalms 112:7)

" He shall not be afraid of evil tidings : his heart is fixed, trusting in the Lord."

THIS psalm is a fine full-length portrait of a godly man. Is it drawn from life ? Did the painter, or any of his contemporaries, sit for this likeness ? " Of whom speaketh the prophet this ? of himself, or of some other man ?"

Neither of himself, it must be confessed, nor of any other man, could the prophet speak all this. This is not the portrait of any mere man that ever lived ; and yet it is a true portrait. Artists paint ideals on canvas, combining in one figure the finest features gathered from many specimens. The result is true to nature ; and yet no living man ever answered to the likeness. The picture represents what man might be, rather than what he is.

Sketches of saints occasionally occur in the Scriptures wanting the blemishes which more or less mar the beauty of every actual life. These representations show what the redeemed may become when they are fully conformed to the image of Christ. They exhibit the new man when he has attained the perfect stature. It is right that the highest standard should be set before us ; but the best has many things to forget and leave behind, and many steps to press forward, ere he gains the prize of this high calling.

The pattern saint of this psalm is happy as well as holy. It concerns us specially to inquire how his happiness is secured while he inhabits a frail body and lives in an evil world. Among other sorrows from which the shield of faith defends him is " the fear of evil tidings." Mark the word ; for there is no promise, even to the most matured saint, that evil tidings shall not reach his ears. He, like his neighbour, is exposed both to the wars and the rumours of wars that shake the most stable thrones. Both the announcement of coming evil, and the evil that has been announced, come upon those that are God's dear children, as upon other people. The sound of the midnight tempest boding evil, and the wreck that it boded, reach the good man as well as the wicked ; and both are like iron entering into his soul. The peculiar privilege that belongs to victorious faith is exemption from the *fear* of evil tidings. Evil tidings, when they come, will pierce a good man's heart ; but in two things he has an advantage over those who know not God : first, he is not kept in terror before the time by the anticipation of possible calamity ; and next, even when calamity overtakes him, he does not look upon it in blank despair. He knows that it is the chastening of a Father, and is sure that love is wielding the rod.

This, then, being the kind and degree of exemption which a godly man enjoys, we must now inquire into the means whereby he attains it. How comes it that evil tidings have not the same terror for him that they have for other men ? Expressly, the text declares, because " his heart is fixed, trusting in the Lord."

This man has a solidity and an independence which others never know. His heart is fixed. It is something to have one's mind made up and settled. No man can be happy as long as he does not know his own mind—does not know what he would be at. " A double-minded man is unstable in all his ways." On the contrary, " if thine eye be single, thy whole body shall be full of light." To have an object in view, and to go straight at it, constitutes in a great measure the difference between a useful and a wasted life.

But while there is very little of either happiness or use-fulness in a life as long as it shifts about from one object to another—one thing to-day, and another to-morrow—it does not follow that all will go well when you have chosen your object, and pursue it steadily. As much depends on the object that the heart is fixed upon as on the fixing of the heart. Even after you get your heart fixed, you may be as far from happiness and safety as before. Your heart is fixed; but what is it fixed on ? On houses and lands ; on emoluments and honour ; on youth, and health, and pleasure ; on wife and children ? Alas ! it is easy to fix on any of these ; it does not require any vigorous act of the will, or any heavy labour of the hands, to fasten your-self to objects like these. Your heart-strings warp them-selves around and through and through these objects spontaneously, when they lie within reach, as ivy clasps, and even interpenetrates, an old wall, without any nail-ing up.

A beautiful object is that same ivy when it has clasped the wall with a thousand tendrils, and covered the wall even to its copestone with woven tasselled green—beautiful as the matted foliage quivering in the wind and glittering in the sunshine. But have you seen the ivy after the old wall has fallen? Then it is a sight that might make the observer weep. Prostrate, broken, torn, soiled, withering— ah, how is its glory gone! And, alas! it cannot be restored. Those tendrils that have grown so closely in, and have been torn so rudely out, cannot now ply into another support, though another and solider support were at hand. The towering and stately but feeble branches cannot now be attached to another prop. Nothing for them now but to be cut down and cast into the burning. Possibly, in another season, the old bare root may send out young shoots again; but it is only by such a death and resurrection that the parasite which held so closely, and was rejected so rudely, can possibly be attached to another and a better stay.

In the fallen, broken, draggled ivy, lying along on the earth, and crushed by crumbling stones, you see the image of a human being whose heart has been fixed on a perishing portion, when that portion has fallen or fled. Woe, woe to those who have grown with, and grown for, and grown into, some tottering wall! When the wall crumbles, what of the life that leant on it? Woe is me! How many heart-strings we see rent in the various calamities of life; and how many heart-strings are preparing for themselves a dread rending, by going for the soul's support into something that is rotten at the root, and will yield to the strain of the next storm!

Look at David's ideal man: not what this man and that man is, but what any man through divine grace may be. See the source of his peace and safety: " His heart is fixed, trusting in the Lord."

We obtain here an interesting glimpse of the true relation in which the children stand to our Father in heaven.

It is a matter of the heart, more than even of the intellect. True religion is not a matter into which a man is driven against his will; it is a matter that he seeks with desire, as the hart panteth for the water-brooks. It is not a demonstration that God is a righteous judge, and therefore the guilty must tremble before him; it is a tasting that the Lord is gracious, and a consequent clinging to his bosom, as a frightened infant clasps its mother's breast. The heart goes to God; the desires of the new nature flow out in that direction: " Nearer to thee, my God; nearer to thee." And then, when you come nigh in the covenant, God is not a terror, but a trust.

The profane and unbelieving are often far out of their reckoning when they try to understand a believer's faith. They suppose that a devout man submits to some dark cold restraint, in order to secure some future expected benefit. Their conception is as near as may be the opposite of the truth. They who get nigh through the blood of the covenant give way to their hearts' longings when they walk with God. If you could by any means convince them that there is no God, the light of this life would be extinguished, as well as the hope of another. Indeed, nothing but a trust in God will keep a human heart near him. We cannot resist the laws of nature in things spiritual any more than in things material. It is a law of nature that the human spirit keeps at a distance from that which it dislikes and dreads. There is no way of keeping our spirit near to God, except by learning to trust him. And conversely, when you trust him, you do not need external compression to keep you near. It is well that the heart should be fixed on the unchangeable and eternal One; for no other anchor for the soul is sure and steadfast.

In proportion as the heart of a believer is fixed on high it becomes looser to all beneath. As it gets firmer hold of things unseen and eternal, it relaxes its grasp of things seen and temporal. A soul cannot be made fast on both sides. " Ye cannot serve two masters." Serving one master, you may have many important and tender relations with fellow-servants. Faith in God does not rend the ties that bind man to man. The expectation of a rest that remaineth does not interfere with needful labour on our present field. You may—you must take many other things into your *hands;* but only one should be permitted to glue your *heart* indissolubly to itself.

The magnet of the ship's compass is in this aspect very like a godly man in the course of his earthly pilgrimage. The magnet on the sea and the believing soul in this life are firmly fixed on one side, and hang loose on every other. Both alike are fastened mysteriously to the distant and unseen, but are slack and easily moved in all their material settings. Precisely because they are unattached beneath, they are free to keep by their hold on high ; and precisely because of their hold on high, they do not turn round with every movement of their material supports.

The magnet is by far the slackest, loosest thing in the ship. It is the only slack, loose thing there. It is not tied to the spars or nailed to the deck ; it is not even laid down and left to the force of its own gravity. An elaborate machinery has been constructed for the purpose of reducing the friction, both vertical and horizontal, to a minimum, and so leaving it nearly as free to move as if it were imponderous. I need not describe the contrivance in detail : suffice it to say, that it is so softly poised on a needle-point in the middle, that if it chooses to fix itself by

its own nature—as it were by the tendency of its heart—
to a known but unseen point in heaven, it is at liberty to
do so, and not obliged to turn with every turning of the
ship that bears it.

The ship rolls from side to side ; the ship pitches, now
her bow and now her stern raised high above the water ;
the ship changes her tack, now going east, and now west,
and anon driving before the wind. All things in the ship
move with her except the magnet of the compass. It
alone keeps ever one attitude, whatever changes of attitude
take place in the ship ; or if it turn partially and momen-
tarily, with the sudden heavings of the labouring vessel, it
is only for a moment—it rights itself again. Steady and
still otherwise, it is when driven for a little out of its
normal attitude that the magnet moves—moves, trembling
and uneasy, until it regains its own place, and there it
rests.

It is thus that a heart is loose to the world if it is fixed
on Christ. It may have needed many rendings to slacken
the heart's hold of things seen and temporal. There are
sometimes more of these, and sometimes less. There are
diversities of operation. Some are more gently set loose, and
some are severed only by the wrenching of God's own
hand, leaving a right arm cut off, or a right eye plucked
out, behind. But whether he comes in an earthquake or
in a still small voice, it is the doing of the Lord, when the
bonds are loosed that bound a soul to the dust, and the
soul, delivered, swings round free to follow the Lord.

But still, however lightly and loosely poised upon its
bearings the needle might be, it would turn with all the
ship's turnings, and never hold its head to the pole, unless
it were magnetized. The needle of the compass is a bit of

steel; but a bit of steel, though rightly framed and nicely balanced, could not serve the purposes of a compass. They take the bit of steel and hang it on a thread at a particular angle to the horizon, and give it a certain stroke with a hammer. Then and thereby it is magnetized. Its nature seems new. There are life and purpose in the iron now, and its life is manifested by a sure fixed pointing to the pole. The freeness of its poising did not make it point to the pole: it is a mysterious change of its own nature that gives it this tendency, and the freeness of its balance in the gearing permits it to obey that tendency without obstruction.

In like manner, the setting free of the heart from all idolatrous cleaving to things seen, though necessary, is not enough. Without it you cannot succeed, but even with it you may fail. Alas! we have seen a man by the strokes of God set adrift from all his moorings on the earth, and yet not fastened by faith to the anchor of the soul within the veil. When all the evil spirits are cast out of a man, it does not follow as a matter of course that he shall take Christ to fill up the empty room: he may leave it empty, until the evil spirits return and regain possession. Weary of the world is not all at once ready for heaven. Except a man be born again, he cannot see the kingdom with his understanding, or cleave to the King with his heart. As the fashioned and poised steel did not turn to the pole before it was magnetized, so the unrenewed heart is not fixed in a trust on God, although all its earthly portion has been taken away. A mysterious touch is needed to bring the heart into unison with Christ, so that it shall ever afterwards point to this pole,—the ministry of the Spirit in regeneration. "Create in me a clean heart, O God; and renew a right spirit within me."

Even after the heart has got its bias, and is by the law of a new nature fixed on Christ, the pointing is not perfect or constant. Many things hinder. The most common cause of the magnet's aberration—an aberration that often causes shipwreck—is an unsuspected mass of attractive matter lying underneath the deck, which draws the magnet from its pole. Alas! even after the heart has been truly turned to the Lord, how often is it drawn aside by certain heaps of stuff that secretly attract it. " Watch and pray, that ye enter not into temptation "—" Set your affection on things above, not on things that are on the earth "—" Demas hath forsaken me, having loved this present world."

There is a comfort which belongs to the children of the kingdom, and yet cannot easily be stated without a risk of soothing the worldly into a deeper sleep. The tumult of griefs and repentings—of regretted backslidings, and eager, agitating returns to the Lord—the fightings without and the fears within—that to a greater or less extent chequer a disciple's life, do not by any means throw doubt upon his interest in the Saviour. These are symptoms of a true faith. While the ship is at sea, the magnet shakes and moves more than any other part of the ship; and that precisely because its heart is fixed on the distant and the unseen. When, by a sudden turn or lurch in the storm, it is driven partially aside, it does not rest there; it immediately begins to struggle back again into its right position. Other objects, when they are turned away with the turning of the ship, continue in that attitude. But the magnet cannot remain averted; therefore, while the ship is at sea, it is constantly quivering. The paradox becomes at once true and easily understood,—because it is fixed it is never at rest.

Souls that have their trust in the Lord are in this way restless. They are always tremblingly struggling back into their right position before the Lord. This is proof of life,—that they rest not in an averted attitude. " Turn us again, O God, and cause thy face to shine ; and we shall be saved."

But perhaps the greatest difficulty and danger to the pilgrim on this part of his course lie in the relations, close and tender, that he must and should maintain to objects lower than the Lord—objects on earth which cannot continue by reason of death. Must one who would have his heart fixed, trusting in the Lord, keep more distant and more cold than others in the relations of kindred and friendship ? No, verily. The heart that is fixed on the Lord may twine round loved ones on earth as closely as the heart that has no hold on heaven. This is possible, but I do not say this is easy. Dangers and temptations lie thick here. Where does the fowler lay his snare ? Precisely on the path that his victim most frequently treads. Among our most binding duties and our purest enjoyments lie some of our greatest dangers.

There is a way of safety, if we have grace to choose and follow it. We must not cling to anything mortal, as the ivy clings to the old wall. There is a possibility of holding fast and yet holding loosely. It is thus that a workman grasps his tool. He holds it fast for an efficient stroke, but he can easily lay it down the next moment.

When a human heart is rightly balanced, the unrestrained exercise of all pure natural affections does not hinder, but rather helps, the faith that fastens on the Supreme. See how the analogous relations have been arranged in the motions of the spheres. The moon does not need to abjure its relations to the earth in order to maintain a supreme allegiance to the central sun. All the planetary bodies revolve round the sun; but that paramount law does not interfere with the circulation of the satellite also, and at the same time, round the earth—the globe that lies nearest to it.

Our moon is as obedient to the sun as any globe in the solar system. Its course around its great centre is as true as the orbit of any planet, and far more beautiful. Whereas the chief planets circulate in a prosaic line, the moon in its movements describes a spiral track, which adds grace and beauty to the landscape of space, as climbing, flowering shrubs relieve the monotony of a forest. The first and great commandment is, " Thou shalt love the Lord thy God with all thy heart ;" and the second, which is like unto it, and consistent with it, is, " Thou shalt love thy neighbour as thyself." If we obtain grace rightly to divide the affections of our hearts as well as the word of God, we shall find that the subordinate relations of time, instead of choking, shelter and cherish the precious seed of a better life. When, through grace, the heart is fixed, trusting in the Lord, the full, free exercise and enjoyment of all pure human relations will be safer for ourselves and more attractive as an example to others than if, in order to make sure of our hold on heaven, we should abandon the duties of time and crush the affections of nature.

The Good Shepherd
(John 10:15-16)

" I lay down my life for the sheep. And other sheep I have, which are not of this fold : them also I must bring, and they shall hear my voice ; and there shall be one fold, and one shepherd."

THE relation between the shepherd and his sheep is employed frequently and freely in the Scriptures to set forth the loving care of Christ on the one hand, and the blessed privileges of Christians on the other. Several aspects of the analogy—some of them unique and peculiar—are presented in this text.

Before we proceed to deal directly with the parable, however, it will be very instructive to glance for a moment at the words which go immediately before it. Here the preface to the parable is greater than the parable itself. Christ tells his disciples first that he died for them, and then that he lived for them. His first intimation is, " I lay down my life for the sheep ;" and his second is, " I have other sheep, and them also I must bring." There is a grand reason why these two are brought together, and arranged in this order. In the plan of this wise Master Builder, the foundation is first laid, and then the superstructure is reared. It is first his satisfying atonement, and next his ingathering ministry.

The estimate that should count resistance to the doctrine of the atonement the chief ingredient in the sceptical spirit of the age would not be far wide of the mark. It is free salvation through the sacrifice of the Substitute that most offends human philosophy in our day. The great Prophet himself, seeing the end from the beginning, and seeing in the end of the world that specific form of enmity to the cross, presciently supplied the antidote in his Word. He speaks first of his atoning death, and next of his ministering life. No effective ministry without a full expiation: on the sacrifice the ministry leans, as a structure on its foundation.

" I lay down my life for the sheep." Here, in a few simple words, is recorded the greatest fact in the course of time. Here lies the reason of the hope that is in believers. " Behold the Lamb of God, that taketh away the sin of the world !" He who clothed himself with a human body clothes his thoughts towards us in forms which, being taken off humanity, fit humanity again. He is the Shepherd, and his people are the flock. The Shepherd lays down his life for the sheep. He takes their place, that they may enjoy his ; he bears their guilt, that they may wear his righteousness ; he endures their curse, that they may inherit his glory. " He saved others ; himself he cannot save." Because he saved others, he could not save himself. If he had come down from the cross we could never have ascended to the crown.

When sin gnaws in your conscience, and the judgment-seat gleams before your eyes, here lies your help. Listen to the voice of Jesus : " I lay down my life for the sheep." From an accusing conscience and a condemning law hide in the suffering Redeemer, as the Hebrews hid under the sprinkled blood till the night of death passed over and salvation came with the dawn.

This is the turning-point; this is the key of the position. Around this spot the conflict of ages has raged. Christ was for this sacrifice, and the devil against it, from the beginning. When the Lord intimated to his disciples that he was about to lay down his life, Peter, or rather Satan within him, replied, "Far be this from thee, Lord." The cross is still to the Jews a stumbling-block and to the Greeks foolishness; but to them that are saved it is the power of God, and the wisdom of God.

In this his greatest plan and greatest work, God has not missed his mark. The Eternal Son has not thrown his life away; he laid down his life to save. I shall trust him that he knew what he did, and did what he meant to do. It is his life laid down that shall support me in my depths. Into this ark I enter when the fountains of the great deep are broken up and the flood overwhelms the world.

After the shortest and simplest announcement of his atoning death comes a description of his saving ministry: "And other sheep I have, which are not of this fold."

1. "This fold:" the seed of Israel—the visible Church of those times. It became Christ to fulfil all righteousness. He came not to destroy the law, but to fulfil. He was born in Bethlehem. He came in the track of the old sacrifices, and came unto his own. The faithful in Jerusalem were waiting for the Consolation of Israel; and at the appointed time the Consolation of Israel appeared.

By his own personal ministry he founded the kingdom in Israel, and left to his followers the task of propagating it through the world. Some of the seed of Abraham were gathered in. The common people heard him gladly, and here and there a ruler also was subdued. At the word of Jesus, living children of Abraham's faith sprang from those stones which then constituted the bulk of his natural off-spring. The Redeemer's soul was from time to time satis-fied as he felt the parched lips of a daughter of Israel pressed to himself, the Fountain of living water. He was filled with joy as he felt branch after branch growing into himself, the Vine, for life and fruitfulness. They got life ––he gave it : both were blessed, but the Giver most. In " this fold" he had some of his flock gathered and sheltered and fed, even during the time of his own personal ministry. But—

2. " Other sheep I have, which are not of this fold." Here the expansive love of Jesus breaks forth. He began at Jerusalem, but he did not end there. Even while his feet stand on the soil of Palestine, the longings of his heart go out to the ends of the earth. He was getting some, but he longed for more ; his appetite was not satisfied. The King is still sending out relays of servants into the high-ways and hedges of the world to compel the poor to come in, that his table may be furnished with guests. After he has gathered into his fold a flock more numerous than the stars that stud the plains of heaven, he still cries, " Other sheep !" " Come unto Me, all ye that labour and are heavy laden, and I will give you rest."

Besides the expansive out-going of the Redeemer's love, you may mark here its all-encompassing sovereignty: "other sheep *I have*." He does not say, I may acquire others at some future time ; he has them already. They were his in the covenant from the beginning, and he held them, every one, at that moment, in distinguishing love upon his heart. At a time when they had not learned to follow him—when they were neither born nor born again—he counts and calls them his. Ah, believing brother, thy soul lay on the Redeemer's heart that day. Thy backsliding hurt him, but did not make him change. Thy sins wounded him, but did not provoke him to let thee go. "I am Jehovah; I change not: therefore ye seed of Jacob are not consumed."

3. "*Them also* I bring." There is no respect of persons with God. Of every nation, and kindred, and tongue will be the multitude, which no man can number, who stand round the throne in white clothing. "Them also." No poor slave will be left out because he is black, or bears the mark of lashing; no servant is pushed aside to make way for his master; no rich or powerful man who cleaved to Christ is kept out at the cry of a mob that envied him. If any were kept back, the Lord would pause as he came across the sky like the lightning—would pause and say, as he beckoned to attending angels, "*Them* also." Gather up the fragments, that none of them be lost. O ye least in the kingdom of God, I have never heard that the law of gravity, God's servant, attended to the worlds and mountains, letting the drops and atoms go because they were small! Be assured God, the master of that law, and of all laws, will not permit his little ones to slip through an opening in his love. "Them also" is a cheering word. I like to hold it in my hand; I like to roll it as a sweet morsel under my tongue, to taste it long and leisurely. Lazarus, with his sores all healed now, must not glide into his old habit of lying at the door; he also must come into the palace of the great King, and there abide. The prodigal, who went far from his father, and remained long, and

had nothing to recommend him when he returned, he also must come in, and come as a son to a father's bosom, without a fear. And these, who only came to Christ when they grew old, after spending their lifetime for the world; and these, who, though they came in youth, came not till they felt the hand of death upon their hearts—come in. The Master stands and says, " Them also." Manasseh, Saul of Tarsus—the blood of the martyr Stephen all off his hands at last—" them also."

" Them *I bring*." He sends none forward to make or find their own way. He goes before them, and bids them follow; he goes with them, and bears them through. They are not alone in trouble; for in all their afflictions he was afflicted, and the angel of his presence saved them. He does not permit them to cross the valley of the shadow of death alone: the High Priest goes into the midst of Jordan, and therefore they pass safely over. " I will fear no evil, for thou art with me." He will not send any disciples to the judgment-seat to make the best of their own case; he will be there before them, and will bring them to himself. Once more it may be recorded, " Then were the disciples glad when they saw the Lord." Those guilty brothers, although they trembled at the first hint of Joseph's power, were, after full reconciliation, glad to find that Joseph ruled the kingdom. When they were convinced of their brother's love, they rejoiced in their brother's regal power. Although I find upon the throne of judgment Him whom I have crucified, yet when he manifests his forgiving love, I shall rejoice with a joy unspeakable to find that all judgment has been committed into his hands. We learn (Eph. v. 27) that when Christ has washed and sanctified his Church, he will present it to himself, without spot or wrinkle, in that day.

He brings his sheep home by going before them. He makes a way through the sea of wrath, that they may safely pass. " I am the way, and the truth, and the life; no man cometh unto the Father but by me." When he brings them to the Father, they are welcome home. " Who shall lay anything to the charge of God's elect ? It is Christ that died."

He brings them through the regeneration into the fold during their life on earth. It often takes much bringing to bring the distant nigh—the prodigal home; but all power in heaven and in earth is given to the Captain of our salvation. He will not fail nor be discouraged. To bring a drunken father home from his cups and his companions may take much power—more than weeping wife and hungry children can exert; but when the love of Christ gets hold of him by the heart, it leads him whithersoever it will. That love has laid hold of a miser, and drawn him from his gold; that love has laid hold of a sinner, whose right hand was bound indissolubly to his lust, and drawn the man to heaven, leaving his right hand behind. " Art thou a king then ?" they said to Jesus, at that unrighteous tribunal; and he condescended to tell them that they had stumbled upon the truth: " Thou sayest." He is a King, and acts in a kingly way: he says, "I bring;" and when his strength is put forth, the threefold chains of the devil, the world, and the flesh give way like threads. He leads; they follow. Thy people, Lord, shall be willing in the day of thy power. At his bringing they come from east and west; at his command the north gives up, and the south keeps not back. Those that cleaved most firmly to the dust fly as doves to their windows, their wings glittering in beauty like yellow gold.

That same bringing power, that rent asunder the chains of sin and liberated the soul, shall prevail to burst the gates of death, and bring the body in life and beauty from the grave. " I am the resurrection and the life," said Jesus : them also—the bodies of his saints, as well as the spirits— I bring with me ; that where I am, they may be.

> " Arise, yea, rise again thou must,
> After a little rest, my dust :
> Thee God thy Maker gives
> Life that for ever lives. Hallelujah !"

4. " Them also I *must* bring." What a word is this ! He commands the winds and the sea, and they obey him : who then can stand over him with authority, compelling him to fulfil his task ? It is the mightiest of all task-masters, his own yearning love. It is not only that he will or may bring his other sheep home to the fold ; he must bring them. He has laid this necessity upon himself in the well-ordered covenant, and the self-imposed necessity is sweet to his soul. "How shall I give thee up, Ephraim?" The Good Shepherd does not know how to abandon any of his flock. The whole body of the ransomed is in Scripture expressly said to be " the fulness of him that filleth all in all." A part of his own fulness would be wanting, if he should leave any fragment behind.

Shreds from this divine necessity of doing good drop down from the Head and beautify the life of the members, as rays from the sun glitter on the leaves of the grove or on the pebbles of the beach. These things that " must be " —these inevitable deep necessities—are the most lovely features of the free. Here is a mother with a sick infant on her knee. The infant's eyes are open, but they see not; they roll at random—lightless, lifeless. The parched lips utter at intervals a faint, uneasy shriek. Thus has the infant lain for several days and nights. The sun has set once more upon the scene, and the city lays itself down to rest. But that mother rests not; although her head is weary, she does not lay it down. Why? Ah! she *must* sit there and hold her child in the safest place, and look into those eyes that give her back now no answering look; she must sit and hold the child till she see the end. An overmastering love compels her, and will take no denial. It is a "must" of this kind, but mightier, that binds the Good Shepherd to bring the most distant and most feeble sheep home to the fold. Can a mother forget? She may; but thy Redeemer will not forget thee, O Zion! The high priest stood in the midst of Jordan till all the people passed over.

Personal Adorning
(1 Peter 3:3-4)

" Whose adorning......let it be the hidden man of the heart, in that which is not corruptible, even the ornament of a meek and quiet spirit, which is in the sight of God of great price."

I N our day some books and magazines devote themselves exclusively to female dress and ornament. When you open them you expect nothing else than pictorial representations or artistic descriptions of the newest fashions and the most admired adornments. But the Bible! when you turn to it, you consider that you bid farewell to all these trifles, and plunge into the deepest things of the human spirit—plunge, in some measure, according to your capacity, even into the deep things of God.

Yet here, in the Word of life, we have fallen upon a text that deals with female attire, condemning one style of adorning, and commending another. Let us listen to what our Maker says to us regarding the most becoming dress and the most effective ornaments. He who formed our bodies, and breathed into them living souls, knows best what we should put on in order to set off his workmanship to the best advantage. Hear our Father in heaven when he tells us what style of apparel will make his children beautiful,

God loves beauty of every kind, both the beauty of nature and the beauty of holiness. How do we know that? Because everything that he makes is beautiful. There is nothing ugly in creation as it comes from his hands. All the works of God are useful indeed, but all are ornamental too. The tree shows lovely flowers before it bears nourishing fruit. Such is creation as a whole. Flowers and fruit are everywhere combined. The sky, whether it is studded with stars by night, or strewn with fleecy clouds by day, is beautiful. The dome of heaven is grander than any that men have ever made. The carpet that covers the ground is studded with flowers, as well as the canopy that overhangs our dwelling. What work of man is so exquisitely ornamented as the leopard's skin and the butterfly's wing? Our works of taste are nothing but imitations, more or less successful, of the patterns which have been given to us in the mount—in the higher sphere of creative art. The chief works of our greatest masters are not original. The sunset, the sea, the landscape, outspread on canvas, and hanging in royal halls, on which successive generations have gazed admiring, are only copies more or less accurately taken from the divine originals.

The works of nature are beautiful on all sides, and on all sides alike beautiful. It is not a bright exterior, and a rough ungainly interior; it is not a polished side to the public road, and a slovenly rubble wall on the shaded side. True beauty is beauty all over, whether any observing eye should see it or not. Nor is the most elaborate design or the most exquisite colour reserved for the most enduring objects. The snow crystals, and the frosted tracery on the windows, are as perfect in design and execution as the monarchs of the forest that outlast fifty human generations.

Man is the chief of God's works, and enjoys most of his care. Man was placed highest, but has fallen from his high estate. He was made most beautiful, but has disfigured himself by sin. When his best work was damaged, the Creator did not give it up, and give it over. He framed a plan to restore. He desires to have his own image renewed. He desires to look upon his world again with complacency, and to call it good.

When the prodigal returned to his father he was in a wretched plight. He bore the marks of his sin and misery. His countenance was wan through want and his clothing was filthy rags. The swineherd bore traces of his mean employment when he appeared again in his father's sight. "Bring forth the fairest robe, and put it on him : put a ring on his finger, and shoes on his feet." The father gave commandment for becoming ornaments as well as the necessary covering. Thus our Father in heaven, when we return to him, sees us defiled and dishonoured ; but he will not permit us to remain in an unsightly and dishonoured plight. He will make his adopted children fit for their place and their company. He will make them like the children of a king. Beggars come to Christ ; but none remain beggars in his presence.

A man of feeble intellect, in the north of Scotland, was wont, like most of his class, to be very slovenly in his appearance. To this weakling the gospel of Christ came in power. He accepted God's covenant love, and found himself a child of the family. Soon after this change the minister met him on a Sabbath morning, and was struck with his unwonted cleanness, and the efforts he had made in his own fashion to ornament his person. Accosting him kindly, the minister said, " You are braw to-day, Sandy."

" He was braw Himsel' the day," replied Sandy reverently; meaning that Jesus, when he rose from the grave on the first day of the week, was arrayed in the divine glory and the beauty of holiness. The Lord on high, who rejoices to receive the little ones, would, methinks, be pleased to see Sandy's Sunday clothes and to hear Sandy's simple answer.

When a gold coin of the kingdom has by long usage lost the image and superscription of the king, they bring it back to the sovereign from whom it originally issued. The king will renew and restore. None other can. But the process cannot be accomplished by rubbing the surface. The defaced coin must be cast into the furnace and melted. Then it is recast, and comes out a new creature. In the act of renewing, the king's image is restored. By such a process, and not otherwise, may God's image be renewed in a soul that has lost it by sin. " Put off the old man, and put on the new."

There is a true analogy between physical beauty and spiritual holiness. In all languages the same names are applied to both. These parallels abound on all sides. For example, truth is like a straight line, and falsehood like a crooked one. Every one comprehends easily what is meant by the great *white* throne. And the fine linen, clean and white, is expressly defined to be "the righteousness of saints."

" This man," said the Pharisees, speaking with their lips a truth which they did not comprehend, " this man receiveth sinners." Yea, *receiveth* sinners. On this side they are poured in sinners ; on that side they emerge saints. Who are these, then, who stand around the throne in white clothing, with palms in their hands ? These are they who entered at the gospel call, in filthy rags, and have washed their robes in the blood of the Lamb.

Peter in this text undertakes to tell how the uncomely may be rendered beautiful. Here is the true adorning; and it is for us, for all. Whosoever will, let him take it. The call of the gospel compels the homeless, naked, hungry wanderers to come into the banqueting hall; and if any one is found there without the wedding garment, his want is due to his own obstinacy, for the King offers it free to all his guests.

Still deeper goes the apostle's thought when he arrives at the details of the recommended ornaments. "Not that outward adorning of plaiting the hair, and of wearing of gold, or of putting on of apparel;"—what then? "Let it be the *hidden man of the heart.*" Strange prescription! when the guests, picked up from the highways and hedges in all their rudeness and rags, must be made fit to sit at the King's table. Get them suitably adorned at once. How? "The hidden man" in the heart of each. So then the ornament which will make human beings really comely is called "the man." What man? The hidden man. He is himself invisible, and yet it is his indwelling that will make the wearer's face to shine.

Adam was the first man. He was beautiful when he came from his Maker's hands, but he was not hidden. He was the visible head of creation when God pronounced it good. Behind him, unseen, was another Man—the original, the pattern Man—in whose image Adam was formed. Adam was but a copy of the divine original. Adam was disfigured by his fall into sin. Then, it was not another copy taken, which might have been spoilt like the first, but the hidden Man himself who came into the world, and revealed himself to restore humanity.

When he had finished transgression and made an end of

sin, and brought in an everlasting righteousness, he ascended again to heaven, and remains hidden from our sight. But he who said, " It is expedient for you that I go away," said also, " Lo, I am with you alway." It is Christ dwelling in a Christian that makes him beautiful. It is not, Lo, here, or, Lo, there;—the kingdom of God is within you. The apostolic expression, " Christ in you, the hope of glory," explains how the hidden man of the heart imparts more than earth-born winsomeness to the countenance and the life of those who walk with God in the world.

There is a whole Christ in every disciple who lives up to his privileges, as there is a whole sun in the cup of every flower that opens to his shining. Suppose the sun should say to the flowers, " Lo, I am with you always," and afterwards remain high in the heavens ; the flowers could not complain that the sun had broken his promise. It is expedient for them that he should remain distant : by remaining distant he is able to dwell in the heart of each, its light and life. It is thus with our Sun of Righteousness : " If any man open, I will come in."

When this ornament is worn in the heart within, its beauty is seen on the outward life. I once met with an unexpected and interesting illustration of this principle in the Gobelin Tapestry Factory near Paris. The web, in course of construction, was suspended perpendicularly from the ceiling to the floor. The operator was concealed behind it. Beside him—for I was permitted to go within the veil to inspect his work—he had a fine picture by a master on canvas. At every thread that he shot through the extended work he took another look of this picture. He was reproducing on the external surface of the web, feature by feature, the picture, in this case of a royal personage, which he kept beside himself under the veil unseen. He continually looked at his hidden pattern, and continually advanced with the visible duplicate, that grew into form and beauty in his hands.

The sight, with the thought which it suggested, startled me. Here is the picture of a true Christian life. The workman's business is to make his visible life an epistle of Jesus Christ. But he must have the model beside himself —within. On this pattern he must frequently look, that he may reproduce outwardly the exact features of the original. When it is Christ in you—" the hidden man of the heart"—some faint but true features of the Lord will be legible on your life and spirit.

In general, a likeness of Christ is in the life of a Christian ; and, in particular, " a meek and quiet spirit." This is not the only ornament which the children of the family put on, but it is one of the most decisive marks of their birthright and their station. It was the feature which the Lord expressly specified when he invited his disciples to imitate his ways : " Learn of me ; for I am meek and lowly in heart" (Matt. xi. 29). As this is the most characteristic feature of a disciple, it is, perhaps, as the world goes, the most difficult to acquire and exhibit. But though it be the chief, it is not the only fruit and evidence of faith. Indeed, if it stood alone, it would not be so precious. It must have others to lean upon. It so happens that in the specific case recorded in the Acts, in which the world outside recognized by the conduct of the apostles that they were Christ's, it was the opposite quality of courage that constituted the distinguishing feature. It was when they saw the boldness of Peter and John that they took knowledge of them that they had been with Jesus.

One of the instructions given by Paul for the conduct of life runs in these terms : " In the midst of a crooked and perverse nation, among whom ye shine as lights in the world ; holding forth the word of life " (Phil. ii. 15, 16). The lantern of the lighthouse has many sides, and it revolves. It does not always present the same side to the observer. The sides, moreover, may be of different colours, so that now the lantern throws over the waters a white, now a green, and now a red light,—all lights and all useful, and all exhibited from the same beacon-tower, but all diverse the one from the other. Thus stand Christians conspicuous—set on a hill, and seen from afar. As they turn round in the varied business of life, they display now one and now another grace of the Spirit ; but if they are true, and not too much blotted by contact with the earth, on every side they give forth evidence that they have been with Jesus.

As a meek and quiet spirit is one of the most useful features to bring out of a believer's life, it is one of the most difficult to get in. When, in the processes of art, a new and beautiful colour is about to be transferred to a fabric, the hardest portion of the task sometimes is to discharge the dyes that are already there. A terrible process of scalding must be applied to take out the old ere you can successfully impart the new. In like manner, the anger and pride and selfishness that have first possession present the greatest obstacle to the infusion of a meek and gentle spirit into a man. If there be a royal, there is certainly no easy, road to this consummation. Nothing will suffice but the old apostolic prescription—" Put off the old man, put on the new."

It is a striking, bold, and original conception, to propose

that an ornament should be hidden in the heart. Ordinarily, we understand that an ornament, from its very nature, must be worn in a conspicuous position. When it is hidden, how useful and valuable soever it may be, it ceases to be an adorning. But in the spiritual sphere the law is reversed. That which is put on makes the wearer loathsome ; that which is hidden within makes him beautiful. Meekness is spoiled when it is set up for show. The bloom was rubbed off from the devotion of the Pharisees when it was exposed at the corner of the streets ; their charity was soured by the sound of a trumpet, like milk in a thunderstorm. The meekness that is hidden is the meekness that adorns. When it is not hidden, it is no longer meekness.

This ornament, moreover, is incorruptible. This epithet is peculiarly relevant. With the exception of the metals and minerals, ornaments are, for the most part, perishable commodities. Rain soils them ; the sun burns their beauty out. In the accidents of life they are worn or torn, or stolen or lost. The rose and lily that bloom on the cheek are not perennial ; the wrinkles of age are creeping on to drive them off and take their place. All these adornings are corruptible. This text recommends one that will never fade. Age makes it mellower, but not less sweet. As it is not a colour of the decaying body, but a grace of the immortal spirit, it will pass unharmed through the dark valley, and bloom in greater beauty on the other side. It will make the ransomed from among men very comely in the eyes of angels, when they stand together round the throne, and serve their common Lord.

One grand concern with buyers is to obtain garments that will last—garments whose fabric will not waste, and whose colours will not fade. There is one Seller in the great market of the world who assures the permanence of his wares. Hear ye him: "Buy of me gold tried in the fire, that ye may be rich; and white raiment, that ye may be clothed." In this apparel the redeemed shall shine, when the sun shall have grown dim with age and the stars fallen from heaven like unripe figs.

Yet another quality is noticed of the recommended adorning—it is *costly*. In the sight of God, and of the godly, it is "of great price." In the market of the world, alas! we, like inexperienced children, are often cheated. We pay a great price for that which is of no value. We are often caught by the glitter, and accept a base metal for gold. He who counts this ornament precious knows its worth.

The righteousness of the saints is dear to God in a double sense. It is both beloved and costly. "Father, if it be possible, let this cup pass;" but it was not possible. "He saved others; himself he cannot save." The price must be paid. The just gave himself for the unjust. The beauty of a new nature and an immortal life for fallen man were bought with a great price. The "unspeakable gift" of God was laid down to obtain it. It cost the Redeemer much to get the "filthiness purged out" of his people, and get them made meet for the inheritance of the saints in light. Nothing shall enter that defileth: the bride shall be adorned to meet her Husband.

The ransomed of the Lord, when they come to Zion, will constitute the crown that adorns their Redeemer's brow. These are the jewels for which he paid an unspeakable price, and which he will wear as his crown of rejoicing in that day.

The practical lesson is very clear and very forcible. We should be fellow-workers with God in keeping off, or casting off, with all diligence, every spot from our own hearts and lives which the Lord that bought us would not like to look upon. "Blessed are the pure in heart: for they shall see God."

The Salt of the Earth
(Matthew 5:13)

" Ye are the salt of the earth."

THIS is a short, pointed, condensed sentence. It gives us much matter in little room. The words were spoken by Jesus, and addressed to his own disciples. Come and let us sit at his feet, and hear him, as it were, speaking them over again. If we come to him as scholars, he will be our teacher still. He will bestow the Spirit at our request, to open the parable and make all its meaning plain. Although the expressions are figurative, they are by no means difficult. The two chief words are, the *earth* and the *salt*. We shall consider them separately, and then apply the lesson from both combined.

I. *The earth and its need.*—It is quite true that the term " earth," when employed in Scripture as a figure to express moral relations, is not always employed in the same sense. Had it stood alone here, it might have been difficult to determine which of several possible meanings should be attached to it; but its connection with the other word " salt " renders such an examination unnecessary. " Salt " stands like a mirror before "earth," to receive and exhibit its precise import. We are not left to guess which of its figurative meanings the word "earth" here bears. The meaning is fixed, and shown to be that which needs purification and preservation. Obviously the earth, considered as requiring salt, is human kind lying in the corruption of sin. It means all mankind; and all lying in wickedness. The Lord Jesus speaks of man, made in God's image, as the head of creation, and speaks of him as tainted by sin. A fly alighted on creation while it was yet young, and its mass became morally a noisome carcass. No portion of the race has escaped the infection. It is, moreover, the law of moral as well as of material corruption, that the evil assumes an aggravated form wherever large masses are collected together. As men multiply, sin increases. The larger the heap of corruptible matter, the more rapidly it decays. Hence the kind and quantity of depravity in large cities.

The use of the single term "earth" in this sense by Him who came to redeem it is calculated to awaken and alarm us. It is not a part of the world that has gone astray, but the whole. This last and chief of God's works—this cornerstone of creation—has fallen from purity. It is corrupt to the core. There is no soundness in it. The only kind of beings on earth that are capable either of holiness or sin have fallen from holiness, and are lying helpless in sin. The earth, as represented by the moral and spiritual being at its head, is altogether an unclean thing.

By birth and nature a part of this corrupt mass, we grow up without uneasiness or alarm, unless and until we be awakened by another voice than our own. The corrupt do not loathe their own corruption. Sinners do not of their own motion grow weary and ashamed of sin. They have no desire to escape from the miry pit; they resist and resent every offer of aid. Although all intelligent beings who are not in the pit, whether they be angels who never fell, or saints who have been lifted up, look on with inexpressible disgust and pity, those who lie unclean in that place of uncleanness are contented with their lot. Corruption is the element of the corrupt. So far from naturally desiring freedom, and welcoming a deliverer, they dread the approach of the hand that would save them. When the maniac's heart was a nest of unclean spirits, his lips cried out, " What have we to do with thee, thou Jesus ?" Holiness, instead of being the inborn delight of the carnal mind, is the object of its strongest aversion. It is in a day of almighty power that the impure are made willing to be led into purity.

Here lies the most dreadful feature of our case : we are not only vile, but vileness is our nature , so that we cleave to it with the strength and steadiness of an instinct. If the case of a sinner in his sin could be justly compared to the case of a man who has fallen into the water, and is in danger of being drowned, all would be easy. To help the willing is a simple task, and is generally successful. But the actual condition of the problem is precisely the reverse. Souls in sin love to be in it; the spiritually corrupt love corruption.

It behoves us to look this matter in the face, and be aware of the desperate state of the fallen, ourselves and our neighbours. It is not by a wish for heaven that the corrupt can escape from their corruption and become new creatures. From its first plan to its final consummation in glory, sovereign free mercy has done all the work of redemption. " Create in me a clean heart, O God, and renew a right spirit within me." The first faint uneasiness under guilt, and the first faint desires to be free, are marks of the Spirit's motion in my heart: let me not quench the Spirit, lest that blessed messenger depart and leave me; let me yield to the drawing which I now feel, and these everlasting arms will draw me more.

II. *The salt and its properties.*—Jesus, addressing his own disciples, said, " Ye are the salt of the earth." A portion of the corrupt mass cannot become the salt to preserve the rest of it. The salt is different from the earth. It is new. It is the work of God in the regeneration.

Those who have been forgiven and renewed are the salt; but why has their Redeemer given them that peculiar name ? What feature of their character, or form of their usefulness, does this figurative expression indicate ? The word teaches us something about the new creature in respect both to what it is and to what it does; a lesson regarding both its *nature* and its *use* lies wrapped in the parable.

In *nature* the new creature is not allied to the corruption that is in the world. It is an incorruptible thing. Left to itself it does not become noisome; it continues pure. There are indeed mixtures of the old man in a Christian while he remains in the body; but the new life from the Lord which has been quickened within him is like its origin and its Author. Although it be lodged among earthly things, itself is not earthly. Although it is sadly true that even a Christian falls frequently into sin, yet the new man created within him " cannot sin, because he is born of God."

As to the *use* of Christ's disciples in the world, the Lord clearly and impressively made known his mind when he

called them "the salt of the earth." This designation
should be as easily and correctly understood as the speech
of a commander who cries aloud to his soldiers, "Ye are
the defenders of your country," as he leads them forward
to repel an invading foe. If we confine our view to what
the Lord has done *for* his people, we shall run away with
half a truth, and convert it into a full error. He does
something for them—something greater than eye hath
seen, or ear heard, or heart conceived; but he does something *with* them too. Nay more: he works *for* them first,
in order that he may work *by* them then. He buys them
off from Satan's bondage with the price of his own blood,
in order that he may have a band of sons and daughters
who shall yield themselves willing instruments unto him,
for his work of righteousness in the world. He redeems
them from their sin, that he may employ them in his own
service. As to the fact that true disciples are of use to
their Lord, the whole Bible is full and clear; and as to the
manner in which he turns their talents to account, a world
of meaning is contained in the one word "salt." When he
has forgiven and renewed some, he places them in contact
with the remaining mass, as an instrument to preserve and
purify it. The errand on which he came is to save the
lost; he is straitened till his work be done; his disciples,
partaking of his spirit, should be straitened too. Paul
greatly longed after certain inhabitants of Philippi whom
he knew; but he longed after them "in the bowels of Jesus
Christ." It was as a member of Christ's body that he felt
that throb of compassion for human kind. It was the
Saviour's own compassion circulating through the soul of
the saved man that stimulated him to zeal for his brethren.

The word of Christ is, as it were, a two-edged sword; it

is a promise and a command in one. He gives what he demands, and demands what he gives. The same master both gives the talents and requires an account of their outlay. He sends none on a warfare at their own charges; but when he has been at charges with any one, and fully furnished him, he does not exempt him from the warfare. " Ye are the salt of the earth." Look to the upper side of that word, and its meaning is—Christ has redeemed and purified his own; look to the under side, and its meaning is—Christians should be in the world witnesses of Christ and winners of souls. Elsewhere this double truth is divided, and both its sides separately displayed,—" Ye are bought with a price; therefore, glorify God."

Now for the lessons.

1. *There is much of the " earth" still.*—The portion that has been broken off and purified is comparatively small; the bulk of the world lies in a state of corruption. The majority of mankind worship the work of their own hands. The nations, without knowing the reason, have rejected the living God, because impurity does not like to come near the consuming fire. It is not an innocent and childlike form of worship into which the nations have fallen. It is evil in its nature and its effects. It dishonours God and destroys men.

But even in countries where divine truth is known, and divine worship set up, great numbers remain almost as deeply corrupt as the heathen. Certain districts of our great cities, and certain classes of our teeming population, live without God in the world. Even within the communion of Christian churches, and within the circle of Christian families, much of the " earth" remains unchanged.

Oh! if there were missionaries ready for the work, the mission field is wide and near. A mighty work must be done ere the earth be penetrated and pervaded by the salt of divine truth, held in the life and conversation of consistent Christians.

2. *There is little of the salt.*—There are not many nations in the world called by the name of Christ; and even of these, comparatively few have actually been transformed into his likeness. Alas! Christians are still a little flock.

But we must beware lest we stumble here on the other side. It would indeed be an error indolently to assume that all are Christians who assume the name; but it would be also an error on the other side peevishly to make the number of Christians less than it is. It is as much our duty to own what God has wrought in the world by his grace as to lament the corruption that still so widely prevails. If it be true on the one side that there is little salt, it is true on the other side that there is a little. There has been a little all along, and the Spirit poured out is at present creating more. While we grieve that the number of true Christians is so small, we ought also to be thankful that it is so great. Many have been added to the Lord in our own day, and he would be offended if we should refuse to own the fact. True Christians are so many that we should greatly rejoice in God's goodness; and yet true Christians are so few that we should not sit down satisfied with the state of the world. The Lord hath done great things for us; whereof we are glad. What has been done should effectually rebuke our repining; but what remains to be done should prevent us from making this our rest. The true attitude of Christians at the present time, on either side, is to thank God for giving us much salt, and give him no rest till we get more. Indeed, the design of our Father in giving us drops is to stimulate our desire for showers. When we are permitted to see sinners coming to Christ by tens, he expects that the sight will send us to his throne with ceaseless supplications that he would arise in the power of his love and draw them to himself in thousands.

3. *There is little saltness.*—We have already pointed out that there is not much salt in the great mass of a corrupt world; and it is our duty now to point out, further, that there is little savour even in the salt itself. Christians are few in the world; and grace is feeble in Christians. The Lord himself, in his lessons on this subject, clearly indicated that even the salt may, in some measure, lose its pungency and power. It is a sad and obvious fact, which may be read on the surface of society, that even true disciples are more or less conformed to the world in which they live. Indeed, it seems, in some cases, to be the specific aim of the " salt " to be as like " earth " as it can. The preserver labours to become indistinguishable from the corruption which it is sent to cure; and, alas! it often labours in this direction with abundant success. Christians, with much trouble and care, disguise their Christianity. The saltness is perseveringly bleached out of the salt, lest the neighbouring corruption should smart under its pungency.

This is not the discontented complaint of one who can see no good among his fellows. It is not a wholesale and indiscriminate sentence of condemnation spoken by croaking lips and guided by a jaundiced eye. It is the truth; and it is plainly spoken, because truth is necessary and salutary. I speak it from the certain knowledge that the case requires it, and with a fervent hope that to speak it plainly will do good. I give forth the warning, not from a despairing but from a hopeful heart. In dealing with the vineyard, I would fain follow the steps of our Father the husbandman: if the tree were hopelessly barren, I would let it alone; but when a tree is bringing forth some fruit, I would like to prune it that it may bring forth more fruit. There is some savour in the salt; but why should there not be more? Great is the bounty of the Giver, and great is the world's need.

What is the rule which secretly, habitually, effectively shapes your conduct? Is it the way of the world, or the will of your Saviour? This is a great question, and it is not necessarily very difficult. We do not drag you through minute details. We ask your attention only to the chief motive power. The flowing stream which drives all the complex machinery of your life—is it the frothy fashion of the world, or the strong deep love of Christ in giving himself for you? The wheel which the fashion of the world drives is, like those of Ezekiel's vision, so high that it is dreadful; but, unlike them, it is not full of eyes round about—it is blind all over. An uncounted number of busy little wheels are dependent on its power. Great are the noise and dust; great the sweat and toil. Do you grind in that treadmill? If you do, you may be weary, but you will not get rest.

> " On the other side of Jordan,
> In the sweet fields of Eden,
> Where the Tree of Life is blooming,
> There is rest for the weary "—

the weary who walk with Christ and work for his cause; but though the god of this world gives his worshippers hard work, he has no rest remaining for them when the work is done.

But the fashion of the world is not only made in secret the real motive power in life ; it is in many cases openly confessed as the rule. Others did the same ; it was common in the place ; what would the world say if we should take another course ?—these and other similar current phrases, like floating straws, show the direction and the force of the current. The plea is worthless. It will not stand in the judgment of the great day ; it will not even stand the scrutiny of common sense. For the food, the drink, the dress, the education, the company, the conduct of yourselves and your children, fling away at once and for ever the fashion of a giddy world, and take as your guiding rule the will of the Lord that bought you. As long as you meanly tread in the track of a corrupt world, you do the world no good. Your salt has lost its savour. To be near you does not trouble an unconverted man. Your way is so like his own that your presence is no reproof. The profane may count you a good fellow ; but Christ counts you an unfaithful witness. On the other hand, if you were enabled to walk in the Spirit and with Christ, your presence would be a reproof to wickedness, your footprints a guide to the wanderer, your faith a support to younger disciples. Salt of the earth, do not let go your savour. Christians, let the mind which was in Christ be also found in you.

4. *The salt is too seldom laid upon the decaying to preserve and restore it.*—Even where there is salt with the savour in it, the benefit is in a great measure lost for want of the needful contact. It is not enough that there is salt here and corruption yonder—salt, it may be, in the square,

and corruption in the lane; unless they meet, the one cannot enjoy the blessedness of receiving, nor the other the greater blessedness of imparting, good. The preserving salt must interpenetrate the body which needs preservation, and lie in contact with all its parts. Thus the Saviour did, and thus should the saved do. He was the friend of publicans and sinners; the friend of publicans and sinners should I also be.

This is the true secret of a home mission. The best Christians are those who are most like Christ. The Holy One came from a holy heaven and dwelt in a sinful world; while there he cast himself in the way of the worst, and wept over them when they would not permit him to come near. Go, ye who are bought by his blood, and bear his name —go, and do likewise. By close communing with the Lord Jesus, keep the savour in your salt; and by close contact with those who are dead in sins, let the earth in its corruptest parts get the benefit of a pungent reproof. Be alternately much with the great Giver, God in Christ; and the needy receiver, a godless world. These are the two things worth living for—getting from the Saviour, and giving to the lost. "Freely ye have received, freely give." It is when Christians have a "savour of Christ" upon their spirit and conduct that they become "a savour of life" to those who are dead in sin.

LESSONS IN FIRST PETER

Peter, an Apostle
(1 Peter 1:1)

"Peter, an apostle of Jesus Christ."

OCCASIONS for critical remarks may occur here and there as we proceed, but I do not propose to introduce any general discussion of cognate subjects as a preface to my work. There is not time nor space for that. It suits my purpose better to plunge at once into the matter of the Divine Word. We do not assume here the position of Israel when first the manna fell—that of the questioner, "What is it?" We assume at once the position of the people after they had tasted it. Being hungry, and seeing the bread from heaven spread out around our tents, we propose to gather and eat —eat, and live thereby. If, through the blessing of God, any gainsayer should be convinced by these expositions, the effect would be incidental : our direct aim is gently to lead inquirers through the open gate into life, to instruct the little ones of the family, and to edify strong men into a still stronger faith.

This letter, like those of Paul and ancient letters generally, throws into its forefront the writer's name and office. The reader desires to know who his correspondent is ; and the practice of placing that information at the beginning

seems more convenient as well as more natural than our
modern method. This man is not now ashamed of his
name, nor of the cause which it supports. He will not
undertake to vindicate all his antecedents; but now he
knows his position and bearings. The latter end is peace.
Peter! the Galilean fisherman; the forcible yet fickle disciple; the cowardly denier, yet the ardent lover and heroic
confessor of the Lord! A number of different and even
opposite qualities go to constitute this man's history and
character. Two kings and two kingdoms strove against
each other for the mastery in the fisherman's capacious
breast. Ishmael, or the world power, had first possession,
and had grown into strength before Isaac, the child of
promise, was born. The son of the strange woman lorded
it long over the heir in Peter's history, as in Abraham's
house; but in the end, the child of promise prevailed, and
possessed all. At the date of this letter, Peter, with all
his force and fire, is on the Lord's side.

"Peter, an apostle." Ah, Peter, is this another piece of
cowardice? An apostle, and no more: are you not the
prince of the apostles? Are you not the representative of
God on earth, and the infallible interpreter of his will?
Are you not the head of the Church, before whose word
Paul and all the rest must humbly bow on pain of perdition?

Mark: if Peter ever possessed these prerogatives, he
possessed them then. He received no subsequent advancement from the Divine Head. If Peter were infallible, what
of Paul who withstood him to the face? Oh the silliness
as well as the wickedness of men! I suspect, however,
that people will never be argued out of Papal Infallibility:
they were not reasoned into it, and we need not expect

that they can be reasoned out of it. The human mind is voluntarily crushed in order to let that dogma in, and therefore it has no power to arise and cast the intruder out again. It is not that men are convinced that the blasphemous pretension is true ; it is that they are given over to believe a lie.

The title which Peter assumes is at once dignified and modest. He assumes all the authority he possessed—all that his Master gave him. If he had a right to more, he should have claimed it, in order to add weight to his word. He was bound to keep nothing back. Yet, according to Romish teaching, Peter and all his successors have from that day to this possessed a divine power of infallible knowledge intrusted to them for the good of the world, and especially for settling all controversies in religion; and they have never told that they possessed the precious treasure,—never known that they possessed it, for that matter, —till now ! " Fie on't, oh, fie ; it smells rank."

The Greek term apostle, and the Latin term missionary, mean the same thing,—" one sent out." Those ministers who dwell at home at ease, however useful they may be in their own place, have no peculiar claim to be accounted the successors of the apostles. The men to whom the Master gave that office thought it needful to offer an apology for remaining in one place a whole year. If any class of ministers more than another had a claim to this distinction, it would have been foreign missionaries.

Moses was a missionary. The I Am, from the midst of the burning bush, first drew him near and then sent him out,—" Come ; I will send thee." From the embrace of the suffering Saviour, in the old time, Moses was sent into Egypt to lead the exodus. From the embrace of the

Saviour more fully manifested apostles were sent out in the fulness of time to win the world. From that glow of divine love Peter issued all on fire—a messenger sent out to seek his Lord's lost and lead them back to his Lord.

By special providence Peter's case has been left on record as a type of the manner in which real apostles are made. Behold the Master (John xxi. 15) bending over him, at once healing the old backsliding and kindling the flame of a new love : Lovest thou me ? lovest thou me ? lovest thou me ? There is some smoke yet in that bundle of flax over which he is tenderly bending : methinks I hear the thrice repeated gentle breathings,—not energetic blasts that might have quenched the feeble spark, but breathings to cherish the dull heat into a flashing flame. Out from this furnace sprang an apostle ready-made, who needed now but to get his specific commission : " Feed my sheep ; feed my lambs."

Apostolic Benediction
(1 Peter 1:1-3)

"To the strangers scattered throughout Pontus, Galatia, Cappadocia, Asia, and Bithynia, elect according to the foreknowledge of God the Father, through sanctification of the Spirit, unto obedience and sprinkling of the blood of Jesus Christ: Grace unto you, and peace, be multiplied. Blessed be the God and Father of our Lord Jesus Christ."

TO the Christians scattered throughout the various provinces of Asia Minor the letter is addressed. The regions enumerated coincide in the main with those in which Paul and his companions founded churches. Did Peter transgress the rule which forbids one missionary to interfere with the sphere and labour of another? No: we may not be able to explain everything, as we are not acquainted with all the circumstances, but we may rest assured there was an understanding between those primitive missionaries. Had Paul by this time been taken away? or had Mark brought word that a letter from Peter to the Asiatic churches would be welcome to the members, and even strengthen Paul's hands, especially with the Jewish portion of the Christian communities?

These disciples were " elect [chosen] according to the foreknowledge of God." What is called the doctrine of Election should not be a stumbling-block to any who acknowledge the divine authority of the Scriptures. There it is, as fully and articulately expressed in the Word of God as it can be in any human creed.

The Bible says they were chosen according to the fore-knowledge of God; and who shall say they were not ? We may well stand in awe on the margin of this unsearchable deep. We may not be able to comprehend it in all its bearings ; but there it is. " Be still, and know that I am God." This great word should make human hearts bow in deep humility, and accept offered salvation all of grace. And as to inferential difficulties, the freedom and responsibility of men are as clearly revealed as the sovereignty of God. " Repent ye," is the commandment ; and the sanction follows it, " Except ye repent, ye perish." So the sovereignty of God does not stand in the way of his free offer and man's full responsibility. He knows his own way through the difficulty. These two ends meet in the deep things of God; and "the day" will reveal the meeting-place. Enough for me : he has said, " Believe in the Lord Jesus Christ, and thou shalt be saved." Even so, " Lord, I believe ; help thou my unbelief."

In this verse the Father is revealed in connection with election and foreknowledge ; the Spirit in connection with the sanctification of believers ; and the Son in connection with the sprinkling of the blood that saves. It is parallel with that word in the Lord's own prayer: " Thine they were ; and thou gavest them me : and they have kept thy word " (John xvii. 6).

While this beautiful introductory salutation, " Grace unto you, and peace," is a formula common to all the apostles, it is also an exact theological definition, rightly dividing the word of truth. The right thing is put foremost here. The living root lies in the ground below, and the fruit-bearing branches tower above it. It is grace first, and peace following it. When God and man meet, it is pardon first, and then a mutual confidence. When he in the Mediator dispenses freely his favour, you in the Mediator draw near without dread. He manifests himself a forgiving Father, and that very thing infuses into your heart the spirit of a trusting child.

" May grace and peace be multiplied." In the Old Testament (Isa. xlviii. 18) there is a promise that his people's peace " shall be like a river"—gaining affluents from either side as it flows, and at the last opening out into " a righteousness like the waves of the sea."

Now, after the designation of the writer and the readers has been given, the matter of the letter begins,—begins with glory to God in the highest. With remarkable unanimity the sacred writers make this their starting-point. From Moses to Peter, the first commandment is glory to God, and the second is duty to men.

There is a distinction maintained in Scripture between " blessed " as applied to God, and " blessed " as applied to men. Although we are obliged to use the same term for both in our language, they are distinct in the Greek. That which is applied to God means to be *pronounced blessed;* that which is applied to men means to be *made blessed.*

Of all the aspects and attributes of the great God, that which first leaps to the lips of this apostle is, " the Father of our Lord Jesus Christ." How real and vivid was spiritual life in those primitive Christians. Faith really dominated. Farm and merchandise receded into the background, and the relations of the soul with God and eternity bounded to the front. And mark how Peter finds it possible to draw near to God: he takes refuge in the Mediator. When he sees God as the giver of the unspeakable Gift, he comes forward with boldness. In point of fact, unless we recognize him in that character, we cannot relish him in any. "*With Him*, how shall he not freely give us all things?" These men were skilful. They knew where consolation lay; they grasped God by his title of Father of our Lord Jesus, and so were enabled to cling in fond confidence as dear children.

There is an amazing wealth and grandeur of thought and expression here. Whence hath this man his wisdom? The fisherman is here the vessel chosen and employed by the Spirit to pour out in all its fulness the gospel of the grace of God. The Epistle at this point where it begins to flow is like one of those infant rivers which burst full-bodied at their birth from a great inland sea in which their waters have been gathered. Unlike the waters of Ezekiel's vision that gathered volume as they flowed, this is a river to swim in the moment that it breaks away from the fountain-head. This testimony from an unlearned Galilean is already a Christian evidence. The book is a witness to itself.

Who is this of whom the prophet speaks?—God.

In what aspect does the Supreme present himself?—As the Father of our Lord Jesus Christ.

What has he done?—Begotten us again; made us new creatures.

From what motive has he acted?—According to his abundant mercy.

By what means has he accomplished this great change? By the resurrection of Jesus Christ from the dead.

To what end in the experience of his people does he thus

work ?—To a living hope burning in their hearts here, and an inheritance incorruptible beyond the grave.

At the opening here made in heaven a great cluster of stars appear. Their united light shines like a sun, and each constituent of the constellation is a separate orb of glory. Nor does the brightness dazzle the sinner's uplifted eye, for it is the glory of God streaming from the face of Jesus, mighty to save.

The Heirs and Their Inheritance
(1 Peter 1:3-4)

"Which according to his abundant mercy hath begotten us again unto a lively hope by the resurrection of Jesus Christ from the dead, to an inheritance incorruptible, and undefiled, and that fadeth not away, reserved in heaven for you."

HOPE is enjoyed here, possession hereafter. But the enjoyment of the inheritance is real, although it is as yet held only by hope. The hope is living. Not only will it surely be substantially satisfied in the end, but even in the meantime it secures the enjoyment. An inanimate cord might bind together the expecting heir and his ultimate inheritance, so that they could not finally miss each other; but a living nerve, extending from the new creature here in the body to the kingdom that is not of this world, conveys even now the revenue of the inheritance before the time, according to the Master's own aspiration, "That my joy might remain in you, and that your joy might be full" (John xv. 11).

How may we be introduced into such a hope? Through the new birth. Peter's doctrine here is in strict accord with the word of the Lord to Nicodemus: "Except a man be born again, he cannot see the kingdom of God,"—neither behold it in living hope now, nor enter it at last. These two terms, "begotten again" and the "incorruptible inheritance," are made for each other, like the two valves of a sea-shell. They shut accurately upon each other, but upon nothing else. Our inheritance by the first birth is neither undefiled nor unfading. To escape the curse of the first birth-right, we must have another birth. The new creature in Christ is joint-heir with him—heir of all things.

The resurrection of Jesus Christ was the closing and culminating act of the redemption that he wrought. If the work had not thereby been completed, it would have been of no avail. The Spirit, through Paul, has clearly borne witness that unless the Redeemer's work had been crowned by his resurrection, our hopes would have been in vain (1 Cor. xv. 17). The meaning is, that the completed work of Christ saves his people from sin, and gives them a right to the eternal inheritance. Those who are born again rise with him into resurrection life. The life that they now live in the flesh, they live by the faith of the Son of God. Earth becomes to these heirs the vestibule of heaven.

The characteristics of the inheritance are all negative. The features that ordinarily go to mar an earthly heritage are enumerated for the purpose of declaring that they do not adhere to the rest that remaineth for the people of God. The inheritance is (1) incorruptible. It is not liable to complete dissolution, like a dead body that returns to dust. It is (2) undefiled. It is not liable to have all its beauty dimmed by some unclean spot falling on its form. Often an earthly inheritance, while its substance abides the same, loses all its attraction for the owner. The eldest son, perhaps, for whom it was fondly cherished, has thrown away his good name. Henceforth the father cannot look with complacency on his green fields and waving woods. A glance at the landscape makes him shudder. His inheritance is defiled. Not so the heritage to which the children of God have, in the regeneration, been served heirs. The inheritance is (3) unfading; its bloom will never wither. It is not subject to alternations of darkness and light, of winter and summer. The Lamb is the light thereof; and there shall be no night there. In exact accord with the imagery of John is the plain, earnest prose of Paul, when life and death were trembling in the balance. To be with Christ was the bright expectation which took all the terror out of death when it seemed very near (Phil. i. 23).

The silence of Scripture, especially in contrast with the coarseness of earth-born systems, is sometimes as emphatic a testimony to its divine origin as its positive revelations. Lights on the shore flash far over the ocean, and conduct the voyager to the land; but they do not reveal to him, while at sea, the particular features of the landscape. It is thus that the Bible exhibits lights sufficient to guide inquirers safe to heaven, but not sufficient to reveal its interior beauties. Those who reach the better land will discover its glories after they arrive.

Some are born to a great inheritance, and yet miss it. In our days thrones are frequently shaken, and their occupants cast off. Princes who were born to a royal heritage wander as exiles in a foreign land. But there are no revolutions in the kingdom of heaven. Every one gets his own there. The laws of nature give a token of the certainty that prevails in the region where the Lord reigns. Although a globule of air were imprisoned for a thousand years within a shell at the bottom of the ocean, the moment its prison-house decayed it would rise sheer through the water, though it were miles in depth, and never halt till it emerged with a bound into its native element, the sky,

Behold a specimen of his power, who has promised " none of them shall be lost."

Here are two keepings promised ; and the two constitute a pair. The inheritance is preserved for the heirs, and the heirs are preserved for the inheritance. Both keepings are needed ; and both are provided in the covenant. The danger was not all over when Pharaoh consented at last to let Israel go. The danger was not all over even when the emancipated Hebrews reached the Red Sea's farther shore. They were saved ; and yet they needed salvation. The returning waters overwhelmed the enemy, and protected their rear ; but a howling wilderness lay between them and their rest. They needed keeping by an Almighty hand, those feeble heirs. They sing. Have they not begun their song too soon ? Are they not hallooing before they are out of the wood ? Have they not something harder than hymns to deal with ? They have ; and yet they have not too soon begun their song. They should rejoice in salvation already wrought, and go forward to work out their own salvation. Getting manna from heaven, and water from the rock, they must tread the rugged path and fight the cruel foe ; and toiling forward, never breathe freely till, in the wake of the forerunner high priest, they pass the parted Jordan, and feel their footing firm in the promised land.

Mighty to Save
(1 Peter 1:5)

" Who are kept by the power of God through faith."

WHAT is done for the heirs while they are here in the body ? They are *kept*. Nothing more is needed here than to give a definition of the word and its meaning. There are various kinds of keeping. It concerns us to define exactly what kind is promised here.

In the first place, it is a keeping within walls and gates. To this meaning the term is limited by the well-known usage of the original language. But even within these limits there are two kinds of keeping, very diverse in design and effect. Stone walls may close around you either for the purpose of keeping you in, or for the purpose of keeping your enemy out. The first is a *prison*, the second a *fortress*. In construction and appearance the two species of fastness are in many respects similar. In both cases the walls are high, the gates strong, and the guards trusty. But they differ in this—that the prison is constructed to prevent escape from within, the fortress to defy assault from without. In their design and effect they are direct and exact contraries. The one secures the bondage, the other the freedom, of its inmates. In both cases it is a *keep*, and in both the keep is strong: the one is strong to keep the enemy out, the other is strong to keep the prisoner in. In the Greek of the New Testament two completely distinct words are employed respectively to designate these two places of strength. Both terms alike signify to guard; but the one (φυλακη) signifies a prison, the other (φρουρη) signifies a fort. The word employed here is not prison, but fort. It is a place strong to preserve liberty, not to take it away.

From David downward, the godly in times of trouble have ever found and confessed that God is a strong tower, in which the righteous are safe. In times of persecution the name is best understood, and the thing most valued: when and where war rages, strongholds are desired and appreciated.

In this life a Christian is safe; but his safety consists in the protection of a fort. He is neither the slave of a tyrant on the one hand, nor beyond the reach of assault on the other. He is no longer in the kingdom of darkness, but neither has he been admitted yet into the mansions of the Father's house. He is in a middle region; and in all that region he is safe, but his safety cometh from the Lord. Before he was converted, he did not get this keeping; and when he is glorified, he will no longer need it. Before he came over to God's *side*, he was not preserved from his enemies; after he is taken to God's *presence*, there will no longer be any enemies to be defended from. But all through this middle passage, between Egypt and Canaan, he needs and gets his Redeemer to be a wall of fire round about him. This is the kind and measure of safe-conduct which the King bestows upon the pilgrim: " I pray not that thou shouldest take them out of the world, but that thou shouldest keep them from the evil." This is precisely what the Mediator asks and the Father bestows.

Some, mistaking the fortress for a prison, refuse to enter it. They give a wide berth to all earnest personal religion, as a dungeon in which, if they should venture too near, they might possibly be immured for life. The enemy of souls, taking advantage of this terror, which is natural to the guilty, sends scouts all over the plain through which the pilgrims are marching, who falsely tell them that this stronghold which the King has built for their protection is a prison in which they will be cruelly shut up. If vice and unbelief slay their thousands, ten thousand fall under the false opinion that to come personally to Christ, though necessary for safety at the end of life, is to dwell in a prison through its course. Believe not this false testimony. " Godliness is profitable unto all things, having the promise both of the life that now is and of that which is to come."

Whereby are the heirs kept ? By the *power of God.* Omnipotence is pledged on their behalf. But it is a different exercise of divine power from that which is exhibited in creation. It is specifically described in Philippians iv. 7 : " The peace of God, which passeth all understanding, shall keep your hearts and minds through Christ Jesus." This is a most interesting and instructive definition. It tells both that in God which he holds them with, and that in men which he holds them by. In him it is " the peace of God " that takes hold ; in them, it is " the heart and mind " that it seizes. God's peace streaming forth through the Mediator, and wrapping itself round the heart and mind,—behold the specific exercise of divine power by which the heir is kept for his inheritance.

Through what means are believers kept ? Through

faith. The cause is God's power; the manner, through our believing. Men are not kept from falling into sin precisely as the worlds are kept from falling away into unlighted space. Both effects are produced by the power of the same God; but there are diversities of operation. In the case of those coursing worlds, it is power on the one side and nothing on the other; it is simple omnipotence. With all their bulk and all their brightness, they lie like clods in the law of God. Worlds were made by God's word; but man was made in his image. Renewed man, living and sensitive, feels his Creator's hand around him, and responds by a reciprocating grasp. This feeble people have no strength, but they make their nest in the Rock of Ages. A believer is not like a god on the one hand, and not like a clod on the other. He does not save himself; but neither is he saved by mere omnipotence. He stands in the middle between these two. He is like a piece of matter in its weakness, but like God in having an intelligent will to choose and refuse. Equally with inanimate matter, he is indebted to divine power for his upholding; but unlike it, he knows his need, and gladly casts his burden on the Lord. God holds him up, and he trusts in God.

Take a glance at these two points now, in their union and relations. They are the two sides, the upper and the lower, of one salvation. The double seal is elsewhere exhibited with both its inscriptions in view: " The Lord knoweth them that are his. And, Let every one that nameth the name of Christ depart from iniquity " (2 Tim. ii. 19). He hath done all things well. He acts as becomes himself; and he exercises also the faculties which he has imparted to his creatures. Nothing unnecessary is intro-

duced, and nothing is left undone. Both on the heavenward side and the earthward side salvation is secure. The
strongest thing in heaven and the strongest thing on earth
are entwined into each other to bear up a believer, that he
may not in time of temptation drop away. The strongest
thing in heaven is the power of God, and that on high
holds fast a Christian; the strongest thing on earth,
removing mountains if need be, and overcoming the world
—the strongest thing on earth is man's faith, and that
below makes fast a Christian. If one of the least of these
should begin to say, Oh! wretched man that I am, my
faith is weak; some day the adversary will gain an advantage over me, and I shall let go my hold,—the reproof and
encouragement are ready here. It is not by your faith
that you are kept, but by God's power. Behold, he that
keeps Israel, he slumbers not nor sleeps. Again, if the
subtle temptation is injected into his heart, If God keeps
me by his power, I need not be at the trouble of keeping
myself,—he will find in this text a scourge ready plaited
to his hand wherewith he may drive the tempter out. My
God, who keeps me, keeps me through my own faith. He
gives me himself to lean on; but he expects me to lean on
himself. If I in carelessness or presumption neglect to
hold, I fall, and my perdition is my own deed.

But in such a case the purpose to escape the trouble of
holding, on the plea that omnipotence is enough, is already
evidence that this soul has no part in the salvation of
Christ. He is a God, not of the dead, but of the living.
If the soul lives, it will grasp its almighty Protector's arm;
and if it does not grasp, the fact is evidence that it lives
not yet. The mother holds her infant, when danger presses;
but the infant, if it is living, also grasps the mother. If it

is dead, it does not; and if it does not, it is dead.   It is the mother's hold of the infant, and not the infant's hold of the mother, that really secures its safety; but if the infant cease to meet the mother, in time of danger, with an answering grasp, the mother will fling the child away— will hide the dead in the earth out of her sight.

Salvation Completed
(1 Peter 1:5)

"Unto salvation ready to be revealed in the last time."

UNTO what end are Christians kept? "Unto salvation ready to be revealed in the last time."

The word is expressly spoken to Christians. The Lord tenderly regards them, and sends them messages of love to cheer them in the house of their pilgrimage.

1. They are kept unto *salvation*, not to perdition. It is the fortress of their King in which they are enclosed to-day; and when at length they are led forth from it, they are led to the palace of the King, that they may be princes there for ever. There are many dark pages of this world's history connected with those who have been long kept in a stronghold, and led forth at length,—led forth to execution. The bridge across the narrow canal in Venice, between the duke's palace and the prison, consisting of a secret path for leading the prisoners to and fro, is called the Bridge of Sighs; and the sight of its solemn gray mass spanning the narrow opening aloft upon the sky, makes the spectator stand and sigh to-day, if he knows some points of its awful history. Many a death procession marched across that gloomy bridge in those gloomy times. Often

the great and noble were kept long in those strongholds—
kept unto a cruel death at last.

Christ keeps his people not in a prison. If the Son
make you free, ye shall be free indeed. He keeps unto
salvation. O thou of little faith, wherefore didst thou
doubt ? Our Lord does not desire that we should pass a
life of terror, as prisoners held over for execution. The
express design of his sacrifice was " to deliver them who
through fear of death were all their life-time subject to
bondage " (Heb. ii. 15). He offers us deliverance from
the bondage of fear. He offers us blessed hope ; he commands us to rejoice in the Lord. When one of Christ's
disciples is led away, it is to life eternal. It is to depart
and to be with Christ.

And many of those who have been by wicked men kept
in prison, and led forth to die, have gone forth with glad
songs, knowing that they would soon be with their Lord.
Argyle's sleep on the night before his execution was
sweeter than that of his persecutors. The hope and joy of
the martyrs in the immediate prospect of complete deliverance have usually been brighter and stronger than other
believers enjoyed, on the principle of compensation which
may be seen running through both the kingdom of nature
and the kingdom of grace.

2. Salvation is *ready*. Salvation has two sides, and
both are ready. One of its sides is in heaven, and the
other is in a believing soul. The kingdom of heaven is at
God's right hand for evermore ; and the kingdom of heaven
is also within you. On both sides it is ready for any
sudden call. On high, Christ's work is perfect ; his
covenant is sure ; his sacrifice has been accepted ; his
people have already been accepted in his righteousness, and

their names are recorded in the Lamb's book of life. They shall not come into condemnation—into judgment—because they have believed in the only-begotten Son of God. They shall not be tried and judged for life at all. That trial is past. They have, in Christ their Substitute, already stood before that tribunal and been approved. The place is ready, the mansions of the Father's house, to receive his children. The company is ready—ten thousand times ten thousand,—all the unfallen, and all the fallen who have been redeemed and taken to glory. Here, on earth, too, the salvation is ready. There is a Christ in the midst of the throne, and a Christ in each Christian indwelling. The salvation is ready within the saved : they have passed from death unto life ; there is now to them no longer any condemnation. They have been sprinkled from an evil conscience, and reconciled to God.

3. The salvation is ready to be *revealed*. Mark this well. It is now concealed. On neither of its two sides is it exposed to the view of men. The finished work of Christ, the prepared home in heaven and the peace of God within a believer's heart—these are both and both alike hidden, secret things.

But these things are, although they are not seen. They are all ready underneath the covering veil ; and when that veil is removed, every eye shall see them. When the Lord shall come again, his coming will be like the morning. As the daylight reveals the green herbs and growing flowers, which the veil of night had concealed, the coming of the Lord will expose to view a new heaven and a new earth wherein dwelleth righteousness. The flowers and forests, the hills and streams, were all there in the night, though they were not seen. They needed not to be made in the morning. They were ready to be revealed. Suppose a creature with the intelligence of a man, but with the term of life allotted to some of the insects—a day. Suppose that creature's life begins after sunset. At midnight and in the early morning watches he looks around, but sees nothing. He reasons, and loses himself in dark speculation. A voice from the abyss above reaches his ear, and tells him that a beautiful, furnished world is ready to be revealed, and will be revealed in the morning. He believes, and waits : the promise is fulfilled. The glory of the world when the sun is up surpasses all his expectation. Such a creature is redeemed man. All is ready. The inheritance needs only to be unveiled. The unveiling only remains for the last time. Now is the time for seeking and obtaining it : then, it only remains that it should be fully displayed.

Rejoicing in Tribulation
(1 Peter 1:6-7)

" Wherein ye greatly rejoice, though now for a season, if need be, ye are in heaviness through manifold temptations : that the trial of your faith, being much more precious than of gold that perisheth, though it be tried with fire, might be found unto praise and honour and glory at the appearing of Jesus Christ."

IN a somewhat formal logical definition Paul declares the kingdom of God to be " righteousness and peace and joy." Gladness is one constituent of a living faith. They are completely out of their reckoning who think that earnest religion means the sacrifice of happiness in this world for the sake of securing it in the world to come. The faith that makes eternal life secure also sheds a blessed light over the life that now is. This may be gathered from the nature of the case. To pass from the condition of a criminal under condemnation to the place of a son and the right of an heir, cannot but gladden a man's heart.

That which the terms of the gospel would lead one to expect appears everywhere in its history. When Philip preached Christ with success in Samaria, " there was great joy in that city ; " and when the Ethiopian treasurer heard and accepted the same message from the same preacher, " he went on his way rejoicing." In our own day the same effects spring from the same cause. There is no feature more distinctly characteristic of present religious earnestness than the gladness which springs in the hearts and shines in the faces of the converts. The absolute identity of results produced by a hearty acceptance of the gospel in the days of the apostles and in ours, is itself a proof that the word of God is a living and reproductive seed—that it " liveth and abideth for ever."

Peter had himself experienced peace and joy in believing ; and writing to the scattered converts, he takes for granted that in their experience like causes would produce like effects. On this point he plants a firm foot ; there is no wavering. He counts on it as confidently as on the sequences of nature, that those who had accepted Christ as their own Saviour were made glad thereby.

Nor is it an ordinary satisfaction, as when corn and wine abound. It is an exuberant, exultant, passionate joyfulness. The term implies an articulate and demonstrative happiness that cannot be concealed. It must reveal itself by leaping and singing. Such, moreover, is its strength and persistence that a great weight of grief will not quench it. " Ye greatly rejoice, though now ye are in heaviness through manifold temptations."

A vivid illustration of this principle appears in Old Testament history. Elijah (1 Kings xviii.) would convict the priests of Baal, and convince the people, by fire from heaven consuming the sacrifice. But first he directs that the wood should be soaked and the ditch filled with water. When the fire burned the soaked wood, and licked up the water in the trench, there was a great demonstration of its power. So here : it is not an ordinary contentment ; it is a joy that burns so fiercely that many waters of grief cannot quench it. The joy overcomes and swallows up the antagonist element, and the presence of the antagonist increases its triumph.

Witnesses, in number constituting a great cloud, have appeared in various ages and in various countries, to show that the joy of faith in Christ triumphed over all the tortures which ingenious superstition was able to invent or the most callous executioners were able to inflict. The hymns which the martyrs have sung in the flames are measures of the strength to which the Holy Spirit may bring the grace of joy in the heart of believers in the body.

The sorrow with which believing joy in those primitive Christians must needs contend sprang from many and various sources. At one time it was persecution for Christ's sake ; at another time it was loss of goods, sickness, bereavement. But when the stream of suffering was swollen by the addition of all these affluents, faith still gave them victory, and they rejoiced in their Lord.

Two circumstances, expressed in two quiet parentheses, come in here to limit the great flood of affliction,—two touching, tender memorials of a Father's pitying eye and all-encompassing arm. These are (1) " if need be," and (2) " for a season." Only if, and when, and as far as there is a necessity for them, are the trials permitted to come at all; and even when they come, their duration is limited. In both cases the Father is himself the judge, and he doeth all things well. Elsewhere in Scripture the believing sufferer is taught the art of diminishing the weight and shortening the term of sorrows. They seem " light " when compared with the exceeding great weight of the glory that shall follow, and " but for a moment " when compared with the eternal rest. It is thus that faith gains the victory over the world. It is on this principle that the disciples, when they find their hearts sinking under trials, say unto the Lord, Increase our faith.

The disciples are taught to regard their sufferings in the aspect of trials ; at once tests to determine whether their faith is genuine, and exercises to increase its strength. It is not faith, but the trial of faith, that is here pronounced to be precious. Precisely because faith is the link by which the saved are bound to the Saviour, it is of unspeakable importance to have faith tested in time and proved to be true. The trial of gold is precious ; for if you sell all that you have, and give away the proceeds for a field that seems to contain the treasure, it is beyond all things necessary to test the glittering heap before the transaction is completed, in order to ascertain that it is really gold. Here the fire and the crucible are the most valuable of all things for the investor. These are his safeguards ; he cannot want them.

In like manner, it is dangerous to venture our eternity on a fair-weather profession ; an assay in some form is essential to determine whether there is life or only a name that we live. The trial of faith by affliction is compared to the testing and purifying of gold by fire. The sufferer, while in the furnace, is encouraged to look up and see a Father in heaven bending over him in all-wise love, and ready to remove the pain as soon as the purpose is effected. The "need be" and the "season" are determined and limited by an omniscient love.

Nor is all over when the trial has come, and burned for a season, and accomplished its purpose here, and passed away. The greatest results will be seen within the veil. When Christ comes the second time to reign, the effect of these trials will appear to his praise. In exact accordance with this representation is the vision of the glorified in the Revelation of John (vii.). Those who stand round the throne in white clothing are described by two leading features, a subordinate and a supreme—they have come out of great tribulation, and have washed their robes and made them white in the blood of the Lamb. Although the one ground on which they enter the kingdom is the atonement made on the cross, yet the tribulation they endured —the trial of their faith for a season through suffering— tells instrumentally with so much effect upon the Lord's glory in their redemption, that it is reckoned worthy of mention among the means of their salvation and their Saviour's praise.

Salvation by Substitution
(1 Peter 1:8-11)

"Whom having not seen, ye love ; in whom, though now ye see him not, yet believing, ye rejoice with joy unspeakable and full of glory : receiving the end of your faith, even the salvation of your souls.   Of which salvation the prophets have enquired and searched diligently, who prophesied of the grace that should come unto you : searching what, or what manner of time the Spirit of Christ which was in them did signify, when it testified beforehand the sufferings of Christ, and the glory that should follow."

THE joy of believing is repeated, expanded, and emphasized.   It is a theme which Peter seems loath to let go.   It grasps his heart and carries him away.   He is passionate about it.   He has no thought of denying his relation to Jesus now.   His wound was thoroughly healed when the Great Physician thrice demanded of him, " Lovest thou me ? " and at the point where he once was weak, he is now very strong.   In this expression of exuberant gladness he obeys the Master's word, " When thou art converted, strengthen thy brethren."

But the object of this strong faith and fervent love is a living Person.   No chain of connected doctrines could beget such enthusiasm in a human heart.   Doctrines, though true and divine, would remain a dead letter if they did not lead a soul to the Saviour.   It is the grand characteristic of apostolic preaching that it constantly presents a personal Christ to sinful men.

Those who simply accept the offered Saviour do not

miss the mark. They receive—that is, they carry off, as the winner in a race bears off the prize—the end and object of their faith, even the salvation of their souls.

We have now reached a subject which in Peter's estimation is of supreme importance. It becomes for him a new starting-point. He expatiates on it in thoughts that breathe and words that burn throughout the next three verses. Surveying the whole course of time, he sees all the lines of Providence and grace converging on this one point,—your salvation. The prophets who were commissioned to promise redemption did not fully comprehend the meaning of their own testimony. We are in a better position for understanding it. In this respect the least in the new kingdom is greater than the greatest prophet of the older dispensation. In the light of the now risen sun we may better perceive both the glory of the luminary himself, and the beauty of the landscape he shines upon, than those morning-stars who promised but did not see the day.

Three distinct things embodied in the testimony of the prophets, yet not completely understood by themselves, are here in succession enumerated :—

1. The grace that should come unto you.
2. The sufferings of Christ.
3. The glory that should follow.

We may learn much by a close examination of these three in their union and relations. A chain of three links gives two joinings. We shall, in the first place, examine the connection between the first and second, and afterwards the connection between the second and third.

"The grace that should come unto you," and "the sufferings of Christ," constitute the first pair. Here, however, we shall gain much by a preliminary critical examination.

In regard to the first member, nothing more is needed than to omit the words printed in italics, not in the original but inserted by the translators,—the words, "that should come." They are not incorrect, but they are not necessary. Let the clause run simply as it is in the Greek, "the grace unto you." The second member runs in the very same form ; and the connection between the two is somewhat obscured by the change made in the translation. Let the original form be restored and retained ; the clause will then read, "the sufferings unto Christ." Thus, by a more simple and rigid adherence to the original in sense and in form, the relation between these two members—which, I doubt not, the Spirit intended to exhibit—is made much more manifest,—

> The grace unto you.
> The sufferings unto Christ.

When these clauses are restored to the simplicity of the Greek text, they exhibit in a very clear light the doctrine of substitution. The grand characteristic of the divine plan, as distinguished from all false religions, and all corruptions of the true, is substitution of the just for the unjust. The Redeemer takes the place of believing sinners, and they take his. He assumes the sin-burden, and with it meets the Judge ; they, freed from their sin, put on his righteousness, and are therein accepted. This is the gospel. This is the thing into which prophets, from Abel to the Baptist, diligently inquired—into which angels strive to look. The eternal Son is made sin for his people, and they become the righteousness of God in him.

The first inexplicable mystery to prophets and angels is "the grace unto you ;" and the second is "the sufferings unto Christ."

Favour from God to the guilty: sufferings poured out on the Holy One—these are the two great wonders on earth, these the two great wonders in heaven. A case which illustrates this aspect of the gospel occurs in Old Testament history. Joseph brings forward his two sons, that he may obtain for them his father's blessing. As the Hebrews counted much on the rights of the first-born, he carefully led Manasseh, the elder, in his own left hand, that the right hand of the aged patriarch might rest on his head; and Ephraim, the younger, in his right, to receive the blessing through the left hand. But the aged prophet, though blind, " crossed his hands wittingly," and laid his right hand on the head of the younger, his left on the head of the elder. Joseph, thinking his father had blundered through blindness, took hold of his hands and endeavoured to reverse the order according to his own idea of primogeniture; but his father, in the spirit of prophecy, persisted in his own method, saying, " I know it, my son; I know it, my son," and gave the greater blessing to the younger child, the lesser to the elder. So, when witnessing angels beheld the goings of their God in the redemption of fallen men, they failed to comprehend it. When they saw the guilty rebels called forward to one side of the throne, and the well-beloved of the Father to the other side, and the Judge of all preparing to pour out his love and favour on the rebels, and sufferings, the due of sin, upon his own Son, we might imagine that they would be inclined reverently, like Joseph, to say, " Not so, my Father; for these are the guilty, and he is the Holy One;" and that the Eternal Father would reply, " I know it, my children; I know it." Ah, he guided his hands wittingly when he apportioned his own favour and love to the fallen who believed, and the sufferings due to sin to his own beloved. This was the fundamental feature of the eternal covenant. The Son had said, " Save from going down to the pit, for I have found a ransom ;" and he added, I am the ransom found.

We need not be surprised that the method of redemption here revealed does not commend itself to the wise of this world, who view it only in the light of this world. It is deep ; it is difficult. Prophets of old, who felt that the revelation of it was passing through their own lips, were amazed and staggered. They returned to the testimony they had delivered, and searched it again. They strove to comprehend what to their understanding seemed incomprehensible. Angels unfallen, too, who seem to have obtained a glimpse of the facts, were unable to determine the reason. This is eminently a spiritual thing. The carnal mind cannot possibly know it. Yet God reveals it unto babes. And it is interesting at this point to remember that the Lord Jesus, during his ministry on earth, gave audible thanks to the Father in a strain of unusual emotion and fervency for this very thing—" That thou hast hid these things from the wise and prudent, and revealed them unto babes."

This is the truth that is able to give peace to a troubled conscience, as the word of Jesus settled the raging sea. He has taken my place to bear and answer for sin ; and he invites me to take his place, that his righteousness may be mine, and I be accepted therein. He is not displeased, but glad, when sinners take him at his word.

No Cross, No Crown
(1 Peter 1:11)

"The sufferings unto Christ, and the glories after these."

ARK now the junction of the second link with the third,—the relation between "the sufferings unto Christ" and "the glories after these." The connection here is as deep and as significant as in the other case. There are many glories in heaven and earth not specially connected with the sufferings of Christ. "There is a glory of the sun, and a glory of the moon, and a glory of the stars." The various gradations and tribes of living creatures, with their members and faculties, wonderfully made, are evidences of the Creator's wisdom and power. But none of these have any place here. This is a glory of a different kind displayed on another sphere,—a glory that excelleth.

The distinguishing characteristic of this glory is that it springs from the sufferings of Christ, as flowers and fruit spring from the root of a living tree. Peter deals here exclusively with those glories that "follow" the sufferings of Christ. No cross, no crown.

Although there had been no cross, there would have been a glory to God from a fallen world. Righteous judgment consuming all the guilty would have been *a glory of* its kind, but not *the* specific glory that springs from the atoning death of Christ. The honour to God that results from destroying the works of the devil, and redeeming the fallen family—magnifying the law, and yet setting free the transgressors—cannot come before the cross, cannot come without the cross.

It is fitted at once to inspire us with awe and to fill us with gladness, to observe how great a place the suffering of an innocent substitute holds in the Scriptures from their commencement to their close. In the Old Testament mainly by symbol, in the New mainly by direct revelation, this one theme pervades the whole Bible. Take this away, and you leave the book like a web when the warp-threads have all been drawn out,—not a web at all, but a heap of tangled threads. Those who cling to Christianity but re- ject the cross, labour in vain. They can extract no glory from its precepts and its examples if they take away the " redemption by his blood ; " for all the precepts and ex- amples are built on that one foundation.

Among the apostles, Peter was peculiarly qualified to teach this doctrine. He received it in an extraordinary way. Besides the ordinary method of instruction by his own word, the Lord burnt this truth into his heart by the most terrible rebuke that he ever addressed to friend or to foe. When Peter, under the influence of true human tenderness, indeed, but also of carnal human pride, ventured to depre- cate the dying of the substitute, saying, " Far be this from thee, Lord," the Master, not content to show him his mis- take as on other occasions of error, flashed in his disciple's face that flaming fire of reproof, " Get thee behind me, Satan." It was thus that he was moved with indignation when any one, either from open enmity or mistaken love, proposed to take away the cross, and so make impossible the crown. Seeing the end from the beginning, the Lord kept in the covenanted course—strove lawfully, that he might win. " For the joy that was set before him, he endured the cross ;" knowing that if the cross were not endured, the glory could not follow.

On another occasion he gave his own suffering the same fundamental place, although circumstances rendered the expression more gentle. When two of his disciples proposed to introduce him to some Greeks, he declined ; and explained the reason why he would not consent to the interview. The cultured Greeks, hearing of his fame, would consent to be taught by the prophet of Nazareth, and carry light from him to their own classic shores. But, like their representatives in modern times, they would accept the teaching of this prophet, and count it enough. On these terms he refused to speak. His answer—sent at secondhand—was, " Except a corn of wheat fall into the ground and die, it abideth alone ; but if it fall into the ground and die, it bringeth forth much fruit." This is precisely the lesson that Peter teaches in our text. The fruit must spring from the dying of the seed ; the glories must follow the sufferings of Christ. That song of white-robed worshippers around the throne is a glory to God in the highest ; but the glory sprang from the cross, for these are they that have washed their robes and made them white in the blood of the Lamb.

The offence of the cross has not yet ceased. The extraordinary fulness with which the atonement is taught in Scripture, in connection with the persistent rejection of it by the wisdom of this world, constitutes the evidence of inspiration. The architect who laid the foundations of that harbour-wall so deep and so broad—deeper and broader than any passer-by would have deemed needful—must have known the strength of the currents below and tempests above to which, at certain seasons, his structure would be exposed. The sufferings of the innocent substitute in the room of the guilty occupy a place for depth and breadth in the Scriptures corresponding to the strength of the wild current that rushes against them in modern times.

Jesus in the Midst
(1 Peter 1:12)

"Unto whom it was revealed, that not unto themselves, but unto us they did minister the things, which are now reported unto you by them that have preached the gospel unto you with the Holy Ghost sent down from heaven; which things the angels desire to look into."

HAVING examined the two junctures which these three links present, and the two pairs which are constituted by these three members, let us now take a parting glance of the whole in one view.

The grace unto you.
The sufferings unto Christ.
The glories after these.

Behold another example of that revealed mystery,—" On either side one, and Jesus in the midst." When Christ was crucified on Calvary, his cross was flanked right and left by a sinner saved and a sinner lost. When his throne of judgment is set, the same phenomenon will reappear, with this difference, that instead of a single sample from either host, the hosts will all be there. Here in this apostle's letter is an exhibition most interestingly analogous. Who is this that stands in the midst here? It is Christ crucified;— " the sufferings unto Christ." On either side of that central object is one, and who are they? On one side favour to the sinful, on the other side glory to God! From the cross stream, right and left, these two distinct but kindred glories—this way pardon to the guilty, that way divine righteousness satisfied and adorned. On no other root do these twin blossoms grow, on no other foundation do these twin pillars stand. Hark, a melody, as the Spirit breathes through the three distended strings of this harp, —we have heard the song before. Then too it was Jesus in the midst. The twin stanzas, radiating both like light beams from the head of the Babe born in Bethlehem, are " Glory to God in the highest, and on earth peace, good-will toward men."

A pictorial, an almost dramatic interest adheres to this brief but pregnant portion of Peter's letter. We have already pointed out, that making Christ crucified the centre, we find the cross supported on either side by favour poured on sinners and glory rising to God the Judge. These are the more immediate surroundings. But extend the radius, and you will find at the greater distance a parallel pair : and the form still is, " On either side one, and Jesus in the midst." Before verse eleventh, where the cross is elevated, you find in verse tenth the prophets promising Christ, and after it in verse twelfth the apostles proclaiming him.

Here is the vision. In the centre stands a throne, and " in the midst of the throne a Lamb, as it had been slain." On the one side a line of prophets stretches from the steps of the throne upwards to the creation of man ; for the Lord never left himself without a witness on the earth. Latest and greatest of the race, the Baptist stands nearest, looking unto Jesus, and exclaiming, " Behold the Lamb of God." Earliest and farthest off, on the eastern brink of time, Abel may be descried, shedding the blood of his sacrifice, and through it seeing Christ's day afar off. Hand in hand they stand this long-drawn line of witnesses, promising a Saviour yet to come. On the other side of the throne stand the chosen witnesses of the Lamb's death and resurrection, reporting the great accomplished fact of the Divine government and of human history, and preaching glad tidings to the world through the power of the Holy Ghost. From the cross in the midst a light streams upward to the very gate of Eden, giving life and meaning to all the sacrifices which, without it, would have been dull and dead; and downward, till the milder light of the first coming meet the lightning flash of the second. All that went before promised, He is coming; all that follow report, He has come. And so in him all the promises of God are yea and Amen.

Incidentally here, an interesting feature of the gospel emerges—" preaching " and " reporting " are identical. To preach the gospel is substantially to report a fact. To tell the now old, old story, and tell it so as to make it ever new—this is the highest style of a gospel ministry. It is finished. The Son of God became the Son of man, that he might take our place, and that we might stand in his. He gave himself, the just for the unjust. His invitation is, " Whosoever will, let him come ; " and, " There is now no condemnation to them that are in Christ Jesus."

Yet another feature is added to the landscape—thrown in near the outskirts, and communicating a tender setting-sun-like glow to the whole canvas—" Which things the angels desire to look into." These holy spiritual beings, flames of fire though they be in ardent and intelligent service to their Creator, could not fully comprehend the redemption of men. They lacked experience. In taking up a difficult idea, no amount of intellectual acuteness can make up for the want of having gone through the case yourself. They had seen, I suppose, that their fellow-creature man had fallen by sin, and yet that the fallen were spared, forgiven, and restored to favour. In the fulness of time they had seen the well-beloved of the Father, whom they were wont to worship, forsaken of the Father, and by wicked hands crucified and slain. This was beyond their comprehension. They stood amazed before the mystery. Saved men have another view-point, and can understand all. Seen from their stand-point, this cloud dissolves into light, and becomes a glory to God in the highest.

In the estuary of a great navigable river, between parallel lines of green hills, a great number of buoys are seen scattered over the surface of the water. You stand on the neighbouring hill-top and see—see, but cannot understand. Some of the buoys are large, some small; some are white, some are red; some are near the shore, and some in mid-channel. They seem to you as if they had fallen from the clouds without order, meaning, or use. But come down from that height; get into a ship that is coming from abroad and making its way home; thread your way through these signals right and left. You will see that they mark the way for the voyager; not the straight, but the deep safe way from the outer ocean to the harbour-home. In some such way might the angels, from their high place, be unable to understand the way of life for the lost, and might desire to descend, and get into our position, and share our experience, so as to taste and see the goodness and wisdom of God in the scheme of redemption.

In the earlier years of the current century, certain *nebulæ*

—shreds of white, mist-like clouds—were familiar to astronomers, hanging in the blue, far beyond the region of our atmosphere—farther distant than the fixed stars. What might these be ? Has a dull, creeping mould or mildew tainted the purity of highest heaven ? At length a new and more powerful instrument was turned in that direction, and, lo, the clouds resolved themselves into innumerable separate stars—shining worlds so thickly strewn, that in the aggregate they seemed a mildew spot on the surface of the azure. If the angels, who are amazed at the sight of sinners spared and the Holy One forsaken, could get a glimpse of the same objects through our instruments and with our eyes, the things that seemed anomalous spots on the universal purity of the Supreme would break out into separate glories—glories that excelled all that they had hitherto known.

Certain it is, that however bright the place of the saints' eternal rest may be, " the Lamb is the light thereof." The method and the means whereby the redemption of lost men has been accomplished will be hereafter the chief study of perfect creatures, and the brightest glory of the Creator God.

Obedient Children
(1 Peter 1:13-14)

" Wherefore gird up the loins of your mind, be sober, and hope to the end for the grace that is to be brought unto you at the revelation of Jesus Christ ; as obedient children, not fashioning yourselves according to the former lusts in your ignorance."

PETER, like his beloved brother Paul, was thoroughly familiar with the relation between *doctrine* and *life*.   In the writings of both apostles these two themes continually emerge in company ; nor is the mingling irregular or accidental.   Everywhere they stand related as roots and fruits.   Out of truth revealed springs duty performed.   Living faith shows itself by the fruits which it bears ; and if it be barren, it is accounted dead.

The link of connection in this passage is brought fully into view : " Wherefore gird up the loins," etc.   At this point the teacher changes his theme, and launches into a series of precepts for practice.   In the preceding portion we have a list of doctrines revealed, and in the subsequent portion a list of duties enjoined.   But it is not enough to observe that these two lie near each other ; they are welded into one like the links of a chain.

The long, connected series of doctrines contained in verses 1–12 seem like the row of jars constituting an electric battery ; and the combined power of the whole is at verse 13th discharged into the field of duty, in order there to generate a force which will send a life spinning forward, " fruitful in every good work." It is thus that doctrines are always in Scripture utilized as the motive-power of duty, according to the fundamental principle laid down by Paul in Romans iii. 31 : " Do we then make void the law through faith ? God forbid : yea, we establish the law."

Activity, as opposed to indolence ; sobriety, as opposed to vanity or vice ; and a cheerful hope, instead of a sluggish despondency,—these are the proper characteristics of one who bears the name of Christ and hopes in his mercy.

The obedience demanded and expected in the gospel is not the mere external act. Dead works do not serve the living God. There is a body, indeed, but there is a soul in it. The precept is not generally " obedient," but specifically " as obedient children." A slave's obedience is not accepted ; there must be a child's love.

We touch here, indeed, a fundamental characteristic of the gospel. We do not first work our way into sonship. We obtain sonship as a free gift ; and then we work to please the Giver, because we love him who first loved us. A true child serves his father not from fear of punishment or hope of reward, but spontaneously from love. It is the child's delight to anticipate and fulfil his parent's wishes : he would be wretched if he were prevented. This, as far as things of time may be compared with those of eternity, is the kind of obedience that our Father in heaven desires and accepts. Thus the expression, " as obedient children," is not merely a figure of speech, but a specific definition of the thing required. Our Father is served by sons, not by slaves,

A clause follows of great significance for us—" Not fashioning yourselves according to the former lusts." The expression occurs only once elsewhere in the New Testament—Romans xii. 2, " Conformed to this world." It is a word with a wide scope ; it is almost a picture. It presents a man bent on some particular pursuit, with body and mind all alert, his eye looking and his hand stretching in that direction. He is, moreover, girt and accoutred expressly for this object ; as a diver or a hunter, each prepared for his work. Ah, Christian, you are acting unlike your name and place when you devote your mind and your energies to worldly lusts ! But in this case a very remarkable epithet is applied to these unworthy pleasures ; they are called " the former lusts." A disciple of Christ is past them ; they lie behind him now. He has done with them.

An epoch is here marked in a human life, and some parts of a man's experience are said to have passed before it. The grand epoch which marks the dates of the civilized world is the birth of Christ. We constantly employ the letters A.D. (the year of our Lord) to mark the age of events. It so happens that in a very precise sense this is the epoch which Peter employs in the text. These lusts were the pursuit of the people's life " before " some specific event. And what event was that ? The birth of Christ in themselves. Before Christ was formed in them, in their regeneration, these lusts occupied them ; but after that event, they were left behind. The apostle's exhortation is, that these vain or vile pleasures should be left, as the tasks of Egypt were left behind the Hebrews when the Red Sea was placed between them and the house of bondage.

It is further said that it was " in their ignorance " that

these lusts had any power over them. A human soul would not succumb to these ignoble masters, unless it were void of understanding. Evil spirits, according to Paul, are "rulers of the darkness of this world:" if the world were not in darkness, they would not be permitted to rule. When a man is mastered by the appetite for wealth, it is in ignorance. He says, "Soul, take thine ease; thou hast much goods laid up for many years." But the Lord replies, "Thou *fool*, this night thy soul shall be required of thee."

I have heard a reflection often expressed by thoughtful country people when they saw a great draught horse meekly submitting to be bridled and led away to labour by a child: "If the brute creatures knew their own strength, they would not submit to the yoke and the lash." These mighty quadrupeds could trample down the stripling that puts bits in their mouths. Yet they submit to whatever their master imposes, ignorant of their own strength. Oh, if man, God's greatest creature, knew his strength, he would not submit to be the slave of vile passions! Strong men in multitudes are in our country led not only to the yoke, but even to the shambles, by the appetite of intemperance. This possessing spirit says to the right arm, Do this, and he doeth it; to the foot, Go thither, and he goeth. Oh that these captives, driven openly in gangs, not through the marshes of interior Africa, but along the streets of British cities, were at last set free!

Hear ye Him: "Come unto me, all ye that labour and are heavy laden, and I will give you rest." Their Redeemer is strong. "If the Son make you free, ye shall be free indeed."

Bought With a Price
(1 Peter 1:15-19)

" But as he which hath called you is holy, so be ye holy in all manner of conversation ; because it is written, Be ye holy ; for I am holy. And if ye call on the Father, who without respect of persons judgeth according to every man's work, pass the time of your sojourning here in fear : forasmuch as ye know that ye were not redeemed with corruptible things, as silver and gold, from your vain conversation received by tradition from your fathers ; but with the precious blood of Christ, as of a lamb without blemish and without spot."

I T is an interesting study to search in the words of the Lord Jesus for the germs of all the doctrines which the apostles subsequently repeated and expanded. Peter intimates that it was in " ignorance " that the former lusts retained their power. He learned this from the Master at Jacob's well. The Samaritan woman, previously to her interview with Jesus, had led a wild, impure life ; but she knew no better till that eventful day. The words of the Lord are very full and precise on this point : " If thou knewest the gift of God, and who it is that saith unto thee, Give me to drink ; thou wouldst have asked of him, and he would have given thee living water."

An invitation to holiness is enforced by an appeal to the holiness of God. Here again the Master has given the cue to his servant in one of the beatitudes,—" Blessed are the pure in heart : for they shall see God." Mark the sweep of the precept : the compass is planted in the centre, and the circle drawn round the circumference of a life. The demand is, " Be holy in all manner of conversation." The meaning is, in all your intercourse with men, in every turning of your history. At home, or abroad ; with your own family, or in presence of strangers ; at work, or enjoying relaxation ; at church, or in the market ;—wherever you may be, or however employed, let lips and life be holiness to the Lord. A life is like a stream issuing from a mountain-lake. The water cannot be of different colours at different places. It cannot be pure at one spot and turbid a few yards further on. If the fountain be transparent, the outflowing stream will be clear over all its breadth. The holiness that is put on, as suitable at certain times and in certain places, is not holiness ; it is hypocrisy. When the streams of a life, as they dispread themselves over the individual history, are found, like the waters of Jericho, to be all bitter, it is not possible, by any medicament, to sweeten portions of them here and there, where travellers may be expected to taste them. There is only one way of cure : a certain salt must be cast into the spring, and then all the water that flows over its brim will be wholesome— all wholesome alike. " Create in me a clean heart, O God ; and renew a right spirit within me."

The warning is addressed to the children of God's family ; and the exhortation to sobriety is enforced by the consideration that they salute as Father him who judges without respect of persons. Neither mistrust of the Father nor jealousy of any brother should have place in this house. Favouritism is a fatal flaw in parental discipline. Seen, or even suspected, it ruins all. But there is no such flaw in the Divine administration. There is great variety of treatment, indeed; but all is regulated by wisdom and love. Absolute confidence in the Father's fairness should banish all fretting from the children's hearts.

This is not your home; it is only a sojourn. The heirs, detained for a time in a strange country, should be watchful lest they contract relations and habits inconsistent with their station and prospects.

To make their actual life solid and true, he bids them remember that they have been redeemed. Here the melody touches the key-note of all Scripture,—redemption is the power that purifies and elevates a life. In entire accordance with this representation, the aspect of redemption presented is deliverance from a frivolous course. True it is that when any one is, in the gospel sense, "redeemed," he is no longer under condemnation; the sentence of guilt is removed, and he is at peace with God. But an immediate fruit and uniform accompaniment of that blood-bought pardon is an emancipation from the bondage of vain and vicious habits of life. "If the Son make you free, ye shall be free indeed."

Those of the Christians who were of Jewish origin were delivered from the intolerable load of rabbinical traditions which had ensnared their consciences and fossilized their lives; and those who were converted Gentiles had escaped the still more debasing idolatry of the heathen, whether Phenician or Greek.

There was no emancipation without a ransom; and the price was not paid in silver and gold. In presence of the ransom actually provided, even these are deemed "corruptible things." Their souls were redeemed from death, and their life on earth from vanity, by "the precious blood of Christ, as of a lamb without blemish and without spot."

The expressions point to the Passover lamb and the exodus from Egypt. Although Israel were a nation that God had chosen and called, they languished in slavery, their days were wasted in making bricks for their masters. Many terrible judgments were sent upon Egypt; but these strokes did not break the captive's chain—they seemed only to weld its links more firmly on his limbs. After the nine plagues had come and gone, emancipation seemed as far distant as ever. Then was the lamb's blood shed and sprinkled on the lintels: a nation of slaves, helpless under the tyrant's hand, but obedient to the word of the Redeemer, crept beneath the sprinkled blood at night, and went out free with a high hand in the morning.

Beautiful and articulate symbol of the true redemption. Terrors of the Lord in succession may tear the flesh and dry up the bones; a law work may keep the conscience for years like the sea in a storm; and yet there may be no peace and no liberty. Without shedding of blood there is no exodus, either to Israel or to us. The law may become a schoolmaster to lead us to Christ; but Christ only can save. I suppose Saul of Tarsus was as much racked and shaken by his self-righteous struggle as Egypt by the nine plagues. The law of God on one side, with the long array of merits on the other to meet it,—the circumcision, and the birth, and the tithes, and the phylacteries, and the long prayers, and the persecuting zeal. There they fought, these mighty adversaries, and poor Saul, body and soul, was the battle-field for contending powers. "O wretched man that I am!" At last came a peace as sudden and as great as the calm that came over the Sea of Galilee when Jesus said, "Peace, be still." But when he cast away all his grand array of merits—cast them away with intense disgust—we do not find that he gathered up another list of better attainments in their stead : " I count all but loss, that I may *win Christ, and be found in him.*" In room of all he obtained one only ; but that one was enough. He learned first in his own experience what he afterwards taught to the alarmed jailer,—" Believe in the Lord Jesus Christ, and thou shalt be saved."

Love on the Spring
(1 Peter 1:20-23)

"Who verily was foreordained before the foundation of the world, but was manifest in these last times for you, who by him do believe in God, that raised him up from the dead, and gave him glory ; that your faith and hope might be in God. Seeing ye have purified your souls in obeying the truth through the Spirit unto unfeigned love of the brethren, see that ye love one another with a pure heart fervently : being born again, not of corruptible seed, but of incorruptible, by the word of God, which liveth and abideth for ever."

A LTHOUGH man was last in the order of creation, he was also first, before all. It was not first a fallible man, and then when he fell an infallible Redeemer provided. First was the Redeemer, the Eternal Son. In his image, off this model, man was made. In order that he may be made high, he is made free. But if he be made free, he will fall. What then ? To prevent the possibility of falling, will he be made low—on the level of the beasts, without a will ? Will he be created, beautiful and glorious indeed, like the stars, but, like them, without the power of choosing, and obliged to be obedient to physical laws whether he will or not ? No ; he shall be made high, so that when he falls, and is redeemed, he will be a glory to God far greater than any that the heavens or the earth declare.

As in regard to the resurrection (1 Cor. xv. 23), so in regard to the original foreordination. It is " Christ the first fruits ; afterwards they that are Christ's." It is not that God created the planets, and then, finding them dark and cold, subsequently provided a sun to afford them light and heat. Rather, he made a sun for his own glory, and scattered satellites around him, that they might circulate and shine in his light.

In the eternal covenant it is first Christ, and then man, with his constitution and his history, to wait upon Christ, as the planets wait upon the sun, receiving his light and reflecting his glory. Foreordained before the world was, the Redeemer was " made manifest in these last times for you." The times we live in are the last. For those who despise the ministry of the Spirit now showing the things of Christ, there remaineth no more sacrifice for sin, no other refuge for sinners.

We have here a very short but very comprehensive creed. " For you, who by him do believe in God." It is parallel with the one given by the Lord himself (John xiv. 1) : " Ye believe in God; believe also in me." The whole matter lies there : come unto God the Father, but come in Christ, the Mediator between God and man. " No man cometh unto the Father but by me ; " and, on the analogy of Scripture, we may safely add, No man will be cast out or kept out who comes in this way to the Father.

We again approach a practical exhortation, and it is a most interesting study to observe how it is surrounded and enforced. This apostle would no more think of laying down a duty without a divine doctrine to enforce it, than an engineer would think of erecting a mill-wheel without a stream of water to drive it round.

The precept in this case is, " Love one another with a pure heart fervently." It is a duty that is very difficult, very necessary, and, when performed, very precious. Before we speak of the precept itself, let us carefully observe how it is flanked on either side for support. Although the moral precepts of Scripture are higher and purer and fuller than any other, they differ from other systems, not so much in their nature as in the motives by which they are enforced. When they propose to throw a suspension bridge across a river, far more labour and cost are laid out in providing the sustaining pillars on either side than in constructing the actual roadway between them. So here it is easy to say, " Love one another ; " but such is the strain which this command puts on human life, that it cannot be supported unless there be faith in doctrines that are divine. More depends on the pillars that support the chain than on the chain itself.

On the one side the precept here is supported by, " Seeing ye have purified your souls in obeying the truth through the Spirit ; " and on the other by, " Being born again, not of corruptible seed, but of incorruptible, by the word of God." Unless these two piers had stood on either bank of the river, founded on the living rock below, the slight rainbow-like line could never have been suspended in the sky. Brother-love may be held up if it is attached on the one side to the consciousness of having purified our souls by the truth applied by the Spirit ; and on the other side to the consciousness of having been born again of the incorruptible seed. Nothing less and nothing else is able to bear the strain.

The structure of the argument might even be presented to the eye on a printed page, thus :—

| Seeing ye have purified your souls in obeying the truth through the Spirit, | *Love one another with a pure heart fervently :* | Being born again, not of corruptible seed, but of incorruptible, by the word of God. |

These two pillars repeat each other, with differences in minor features, as was meet. Both express the new birth, and the means by which it is accomplished. In the first, however, man's own activity is more prominently presented; and in the second, God's sovereign power. The same difference may be observed between the parable of the Prodigal, which presents the human side of redemption, where man is active, and the parable of the Lost Sheep, which presents the Divine side, where the Redeemer does all.

The instrumentality of conversion is in both cases substantially the same—the word and Spirit of God.

In the precept itself there is one feature which demands and will repay a careful examination. The term "fervently," although it gives the meaning of the original, is not a literal translation. It means extended, or on the stretch. It conveys the idea of a constant tension such as is supplied in machinery by a steel spring. In one department of a sewing machine all depends on the thread being kept constantly tight, so that the moment any slackness occurs, the loose portion is picked up instantly and without fail. If that operation were left dependent on the watchfulness and quickness of a human operator, it would entirely fail. The worker would grow weary, would forget, would hasten to tighten the thread after the time was past, and all would go to wreck and ruin. But by entrusting the watch and the work to a bent elastic steel wire, an absolute infallibility is secured. The watcher never forgets, the worker never wearies. The work is done perfectly, and always done at the right moment. The spring is always on the stretch, and never misses. Though it is obliged to watch the slackening, and pull the thread instantly tight, a hundred times a minute, all day long for twenty years, it never once forgets or fails.

The precept requires a love of this sort—watching and working in a Christian's heart. If you need to remember your duty every time that a sudden injury occurs, you will not be in time with the soft answer that turns away wrath. Before love has gathered itself up, and determined on its course, the opportunity will be past. The disciple of Christ will appear as irascible, passionate, and revengeful as other men. There must be a spring—a law of love set once for all as a faculty of the new heart, that will operate instantaneously and uniformly.

The disciples thought it was a burdensome and irksome task to forgive an injurer seventy times seven injuries. Such indeed it would be, if you needed every time to reason the matter out and spur yourself on to duty. If the spring is not on, loops will fall, and the web will be spoilt. But the spring-love, once inserted as a faculty of the regenerated heart, will catch and keep every opportunity like a law of nature.

Man and His Glory
(1 Peter 1:24-25)

" For all flesh is as grass, and all the glory of man as the flower of grass.
The grass withereth, and the flower thereof falleth away : but the word of the
Lord endureth for ever.   And this is the word which by the gospel is preached
unto you."

THESE verses institute a comparison and bring
out a contrast between the natural life and the
spiritual.   Every son of man is *born* into one
life, and every son of God is *born again* into
another.   There is a mystery in every man, but a greater
mystery in every Christian.   Nature is deep, but grace
is deeper.

This is not a contrast between the carnal and the spiritual mind.   Of these it cannot be said that the one is
short-lived and the other enduring.   Spirit does not die,
whether good or evil.   The two lives brought into contrast
here are the natural life of man in the body, which soon
fades away, and the new life of the regenerated, which will
for ever flourish.   These two lives are not in all their
aspects opposite, for the same person may at the same time
possess both.   When a man is born of the Spirit, he is not
then and thereby stripped of the life which belongs to the
flesh.   Every child of God, from the day of his conversion
till the day of his death, possesses and enjoys both.   He

holds them, however, by different tenures : the first or natural life will soon depart ; but the new or spiritual life will be his for ever. The " word of God," as the seed of the new life in believers, " endureth for ever." That word is " Christ in you, the hope of glory."

The analogy employed is exact and full and beautiful : " All flesh is as grass, and all the glory of man as the flower of grass." The figure fits so well that we may venture to make a close inspection, and institute a minute analysis. The comparison of human life generally to the herbage of spring contains two distinct but corresponding parts, expressed in the usual manner of Hebrew poetry. First, we have the simple, broad, and comprehensive intimation, " All flesh is as grass ; " and then a more special analogy rising out of it, as the flower springs from the stalk, " The glory of man is as the flower of grass." Man is like the grass, and his glory like its flower. Life is short, and the period of its perfect development is shorter still.

The analogy in its first and more general form requires scarcely any exposition ; no comparison could be more true, or more obvious. Mankind are like the herbage of summer, which will wither at the turn of the year, although no accident befall it, and is liable to be crushed before its time by a wild beast's foot, or cut through by the mower's scythe. A human life passes through the same stages as the herbage of a season : it has a growing spring, a ripening summer, and a fading autumn. The history of a man consists of a gradual growing to maturity, and a gradual declining to the grave. Such is his best estate, when no accident cuts him off in mid-time of his days. This is the mirror which truly reflects the image of " all flesh." So pass the threescore and ten years which sum up the pilgrimage. It is like a dream when one awaketh : it seems very small when it is nearly done.

But if this is true of the flesh—the sensitive nature which man has in common with the brutes—what shall be said of all his distinguishing features as a moral and intelligent being ? Although the mere flesh is evanescent, what of the glory wherewith his Maker has crowned his head ? The text has two things to say of this glory,—the first, that it greatly excels in worth and beauty the animal structure on which it grows ; the second, that it is still more short-lived. If all flesh be as *grass*, all its glory is only as the *flower* of grass. Two characteristic features distinguish the flower from the herbage,—greater brilliance, and a shorter day. The herbage lives long and grows far ere the blossom appears ; and the blossom, although more beautiful than the supporting stalk, fades and dies before it. The flower is indeed the glory of the grass ; but it comes up later, and withers earlier. What shall we say, then, of all that is peculiar to man—of all that distinguishes him from the beasts of the field—of that human face divine, and that articulate speech, and that calculating mind, which mark him off as chief of God's creatures here and ruler of his world ? Can the glory of man be compared to the herbage as well as his sentient nature ? No ; for though it is more brilliant while it lasts, it is sooner over. The distinguishing excellence of human nature is not like the grass ; it is only like the flower of grass.

Beauty of form is one of the distinguishing glories of humanity. In our species beauty of person is the rule and tendency of nature, although particular features in individuals may by various accidents be more or less obscured. It has pleased God our Father so to arrange the features of our frame, and so to constitute our minds, that we count them comely. We admire the flower of the herbage, and devoutly see in it the Creator's wisdom. Shall we not look with deeper interest on a lighted human countenance, and see in that glory of man a glory to the Lord ? Loathe as much as you will the moral depravity which converts all a Father's gifts into instruments of evil, but reverently acknowledge the mark of his fingers in the model of man.

This glory does not last long. It is a flower—fragrant, attractive ; but it withers soon. Man's life is short, but the glory which grows on it is shorter. The flower is later blown and earlier faded than the frail green stem that bears it.

But the beauty of the new creature in Christ does not fade like a flower. It is an interesting speculation— though it can be nothing more—to imagine the beauty of man unfallen. The peculiar sweetness sometimes imparted to the countenance of an ordinary person by the sudden influx of a " great peace " in periods of spiritual revival, suggests the probability that we lost by sin an external loveliness so great that we lack now the power of conceiving fully what it was. But, great though the loss be, Christians sorrow not over it as those who have no hope ; for their gain is greater. Where sin abounded to mar, grace will much more abound to renew. Whatever is lost by sin is more than restored by redemption. The risen Christ is glorious, and risen Christians will be like him. Humanity redeemed will be humanity perfect. As the idea of man in the mind of God from eternity, will be the man who shall stand before the white throne, accepted in the Beloved.

I would fain realize the beauty of the resurrection body, as well as the spiritual purity of the saints in light. How beautiful man will be when there is no longer any seed of corruption in his body, or any enmity to God in his soul! I think a true Christian sometimes halts painfully in his pilgrimage for want of this ingredient in his hope. The redemption of the soul is indeed the most precious; thereon all other blessings depend; but among the good things that go in its train, the perfection of the redeemed body is a consoling hope—a consolation which Christians greatly need in this vale of tears. "How bright these glorious *spirits* shine!" Yea; but when Christ's work is completed, they will be embodied spirits. How bright these glorious *bodies* will shine also, when mortality shall be swallowed up of life!

Christit in You the Hope of Glory
(1 Peter 1:25)

" But the word of the Lord endureth for ever. And this is the word which by the gospel is preached unto you."

I N contrast with the fleeting life of man, "the word of the Lord endureth for ever." Every creature after its kind. The life that springs from the word will, like its origin, be immortal. But we cannot reach the full meaning of the message here, if we think only of the written word, or even of the mind or meaning which the Holy Spirit expresses thereby. These are only the clothing : it is Christ himself that is wrapped therein, and presented to us. It is from John that we learn most fully the relation of the Scriptures to Christ. " The Word was made flesh, and dwelt among us." The corn of wheat which must fall into the ground and die is the speaker himself. He was at once the sower and the seed ; he was at once the offerer and the sacrifice.

Nowhere else does the prophecy of the text find its full meaning. The Word that endureth for ever is the Word that was with God, and was God. This comes out with great clearness and force in the example of his own preaching in the synagogue of Nazareth recorded in the Gospels (Luke iv. 16–21). When he had read the text from the

Scriptures, he closed the book and gave it back to the attendant. As soon as the book had delivered its message, it was laid aside, and he presented himself to the congregation as the fulfilment of the prophecy. His sermon consisted in permitting the prophet to pronounce the promise, and then exhibiting himself as its fulfilment. No other preacher, either false or true, ever acted thus. To do so would in any mere man be a measure of pride and arrogance that even the boldest has never attained. Only He whom the Father sent into the world could stand in that breach. The weight would crush any creature. This alone is proof of his divinity. If any should dare to assume that position, the height would make him giddy, and his life would reel into all manner of extravagance.

Again, referring to the ostentatious assiduity with which the Jewish doctors searched the letter of the Scriptures, he tells them that in so doing they allow the kernel to slip through their hands, while they vainly strive to live upon the shell : they—the Scriptures—" are they that testify of me ; and ye will not come unto me that ye may have life." From the beginning to the end the Scriptures are the vehicle which contain and convey and deliver Christ. Christ in the Scriptures revealed is the Word of God,— the mind of God toward lost men, expressed and embodied.

The same central truth is taught in many places and in many forms by the Lord : thus, " He that eateth me shall live by me ;" " I am the vine, ye are the branches."

" And this is the Word which is gospelled unto you." It is not so many doctrines, and so many precepts, logically strung together and intellectually understood. It is the ever-enduring Word that is given by God, and accepted in

faith by man. When the Lord articulately on appeal de-
cerned between the sisters Martha and Mary, the distinction
he drew was between the *many not needful* and the *one
needful*. His judgment is, " Of one there is need ;" and
Mary had fixed her choice on the one when she sat at his
feet. In the case of Paul, too, it is made marvellously
clear that what God gave, and he accepted, was the Word
in person. Taught by the Spirit at length, he flung away
all his long-cherished righteousnesses, naming them one
by one, and casting them away with loathing as filthy
rags. But when he comes to tell of the new portion
for his soul that he obtained instead of his cast-off
merits, he does not give a list of many good things that
took the place of the evil ; he counted all loss for *Christ*
(Phil. iii. 7).

It is this that constitutes the " gospel "—the good news.
No number of good things would serve our turn. " There
is need of one." But that one is enough. It is finished :
He hath done it all. All things are yours, if ye are Christ's.

But the gospel is preached " unto you." Unless we personally, one by one, appropriate for ourselves " the gift of
God," there is no transaction. It is not Christ in heaven,
Christ in the Bible, Christ in the confession, but Christ
in you, that is the living hope of glory. The expression
here is parallel with that which is employed in the report
of Philip's address to the Ethiopian treasurer — " He
preached unto him Jesus." On both sides the parallel
holds good ; both subject and object are identical. What
did Philip preach ? Jesus ; that is, as represented by Peter,
the ever-enduring Word. How did Philip preach that
Word ? " Unto him." So here, " unto you."

This is a great and pressing point. It is, indeed, the

turning-point. In the sphere of life it is the article of a standing or a falling man, as in the sphere of doctrine justification is the article of a standing or a falling Church. In some countries and at some periods there has been a disastrous divorce of these two whom God hath joined. Sometimes there has been much preaching of Jesus—of the Word—without the application of the truth to persons. It seems to have been the gospel poured into the air, and not " unto you." The expression conveys the conception of a human soul being the vessel into which the eternal Word is poured. Now, though the Word be preached truly and abundantly over all the land, it will save only those into whom it is poured. Though much water be poured out, it will not benefit the vessel that stands shut, and empty, and dry. It is the old, plain truth : " Believe in the Lord Jesus Christ, and thou shalt be saved." The two essentials are the Christ and thou ; that which saves is Christ unto thee. It is parallel with the Lord's own word to Peter, " Simon, son of Jonas, lovest *thou me ?*"

The spiritual quickening which is spreading over the land, and arresting the regard both of the Church and the world, touches mainly this point. It is not a greater or a better gospel, but the old gospel more specifically pressed home upon persons. It is the gospel *unto you.* In as far as there is an advance, I think it lies very much in this,—that Christ is brought into contact with the individual soul, and these two are left to wrestle, like Jacob and the angel. The Christ " apprehends " the lost man as the shepherd grasped the lost sheep when at last he found it,— apprehends him, and will not let him go : the lost man, conscious that the Christ is " apprehending " him, conceives from that fact a new hope, and, in turn, " apprehends " his

Apprehender, with the life and death cry, " I will not let thee go, except thou bless me." The King suffers this violence, and delights to suffer it ; and the violent gain Him by this force. Hence the frequent glad announcement, as the wrestler emerges from the conflict, " I have found Christ."

Prescription for Living
(1 Peter 2:1-2)

" Wherefore laying aside all malice, and all guile, and hypocrisies, and envies, and all evil speakings, as newborn babes, desire the sincere milk of the word, that ye may grow thereby."

THIS is not a converting word, but a word for the converted. Here are precepts for practice. The deep things of God, both in the covenant of grace and in the conversion of men, have been fully set forth. But these are not left merely as the materials of a creed; they are employed as the power that shall purify the life.

The particle "wherefore" is the visible link that connects doctrine and practice. Ye have been forgiven and renewed; therefore put off the evil and put on the good. "Ye are bought with a price; therefore glorify God in your body, and in your spirit, which are his." "Let every man that hath this hope in him purify himself even as he is pure."

In accordance with the facts of human experience, and with the whole analogy of faith, the precept here is two-sided. It points at once to the evil that must be discarded, and the good that must be admitted in its stead. That which has first possession must be expelled, in order that the faculties of the new man may have room to expand

and operate. Following the order of nature, the apostle first names the tenants in possession, and serves them with a writ of ejectment.

These are arranged in three compartments, with the universal "all" attached to each.

1. All malice.

2. All guile, and hypocrisies, and envies.

3. All evil speakings.

The first term is general. It indicates the soil in which the roots of bitterness grow—badness. The group of three under the second head represent evil thoughts teeming in the heart, like invisible seeds that lie in the ground ready to spring up on the first favourable opportunity. And the third is the issue of the inner thoughts by the readiest channel upon the outward life.

Alas, evil speaking floods the world as some weeds cover the fields in early summer! My heart was made sad in some journeys last year, as I saw many large tracts of grain almost hidden by a yellow sea of flowering weeds. For the time you think it is not possible that any of the corn can come to perfection. Even there, however, a harvest is reaped; but the harvest would have been heavier, if the fields had been clean. Evil speaking, like one dominant weed, covers the surface of society, and chokes in great measure the growth of the good seed.

Christians, ye are God's husbandry—ploughed field: put away these bitter things in their seed-thoughts and in their matured actions, that ye may be fruitful unto him. If the multitude of words spoken by professing Christians in disparagement of their neighbours were reduced first by the omission of all that is not strictly true and fair; and next by the omission of all that is not spoken with a good object in view; and next by the omission of all that, though spoken with a good intention, is unwisely spoken, and mischievous in its results;—the remainder would, like Gideon's army, be very small in number, but very select in kind. The residuum would consist only of the testimony of true men against wickedness, which truth and faithfulness, as in God's sight, compelled them to utter.

The positive precept that follows is conceived and expressed in the form of a most interesting and obvious analogy. " As newborn babes, desire the sincere milk of the word." The terms translated milk of the word certainly and simply mean, milk not in a literal but spiritual sense. It is the same epithet that is employed (Rom. xii. 1) to signify that the service or divine worship expected from Christians is not material offerings of sheep and goats, but a reasonable—that is, a spiritual in contradistinction from a material—service. It is an act of the human soul, worshipping God a Spirit, through faith in the one Mediator. So here, in making use of the word milk, the apostle does not leave it to be inferred, he expressly intimates that it is spiritual milk he means. And by further introducing " babes " into the analogy, he more clearly explains his meaning to be the food provided and suited for the young spiritual life, corresponding to the food provided in nature for a new-born child.

Spiritual hunger and thirst are as real as the corresponding appetites of the body, and as commanding. Saul of Tarsus, when that new hunger began its cravings in his soul, abandoned material food and drink for three whole days. The spiritual hunger was stronger than the natural, and overbore it. Such also was the experience of the Master himself when " he waited at the well of Jacob." Though hungry, he declined to eat the bread his disciples offered, because his appetite for another bread overbore and for the time silenced the appetites of nature. He was so satisfied with the act of imparting salvation to a lost sinner, that he forgot to eat his daily bread.

So then the prescription which this beloved physician administers to invalids is spiritual or soul milk. We are not at a loss to understand his meaning; for Christ has presented himself alike to the newly converted and the experienced as the food whereby they must live and grow. " Except ye eat the flesh and drink the blood of the Son of man, ye have no life in you." As new-born babes desire the milk, and drink it, so the born again come to the Word, and get out of his fulness the supply of all their need.

Observe now the relation in which the negative and the positive stand to each other. Although the precept about putting off first meets our eye on the page, the act is not represented as taking precedence in point of time. It is neither first put off the evil, and then admit the good; nor first take in the good, and then get quit of the evil. The language of the text determines that the two acts are strictly simultaneous. The form of the sentence is—" Laying aside these, desire this." This is scientifically correct as well as scripturally true. The coming of Christ unto his own—to the throne of a human heart—" is like the morning." And how does the morning come? Is it first that the light comes, and then the darkness departs? or first the darkness departs, and then the light advances? It is neither. As the light advances, the darkness recedes. The processes are strictly simultaneous; but in nature the advance of light is the cause, and the departure of darkness the effect. Such, also, is the rule in the spiritual sphere.

It is indeed true that evil must depart to let in the good; but it is the advance of the good that drives the evil before it. Christ is the stronger who overcomes the strong, and casts him out, and reigns in his stead.

To take in the milk and retain also the envies and evil speakings, will give neither comfort nor growth. The effort to mingle these opposites mars the happiness of many a life, and distorts all its testimony for the truth of the gospel. To pour in the milk on the head of these manifold corruptions still retained and cherished, produces neither health nor strength. The milk so mingled sours, and so disturbs. No man can serve two masters. As David's house waxes stronger, the house of the deposed and apostate monarch must wax more feeble.

Living Stones
(1 Peter 2:3-5)

"If so be ye have tasted that the Lord is gracious. To whom coming, as unto a living stone, disallowed indeed of men, but chosen of God, and precious, ye also, as lively stones, are built up a spiritual house, an holy priesthood, to offer up spiritual sacrifices, acceptable to God by Jesus Christ."

HERE Peter walks closely in the Master's footsteps. He intimates that all his expectation of growth in the new life of his friends depends on their experience of forgiving love in their own hearts. He proceeds on the supposition that they have " tasted that the Lord is gracious ;" otherwise he has no expectation of fruit. So taught the Lord himself, when he said, with reference to the relation between the vine and its branches, " Without me ye can do nothing." The actual performance of duty depends on the receiving of pardon, as an effect depends on its cause. In the gospel it is not, Do in God's service, then and therefore you will receive from him ; it is, Receive from him, then and therefore you will be enabled to serve him. It is the branch in the vine that is fruitful.

In the affluent imagery of this fisherman apostle, we are introduced somewhat suddenly here to a new analogy. Dismissing the conception of infants with their sure strong instincts for their mother's milk as the means of life and growth, he steps with all the ease of a master into the widely different yet perfectly congruous conception of a house growing from its foundation to its summit, by the preparation and piling up of many stones. The figures here crowd upon one another, and yet all contribute to the exactitude and completeness of the idea. To the notion of many stones constituting one edifice, is added the idea of life in each separate stone, and the consequent increase of the edifice being a spontaneous growth instead of an operation performed on inanimate matter. And then the conception of a priesthood is added to that of the temple in which they serve, that another aspect of the kingdom may be included in the picture.

" To whom coming." This is in harmony with the whole gospel. It is always and everywhere, " Come unto me." The corresponding complaint of the Lord against the Jews is, " Ye will not come unto me that ye may have life." But here the " coming " is applied to a stone, that enters as a constituent of an edifice. The figure requires that we should conceive of a stone carried to the spot by human hands. So much the worse for the figure if it make any such demand. We are learning here at the feet of a teacher who is bent, not on maintaining the rules of rhetoric, but on conveying to men's minds the saving truth of the gospel. The form must yield to the substance. When nature fails to convey the whole lesson, the lacking part will be given contrary to nature ; and so the stones are " living stones." They represent living souls,—a people made willing in a day of Divine power ; therefore the rhetorical unity of the analogy must be broken, in order to maintain the unity of the faith.

Both the rock which constitutes the foundation, and the stones which are laid on it, are living. The Christ to whom they come, and they who come to him, are living stones; and thus the house grows, like the vine and its branches. As the vine grows into the branch and feeds it, and the branch grows into the vine and draws from it sustenance, so the living foundation attracts the stones, and the stones, by that mysterious attraction made living, come to the foundation, and grow into an holy temple.

It is worthy of notice here that the growth of a tree and the construction of an edifice are very closely and very frequently united in the Scriptures, in order to exhibit the nature and result of the new life in a soul. We give two specimens, one from the Old Testament and the other from the New : " That our sons may be as plants grown up in their youth ; that our daughters may be as corner stones, polished after the similitude of a palace " (Ps. cxliv. 12). " Ye are God's husbandry ; ye are God's building " (1 Cor. iii. 9).

The foundation chosen by God was rejected by men. He came unto his own, and his own received him not. This rejection by the Jews was indeed the preconcerted mark by which the faithful should recognize the Messiah. " He was rejected and despised of men." On this foundation resting, each living stone is a temple, and all the living stones together constitute the universal Church.

As Christ himself is at once the offerer and the sacrifice, so a Christian is at once the temple where God condescends to dwell, and the consecrated priest who presents offerings there. Ye offer up spiritual sacrifices. In the Epistle to the Romans, we find that the bodies of believers—this life, with all its faculties and powers—are the living sacrifices that God will accept at the offerer's hands, as distinguished from the dead offerings of a former dispensation.

Two qualities in New Testament worship go to make it acceptable. One is, the offerings must be spiritual, not material; the other is, they must be presented through the one Mediator between God and man. Only spiritual offerings can be acceptable. Bodily service has no merit. No amount of material gifts contributed can avail the opulent worshipper, and no degree of self-inflicted torture can avail the devotee who is courageous but poor. Vestments and candles and incense are out of place under the gospel. God does not regard them; they have no value in his sight, except a value on the wrong side, as marking men who have departed from the simplicity of Christ. Beware, ye who labour in the fires to produce these mechanical and dead sacrifices. The answer prepared for your appeal is,— " Who hath required this at your hands?" God calls for spiritual sacrifices. Christ taught with marvellous clearness that under the New Dispensation the acceptance of worship does not depend on place and form, but that men must everywhere worship in spirit and in truth. It is the human soul, in contact with the Father of our spirits, worshipping, loving, serving,—this only is acceptable.

But even this, in order to be acceptable, must be all presented always through the one Mediator between God and man. The office of the Holy Spirit in the word is to take of the things of Christ and show them unto us. Here is a thing of Christ which the Spirit clearly shows. He is the Daysman, laying his hand upon both, to obtain acceptance for our worship or work. Even the most spiritual sacrifices are acceptable only through Jesus Christ.

The announcement from above is, " Lo ! I am with you alway." Let our heart's answer echo up to him that speaketh—" Even so, come, Lord Jesus." It is not his name as a dead letter in our creed, or his name as a sound at the termination of our prayer, but himself in simple faith accepted, dwelling in our hearts, and ever presented unto God as our righteousness, not only when we bow the knee in prayer, but also in all the turnings of life. " Which hope we have as an anchor of the soul, sure and steadfast, within the veil." Let the line be ever tight that unites the ship tossed on the sea of time to the anchor within the veil, until the soul, saved from shipwreck, get an abundant entrance into the Lord's presence, and so the need of an anchor be felt no more.

The Chief Cornerstone
(1 Peter 2:6-8)

" Wherefore also it is contained in the scripture, Behold, I lay in Sion a chief
corner stone, elect, precious : and he that believeth on him shall not be confounded. Unto you therefore which believe he is precious : but unto them
which be disobedient, the stone which the builders disallowed, the same is made
the head of the corner, and a stone of stumbling, and a rock of offence, even to
them which stumble at the word, being disobedient : whereunto also they were
appointed."

THE Scriptures did not determine the provisions
and character of the covenant of grace : rather,
the provisions and character of the covenant,
arranged in the Divine counsel before time
began, gave shape to the promises and ordinances of Scripture. Because matters were so ordered in the plan of
salvation, therefore also that same ordering was given in
the Scriptures. In particular, because, in the purpose of
God, the eternal Son undertook to redeem his people, the
promises of his coming were given in the prophets, to keep
the eye of faith from the beginning ever looking unto
Jesus.

The eternal God has laid this foundation : we need not
fear to trust it. He hath done all things well. It was
laid in Zion : it pleased God to select one family, and constitute them the custodiers of his oracles, for distribution
through the world in the fulness of time.

The chief corner stone is chosen and precious. The word means dear, as in the case of the centurion's servant, who was dear unto his master. The well-beloved of the Father was chosen for this service, and sent into the world. Much of the power which the gospel exercises on stony hearts to break and melt them lies here. God spared not his own Son : the gift was, in human language, unspeakable. It is the preciousness of his gift that imparts power to his invitation. As soon as an anxious inquirer realizes that God, in order to save a soul from death, gave up his Well-beloved, the melting begins, and the hard stony heart flows down like water. It is not that God was hard and unforgiving until Christ, by his suffering in our stead, propitiated his favour. This conception grasps even the glorious gospel by the wrong end, and turns it upside down,—turns the truth into a lie. The opposite is the truth. Such was the love of the Father to the lost, that he spared not his dear Son, but gave him up to die, the just for the unjust. The mercy of God to sinners is the cause, not the effect, of the incarnation and sacrifice of the Son.

" He that believeth on him shall not be confounded." It seems to point to the flutter and confusion that must overtake the guilty at the appearing of the Judge. Those guests who wore the wedding garment were not put about when the footfall of the king was heard approaching. They were adorned with the robe that the king himself had chosen, prescribed, and bestowed. They knew that he would be well pleased with his own. This is the shadow of that confidence which calms and keeps the hearts of believers when they have put on Christ. They know that God is well pleased with his own beloved. There is no confusion of face for those who are found in him. " There is therefore now no condemnation to them that are in Christ Jesus."

It was well for Paul that he cast away with loathing the long array of merits in which he formerly trusted. For if he had been placed before the great white throne with those filthy rags for covering—his birth and baptism, his orthodoxy and his zeal—he would certainly have been confounded in the presence of the Judge. He learned in time to loathe these filthy rags, and he passionately put them off, counting them loss for Christ, his new portion,— his only and sufficient righteousness.

Nor is it merely a confidence in the great day; it is also a firm footing and a glad song at every stage of the pilgrimage on earth. Alas, the life-course of a sinner unforgiven is like the flutter and fright of a painful dream, where the feet sink in mire at every step,—where the opening is so narrow that you cannot pass through, and you experience a sense of suffocation as you vainly repeat the effort.

I observe with glad gratitude that no other condition is attached to this confidence than the one—believe on him. The Spirit has not said, If you belong to this or that ecclesiastical corporation, or have received ordinances at the hands of self-styled successors of the apostles, you shall not be confounded. I admire the liberty wherewith the Son has made his people free. He that believeth on him—this condition, and none other! In presence of this divine decision, seen like the sun in its own light, how can a puny, ignorant, sinful man, strutting about in an authority derived only from equally puny, ignorant, and sinful men who lived before him, dare to set up other conditions of peace with God!

"Unto you therefore which believe he is precious." He is now summing up the results of the preceding argument. The term here is not the same as that which is rendered "precious" in verse 4th. There it is the adjective; here it is the corresponding noun, and means "the price." It is the word employed to designate the thirty pieces of silver (Matt. xxvii. 6); "it is the price of blood." It is true that Christ is "precious" to them that believe; but more than that lies in the word. He is their price—the price paid for them, and by which they were redeemed. They were, according to Luther's rendering, "bought dear;" and he who became their ransom is, in the other and cognate sense of the term, "dear" to their hearts.

It is eminently worthy of notice that over against "believe" in verse 6th stands, not its exact correlative "unbelieving," but "disobedient." They who receive Christ believe: you would expect to read conversely, they who reject him are unbelieving; but instead, you read that they are disobedient. People raise a great debate upon the question whether a man is responsible for his belief, and whether he can be condemned for not believing. Quietly this debate is all quashed here by the representation that unbelief is disobedience. Unbelief is indeed the root, but the outgrowth is disobedience. As you can more easily push over a tree by applying force to its lofty head, than by acting on its stem near the ground, so the matter is more easily settled by reckoning unbelief as disobedience. This is a matter which we must leave with the conscience of the individual. Sincere inquirers after truth, God will hear and guide; those who cannot believe, because they have in their hearts a foregone conclusion that they will not obey, God will judge. Every man is his brother's keeper, for loving, patient effort to lead him into truth ; but no man is his neighbour's judge. To his own master he standeth or falleth.

In regard to the expression, " Whereunto they were appointed," all that I can suggest towards its interpretation is, that it corresponds with and balances the clause in verse 6th, " I lay in Sion a chief corner stone." The same word is employed in both clauses. " Appoint " here is not the word which signifies choose, or determine. It is simply place, or lay down. The two clauses are the complements of each other. He who lays down the corner stone, also lays down these men in their lives before it. He places them in each other's way. Whatever may be taught elsewhere in Scripture on cognate topics, as far as I can see, all this passage teaches is, that the corner stone, and these rejecters, were by God placed reciprocally in each other's path. The stone is set before them, and they are set before it. There is no possibility of evading a decision. This stone must be to them one of two—must be either the foundation on which a believer's hope shall securely rest, or the stone that in judgment will fall upon them and crush them as enemies. " Choose ye this day whom ye will serve : as for me and my house, we will serve the Lord."

The Lord's Treasure
(1 Peter 2:9)

" But ye are a chosen generation, a royal priesthood, an holy nation, a peculiar people."

THE last of these four expresses the aim or object pursued and attained ; and the three preceding reveal the steps or means by which that end is reached. We shall accordingly examine the last first. The central object here is the special designation given to the Lord's redeemed as his " peculiar people." On this point in the middle we must plant our compass, if we would trace to any good effect the circumference of the verse, explaining alike what goes before and what follows.

At this stage the view-point of the observer is changed. Hitherto we have been considering redemption as some good thing which we obtain from God ; now we must think of it as some good thing that God obtains for himself. In this case the Good Shepherd has lost some of his own sheep. He is not willing to want them. He leaves the un-strayed safe on the pasture, and goes after the wanderers until he find them ; and when he has found them, he bears them back rejoicing.

Some years since the son of a wealthy English family was seized by a band of robbers while he was making a tour in the mountains of Greece. Through some mis-management the ransom demanded was not promptly paid, and the men, in revenge, killed their captive. There was a great deal of trouble with the Government of Greece ; but nothing could restore their beloved child to his be-reaved family. They had agreed to pay the stipulated sum, and they remained inconsolable because that ransom, instead of reaching the robbers, returned to their own hands. Their money came back, but they lost their son.

More recently, a young man was similarly captured and held to ransom by bandits in Italy. The parents, in this case, succeeded in paying the price, and redeeming their son. From this completed transaction two distinct joys sprang—one, the joy of the child in gaining his liberty ; the other, the joy of the parents in obtaining their child.

Hitherto we have been thinking of redemption through grace as the first of these joys; now we think of it as the second. In the preceding verses we have stood on the view-point of the ransomed captive ; now we stand on the view-point of God who redeems. " This my son was dead, and is alive again ; was lost, and is found."

Literally and fully the expression is, " A people for his peculiar property." The idea is transferred from the Old Testament : " Now therefore, if ye will obey my voice indeed, and keep my covenant, then ye shall be a peculiar treasure unto me above all people " (Ex. xix. 5).

The word " peculiar," by which the thought is expressed in English, we derive directly through the Latin, and the use of the term in the secular life of the Romans will throw light on its meaning here in the spiritual sphere. The system of slavery prevailed in the Roman Empire. It interpenetrated all society. An elaborate code of laws had sprung up to regulate its complicated and unnatural relations. The slave, when he fell into slavery, lost all. He became the property of his master. But if he served faithfully, law and custom permitted him to acquire private property through his own skill or industry. A man might, for example, hire himself from his owner, paying him so much a day. He might then employ himself in art or even merchandise, and if successful, might soon accumulate a considerable sum. Some slaves, in this manner, purchased their own liberty, and raised themselves to a high position. Now the savings of a slave, after satisfying the demands of the master, were called his *peculium*. The law protected him in his right to this property. It may be supposed to have been very dear to the poor man. It constituted his sole anchor of hope. He cherished it accordingly. From this a conception and expression have been borrowed to show the kind of ownership that God is pleased to claim in the persons who have been won back to himself after they were lost.

He had made man in his own image and for himself. For him he had formed and furnished the world. Man, made last, made best, was the chief of the Creator's works. That chosen, cherished portion was lost and enslaved. The Father was not content to leave his child a captive in the enemy's hands. He provided a ransom. The ransom was paid. The slaves set free returned in number and purity like dew-drops from the womb of the morning. The darkened and denuded heavens were studded again with stars. The portion regained became dearer than ever to the Redeemer. These sons and daughters of the Lord Almighty became a " peculiar people." They were God's own cherished treasure in a closer sense than any other creature of his hand.

The same language is frequently employed in the New Testament, to indicate that while all other beings and things belong to God, human sinners redeemed by the blood of Christ are in a higher sense his own—the treasure in which he delights. When Paul is commending the church at Ephesus to the special care of its own elders, he reminds them that God had purchased that church as his own peculiar treasure, by the price of the Redeemer's blood. The circumstance that they are so peculiarly precious to the Lord that bought them, is given as the strongest reason why the under-shepherds should faithfully feed the flock.

While therefore it is right to stand on the earth below and look up to redemption as a boon which the ransomed obtain, it is right also, in proper place and time, to reverse the view,—to come up higher, and look as the Redeemer looks upon the portion he has won. Those whom he has bought with his blood are his treasure, his portion, his reward. He rejoices over them with a joy that is unspeakable and full of glory. He keeps them as the apple of his eye. It is a great thing that my Redeemer is mine; but it is still a greater, if I can attain to it, that I am his.

Way and Fruits of Redemption
(1 Peter 2:9)

" But ye are a chosen generation, a royal priesthood, an holy nation ; that ye should show forth the praises of him who hath called you out of darkness into his marvellous light."

WE proceed now to trace in this scripture the steps by which this great end is attained. The goings of the Lord are glorious—the goings by which he achieves for himself his own peculiar possession. The steps as written here are three: " A chosen generation, a royal priesthood, an holy nation." Father, Son, and Spirit appear working here. In that same eternal counsel where the constitution of man was determined, the redemption was provided too. There is more in the purpose of redemption than pity for the perishing. It is much to learn that God is merciful, and that the gift of Christ is the outcome and the evidence of his compassion. That is deep ; but a deeper lies beneath it. It was good for the lost sheep that through the pity of the tender shepherd it was brought back to the fold ; but it was better for the owner that he got back his own. There are two revolutions of the earth, a less and a larger. It revolves round itself, and it revolves also round the sun. To revolve round its own axis is great, but to circulate round the central sun is inexpressibly greater. In some such manner and proportions seem related the two gains—the gain of the ransomed when he is saved from death, and the gain of the Redeemer when he wins his treasure.

1. "A chosen generation," or race. This is the beginning. The spring of all is in the Father's purpose.

2. "A royal priesthood." The Mediator's hand is revealed here. This is the Daysman's place. He makes them kings and priests unto God. They are accepted in the Beloved, and in his birthright they reign.

3. "An holy nation." This is the work of the Sanctifier. The baptism of the Spirit cleanses. This is "the washing of regeneration, and the renewing of the Holy Ghost."

Chosen by the Father, this is the favoured race; ransomed by the Son, their guilt is taken away, and they are delivered from bondage; sanctified by the Spirit, they are meet for heaven. These three steps in the same order are exhibited in the Lord's intercessory prayer (John xvii. 6),—

"Thine they were " = a chosen generation.

"Thou gavest them me " = a royal priesthood.

"They have kept thy word " = an holy nation.

I suppose Peter listened while the Master spoke that prayer aloud. It was there he found the germs of the grand theology which he teaches here. These Galileans were not original in their conceptions and dogmas. They teach us in their Epistles what they learned at the feet of Jesus.

To what uses will he put his peculiar and cherished property, now that he has obtained it at a great price. His intention in that regard is written here at length, "That ye should show forth the praises of him who hath called you out of darkness into his marvellous light." This is the uniform testimony of Scripture. "Arise, shine; for thy light is come." "Father, I am glorified in them." "Epistles of Jesus Christ, known and read of all men."

That ye should show—should "angel forth"—his praise. Do it with your lips, where and when an opportunity may occur, as when the Lord directed the restored maniac to tell them of his own house what great things God had done for him. But in any case the delivered captives should in their lives be witnesses to the Lord that bought them. Israel, after the exodus, turned the great facts of their deliverance into psalms. So here, the experiences through which the saved are led are suggested as the material of their praise. He hath effectually called us out of darkness into his own marvellous light. Say this, and sing it too. They have been called out of darkness ere their mirth began: while they were in the darkness they did not sing about it. Before they heard his call they spake nothing in his praise: as long as they were deaf they were also dumb. They make a song about the darkness after they are in the light. Israel made psalms on Pharaoh and his warriors after they saw them sink as lead in the mighty waters.

Suppose a person has been born and has passed his life hitherto in the recesses of a mine. He may have heard companions telling of a glorious light in the heavens, and a lovely landscape spread out beneath it. Some dim conceptions the captive may have entertained of day, based on multiplying many times in conception the oil lamps that guided his steps in the narrow galleries. But when at last he is brought up "out of darkness into light," he learns the meaning of both. He sings now intelligently, for the first time, both of the darkness from which he has escaped, and of the light into which he has come.

The redeemed of the Lord, when they are brought out of darkness, behold the Light of Life in the face of Jesus. It is that light off the face of Jesus streaming down into their dungeon that drives the darkness away.

The Warfare
(1 Peter 2:11)

"Dearly beloved, I beseech you as strangers and pilgrims, abstain from fleshly lusts, which war against the soul."

HERE we suddenly step down again into the arena of practical duty,—the conflict which must be waged through life against multiform vice. But, Peter, you gave us an exhortation on that head a few lines further up. After the practical warning, "Laying aside all malice," etc., you led us into the deep doctrines of the covenant, and made us almost forget that there is still a world and wickedness. Again you revert at a spring to the old subject, "Abstain from fleshly lusts." Has the ardent apostle forgotten, and glided off the track? No; he knows where he is: he is about the Master's business. "The Lord said unto Peter, I have prayed for thee ......When thou art converted, strengthen thy brethren." He is in the act of obeying that injunction now. He knows by bitter experience, that after making a good confession, a man's heart, if left to itself, will fall again into deep sin. "Thou art the Christ, the Son of the living God." Blessed art thou, Simon Bar-jona; that is a grand and full confession. But Simon's warfare is not yet accomplished. He thought it was; but he was mistaken.

" Though all men forsake thee, yet will not I." Hear him! He is hallooing before he is out of the wood. The next time you meet him, he is cursing and swearing : " I know not the man." This time the apostle does not fall into the mistake of counting the battle won as soon as the soldier has got his armour on. He returns to the charge, on the assumption that the enemy is not dead yet. Another blow : " Dearly beloved, I beseech you as strangers and pilgrims, abstain from fleshly lusts, which war against the soul."

His doctrinal discussions are always followed up by warnings and precepts for practice. Like other good soldiers, he takes advantage of everything that promises to further his object. Human affections are pressed into the service : " Dearly beloved." The power of love is like the power of gravity. It surrounds the greatest, and yet grasps the least. It keeps a mountain steady on its base, and balances a dew-drop on a blade of grass. How often do human beings labour in the fires to accomplish their objects, and fail for want of this greatest ally ! This is as if manufacturers should abandon steam, and revert to the strength of human arms. Love will do effective service at every turn, and on any material. Call love to your aid, and it would be hard to say what barrier you will not surmount.

" As strangers and pilgrims." Another weight thrown in to increase the vantage on the side of right. In military monarchies it has always been the policy to employ the soldiers far from home. When the Austrian Empire was a conglomerate of many nationalities, German regiments were sent to campaign in Italy, and Italians served in Germany. When the men had not a home to care for, they were more completely at the disposal of their leaders. This is Peter's idea here. Christians are not at home in the world. There is less to distract them. They should be better soldiers of Jesus Christ. The more loose their hearts are to the earth, the more firm will be the anchor of their souls on high. Conversely, the more they are attached to their home in heaven, the less will they be entangled with the wealth and the pleasures of the world. The same contrast is exhibited by Paul when he brings the two classes together, in order to exhibit their opposite courses and ends. This class mind earthly things; that class, on the contrary, have their citizenship in heaven (Phil. iii. 18–20).

These desires that belong to the flesh are adversaries of the soul. There is a difference between a war and a battle. It is not a random stroke; it is warfare on a plan. A battle may be won, and yet the victor be overcome ere the war be over. The first French emperor gained several great battles in the Russian campaign; but his army was not only vanquished, it was almost annihilated in the end. It is thus that certain appetites and passions, although once and again overcome by a resolute will, return to the charge, and watch their opportunity. It is not a battle, and done with it; the vanquished foe often enslaves his conqueror. A young man in modern society must do battle for his life with strong drink. He can taste it freely and stop in time. He despises the weak who seek safety in flight and abstinence. He knows what is good for him, and will not allow himself to be overcome. He obtains a good many victories, and counts himself invulnerable. But the wily foe persists. By little and little a diseased thirst is generated. The enemy now has an accomplice within the castle gates; and in the end the strong man, like Samson with his eyes out, grinds darkling in his enslaver's prison.

For the Lord's redeemed it is not a hardship but rather a privilege to be strangers and pilgrims. The last step of the pilgrimage is the entrance into home. If here we have no continuing city, all the more intently will we seek one to come. If this is not our rest because it is polluted, into the rest that remaineth for the people of God nothing shall enter that defileth. " Fear not, little flock; for it is your Father's good pleasure to give you the kingdom."

The Witness of a Pure Life
(1 Peter 2:12-13)

" Having your conversation honest among the Gentiles: that, whereas they speak against you as evil-doers, they may by your good works, which they shall behold, glorify God in the day of visitation. Submit yourselves to every ordinance of man for the Lord's sake."

H AVING your conversation honest." Both terms need some explanation. Both words come from the Latin, and have in process of time greatly changed their meaning. In modern English, conversation means the talking of two or more persons with each other; but the sense in the text is, the whole habit and life-course of a person,—his character, and temper, and conduct in presence of his fellows. You are exposed now on this side and now on that,—now to one observer and now to another. See that the whole circumference of your life be wise and pure and true. At all times, and in all circumstances, walk circumspectly, for you never know who may be looking on. The modern meaning of honest is, that you do not cheat in a bargain; but as used here, and in ancient times generally, it signifies beautiful,—first a material and then a moral winsomeness. These two terms in conjunction convey the precept, Let all the circumference of your life shine in the beauty of holiness. Alas! bid this dull earth shine like a star of heaven!

There is nothing impossible there. In very deed this opaque globe does shine as a star, not a whit behind its neighbours in brightness, when it receives and reflects the sunbeams. To have commanded the house of Israel to shine as a light to surrounding nations would have been an impossible requirement, if the precept had not been mated with a promise. But as the record runs, it is a reasonable service that is demanded : " Arise, shine ; for thy light is come, and the glory of the Lord is risen upon thee " (Isa. lx. 1).

This precept given by Peter is on both its sides the echo of Isaiah's words. A light is needed because darkness reigns around. Peter desiderates a beautiful life among the Gentiles ; and Isaiah expects that, when Israel basks in the favour of God, the Gentiles shall come to their light. It was in the same spirit that the Lord promised to the eleven before the Pentecost, " Ye shall receive power, after that the Holy Ghost is come upon you : and ye shall be witnesses unto me."

The nations sat in darkness, and the disciples of Christ were commissioned to go out as lights in the world. One day, the people of Lystra brought a garlanded ox, and would have sacrificed to Paul as a god ; another day they stoned him, and left him for dead. Such was heathenism at its best.

It is a characteristic of true faith that it has positive hope. It does not despair even when things are at the worst, for it trusts in God. It is not enough that the primitive disciples should repel surrounding, assailing evil, and hold their own. They expect to make aggression and to gain a victory ; to turn scoffs into hymns of praise, and enemies of Christ into zealous disciples : " That, whereas

 Parables of Our Lord

they speak against you as evil-doers, they may by your good works, which they shall behold, glorify God in the day of visitation."

It is not by the loudest debate and profession that these conquests can be made. It is not by what Christians say, but by what Christians are, that they can win the neighbourhood. The call is not so much to give evidence, as to be witnesses. What the adversaries see will be more effectual to convert them than what they hear. It is by their " walk " that Paul distinguished certain persons at Philippi as enemies of the cross of Christ; and it is by their walk that true disciples may most effectually challenge recognition as its real friends.

Still further the precepts run down into detail. Submission to magistrates is prescribed as a Christian duty. Considering the time and the circumstances, this is a remarkable feature of the New Testament Scriptures. They are in favour of authority, but not of tyranny. The gospel fosters liberty, but does not suggest insurrection. Witness the emigration of the persecuted Puritans from England to America. These men would not resist constituted authority; but neither would they allow themselves to be crushed by a despot, as long as a remedy, which they could with a good conscience adopt, lay within their reach. The results will tell with decisive effect on the future condition of the human race.

Ordinances of man should be obeyed, but they stand not on the same level with ordinances of God. Divine laws that directly appeal to the individual conscience must be obeyed absolutely and at all hazards; ordinances enacted by the civil legislature are binding also when they do not come in conflict with a higher law. If any man resist a civil enactment, regularly made and enforced, it is at his own peril. He must in that case make very sure that the law of God forbids obedience.

The principle that we must obey God rather than man, is precious not only as a religious truth, but as the firmest safeguard of national liberty. But there is an application of that principle in vogue in some quarters of Europe which is a caricature of truth and decency. When the Pope issues an order to the subjects of a king, or the citizens of a commonwealth, which is directly at variance with the laws of the State, and Papists claim the liberty of obeying their spiritual head in defiance of their country's law, under authority of the rule, Obey God rather than man, they offer an insult to the common sense of the community, and to the real authority of the divine Word. It seems degrading to the dignity of human nature to be obliged even to maintain an argument on this question. The citizen who profanely identifies the random and passionate assertion of a foreign priest with the word of the living God addressed to the souls that he has made, does not deserve an answer. When he violates the " ordinance of man "—the legal statutes of the constituted authorities —on such grounds, he must even be left in prison to meditate on the consequences of his crime.

How honest old Peter would have stared, if any one had proposed a qualifying clause at this point of his Epistle, to the effect that any one should be at liberty to resist the ordinance, provided a priest in Rome, claiming to be Peter's successor, gave him permission !

Submission to Authority
(1 Peter 2:13-16)

"Submit yourselves to every ordinance of man for the Lord's sake: whether it be to the king, as supreme; or unto governors, as unto them that are sent by him for the punishment of evil-doers, and for the praise of them that do well. For so is the will of God, that with well-doing ye may put to silence the ignorance of foolish men: as free, and not using your liberty for a cloke of maliciousness, but as the servants of God."

THE passage 11–16 is a group of practical precepts. In a preceding portion Peter had taught the doctrines,—" What man should believe concerning God." Here he applies himself to conduct,—"What duty God requires of men." Observe in what manner the Scriptures teach and enforce morals. The rules are specific and minute ; but these, if left alone, would lack power—they would remain dead letters. In order to give life and force to his precepts, the apostle binds them at every joint not only to religion, but to God. Four times in this little bundle of precepts the personal living God comes in as the present power to enforce obedience :—

Verse 12. " That they may glorify God."

Verse 13. " For the Lord's sake."

Verse 15. " For so is the will of God."

Verse 16. " As the servants of God."

A great sheet is let down, full of miscellaneous duties, knit at the four corners, not to heaven merely, but to the living God. This Bible stands alone; no book at all approaches it. It brings God as close to the whole of human life as the air is to the surface of the earth and the bodies of men; and this not in terror but in paternal love. Christ is the mediator, and he is the gift of God to the lost. It is not that a sacrifice was offered in order to deliver the guilty from punishment, and leave him in a place of safety. The Deliverer abides with his redeemed for hope and holiness: " Lo, I am with you alway"—always to sustain, direct, and comfort.

God desires to be not only the author of a salvation sent from heaven, and the receiver of the ransomed into rest, but also to be in the life of his people here, compassing them about with his favour, as the air, and supplying them with the breath of life. Like the veins interspersed through a leaf to strengthen its weak points, the peace of God runs through a Christian's life, to keep his heart and mind.

The motive supplied refines and elevates the duty, however lowly may be the sphere of its exercise. Do it for the Lord's sake; and then the life is sublime, though it be worn out in menial occupation, or crushed by unjust laws.

The various classes of magistrates are noticed, to show that obedience is due, not only to the supreme, but also to the delegated authorities. Civil government is recognized as a divine institution, and obedience is simply enjoined as a duty, although in point of fact laws have often been unjust and rulers have acted unlawfully. These, and similar precepts elsewhere in the New Testament, constitute a standing evidence that the writers spake as they were moved by the Holy Ghost. Peter and Paul were hunted by the magistrates of the empire, like wild beasts, until at length they were hunted down; and yet no bitter word escapes from their lips. Other ships reel and stagger, like drunken men, on a stormy sea; but this vessel alone moves straight and steady. That very fact proves that she is not leaning on the waters like the rest, but is sustained in the air above them.

"This is the will of God concerning you." Blessed news! I delight to learn that God in heaven has a will about me, and the manner of my life. Cheer up, fellow-pilgrims, he careth for us—he whom the hosts of heaven adore. It elevates my life to know that its smallest joys or sorrows concern the King Eternal. This is a kindlier doctrine than any theory of atomic development.

And as there are many ignorant and foolish men going about, making a very great noise because of their folly and ignorance, it seems that one part of God's will concerning Christians in the body is that they should silence these noisy fellows. How? Shall we smite with the sword? That was the method which this same Peter once proposed —and not only proposed, but practised. He valiantly cut off the ear of a servant of the high priest, in order to silence him. Ah, Peter, you will not silence your adversaries in that fashion. Two can play at that game; and in a very short time they will silence you. But now, when the Holy Ghost has come upon him, the impetuous Peter has received power to be a true witness unto Christ. He would still have these adversaries silenced, but he knows a better method of doing it now: silence them "by well-doing." Such is the principal weapon used in this holy war.

"As free, and not using your liberty for a cloke of maliciousness." While he certifies their right to freedom, he gives faithful warning against the tares that often spring among the precious wheat. Many abominations are wrought in this world in the name of liberty. The apostle has a particular species of hypocrite in his eye. Foreseeing that this kind will infest the Church, he blows a blast to drive the chaff away. This man has assumed the name of Christian, and joined himself to the visible Church. He is accountable only to God ; he is not bound by the laws of human magistrates. In virtue of being a king and priest unto God, he is not obliged to be submissive to the laws of men. This kind of pretender has often strutted about on the stage of history, and brought shame upon the Christian name. He gets no countenance here ; he is articulately condemned by the spirit of prophecy in Peter's word. In the Scriptures great pains are taken to show that faith is not against authority and order ; and yet it is made perfectly clear that whenever human ordinances traverse the law of God for the conscience of the individual man, they must give way. Can the line be always correctly drawn between these two jurisdictions ? The line is not in itself uncertain or obscure. It is like the horizon line between the air above and sea and earth below : it is a well-defined boundary ; but men do not always clearly see or faithfully keep it. In our own country, in past times, dreadful conflicts have raged on this border land. Power lay on one side, and martyr courage emerged on the other. The strife has made our history sublime. None of the sufferings are altogether lost. All past experience will contribute to clear the clouds from the horizon, and introduce the brightness of the latter day.

The Dignity of Man
(1 Peter 2:17)

" Honour all men."

T HE first three precepts of this verse constitute an ascending series, and the series is complete. It begins on earth, and ends in heaven. The Spirit in this word specifies the kind of affection that is due respectively to three different objects, lying in three distinct spheres. The first and lowest of these objects is humanity, as it is,—all mankind ; the next above it is the redeemed from among men who are still in the body ; and the highest is God. One kind of regard is due to human beings as such, however low their state or bad their character ; another kind of regard is due to those who are born again, and have become sons and daughters of the Lord Almighty ; and yet another kind of regard is due to the Creator of all, the Recreator of his own.

Instead of " honour," I shall employ the term " value," as equivalent to " esteem," which the translators have given in the margin, and which expresses more precisely the sense of the original. I retain the term " men," as in the text, although the noun is not expressed in the Greek, because in the circumstances the masculine adjective is equivalent.

Let us now place the emphasis successively on each of these three words, and the lessons will emerge in their natural order.

1. *Value.*
2. Value *men.*
3. Value *all* men.

1. *Value.*—The root on which the expression grows is "a price." This original meaning adheres to it with more or less of strictness through all its forms and all its applications. It is the word which in Matthew xxvii. 9 has been translated "value,"—"They took the thirty pieces of silver, the price of him that was valued, whom they of the children of Israel did value;" and "honour," in Matthew xv. 4,—"Honour thy father and thy mother." Honour, as it is usually understood, is only the external expression of the value which in your heart you may have set upon an object. You weigh the worth of a man, and honour him accordingly. The estimate fixed by the judgment determines the honour expressed by the lips.

Although the three precepts of this verse are separately presented to the mind, they are bound into one for the power to produce obedience. Where the two higher fail, the lower cannot succeed. If the fear of God and the love of the brotherhood be wanting or weak, the estimate of humanity will go far astray. And it is error in the estimate of man that practically distracts the world. Some get too much honour, and others too little. These extremes throw the machinery of society out of gear. Hence the adulation of the great; hence the oppression of the poor. The man who is godly and brotherly is also humane. He who sets a proper value on the higher things sets a proper value also on the lower. Look on men—the human race at large—in the light of the fear which you owe to God, and the love which you cherish towards the brethren : thus you will neither meanly flatter nor coldly neglect ; you will count the meanest a man, and the mightiest no more.

2. Value *men.*—Here God our Maker has left us an example that we should follow his steps. Both creation and redemption teem with evidences that God sets a high value on his creature man. All the relations and uses of minerals, plants, and animals have been arranged for man's benefit ; for no other creature is capable of observing or turning them to account. All the rich furniture of the world bears obvious marks of having been constructed for the convenience of its chief inhabitant. The house was arranged, and all its furnishings completed, and living creatures destined for servants provided, before men, the children of the family, were brought home. All that the Father did in constructing this earth and these heavens he did for our sakes.

But the grandest evidence of the value which God sets on man appears in the mission, ministry, and sacrifice of Christ. So high in heaven was the estimate of even ruined man, that when no other price could buy the captive back, the Son of God gave himself, the just for the unjust.

A jewel has dropped from the wearer's neck into a deep and filthy pool. The owner, looking on it from aloft, loathes the fetid object, and loves it too,—so loves it, in spite of its loathsomeness, that rather than lose it, he plunges into the polluted deep, wades among its filth, and feels for his treasure. If he find it, he goes home rejoicing; and when the jewel has been burnished again, he rejoices more than ever to see it on his own breast, receiving bright glances from the sun, and throwing them back as bright.

In some such way, making allowance for the difference between the finite and the infinite, did Christ set a high value on men, though they were fallen and polluted. In some such way does he now rejoice over those whom he has rescued from perdition and carried into rest.

Value highly immortal beings made in their Creator's likeness, and capable yet of living to his praise. We act according to our estimates. Estimate humanity aright in the habit of your hearts, and your conduct will fashion itself naturally accordant, as a river finds its way to the sea. Value the whole man, and not merely a part. In particular, and for obvious practical purposes, value his soul as well as his body, and his body as well as his soul. So did Christ; and therefore so should we. The body's sufferings did not occupy his attention to the neglect of the soul's sins; the soul's sins did not occupy his attention to the neglect of the body's sufferings.

As the legs of the lame are not equal, a one-sided philanthropy is abortive, whichever side it may be. You cannot do good to the poor by merely supplying his material wants. Unless you lift his spirit from despair into hope, and lead his spirit from darkness to light, your gifts go all into a bag with holes. You must be always giving, and yet he is never full. On the other side, the ordinary path to the soul lies through the body's senses; and all your efforts for spiritual good may prove abortive, if you do not clear material obstructions out of your way.

Do good to the whole man as you have opportunity. Neglect not to entertain those strangers that step about in human form upon the earth, for in so doing you entertain angels unawares,—fallen, indeed, but capable yet of a glorious immortality.

No Respecter of Persons
(1 Peter 2:17)

"Honour all men."

VALUE *all* men.

There is no respect of persons with God, and there should be none with men. When you fail to value aright any man or class of men, you are fighting against God, and will certainly be hurt. He that falls upon this stone shall be broken. Action and reaction are equal and opposite. Suppose you and your neighbour are walking abreast on a pavement of pure ice; and suppose you put forth your strength to push your neighbour off the way on one side. You may, perhaps, succeed; but the same effort at the same time has pushed yourself as far from the path on the other side.

The operation of this principle may be seen in all ranks and in all places. Wherever and whenever a man fails to give a neighbour his due, he thereby to the same extent injures himself. The machine of Providence brings vengeance on the transgressor, as its awful wheels move round.

Take an example from the treatment of negro slaves in our own colonies and in the States of America till lately; in other places of the world still. White men cannot push black men aside from the right position without pushing themselves as far from the right character. The loss which they suffer is greater than the loss which they inflict. As it is more blessed to give than to receive, so it is more cursed to deprive another of his rights than to be deprived of your own. I would rather have my condition deteriorated by another's violence, than my character deteriorated by my own sin.

Man's foundation is not like the everlasting hills. It is not in his power to push another and yet not move himself. The oppressor and the oppressed are by the same operation equally, although in opposite directions, depraved. As far as the slave is pressed down beneath the level into brutish indifference, so far is the master thrust up above the level into supercilious pride. As deeply as the vice of meanness is scored into the black by the lash, so deeply is the vice of arrogance scored into the white by lashing. Those are injured by suffering oppression, and these by inflicting it. Nothing is gained by a false estimate of the value of any man. The circles of Providence, like the celestial bodies, correct aberrations, and right themselves as they go round. The same sleepless eye, and the same avenging arm, are over masters and servants in the economical relations of our own land.

Value the young. How precious these germs are! These spring-buds are lovely to look upon, but their worth is greater than their beauty. An immortal life is opening there; heed it well. Proprietors rear strong fences round young trees, while they leave aged forests to take their chance. Permit not the immortal to be twisted at the very starting of its growth, for the want of such protection as it is in your power to afford. By failing practically to value little ones at their real worth, we both suffer and inflict an incalculable injury. They will be the men and women of the generation when we become children again. If they grow crooked for want of our care to-day, we shall lack support when we are too feeble to bear our own weight.

Don't spoil these tender, precious things. Tell them no lie. Speak no vile or profane word in their hearing. Let no drop fall on that polished surface, which may eat like rust into the heart, and become the death of a soul.

Value the poor and ignorant. In that state Christ valued you, believer. He did not pass you because you were worthless. He came to make you rich in grace, and to rejoice over you then.

Value the rich. We speak here not of the Christian brotherhood, but of humankind. Many of those whom the world call rich are selling themselves for vile stuff. They give themselves for money and show. The rich man's soul is more precious than all his riches. If he cannot estimate the things at their proper worth, you can, and should. He is as precious as the poor, and will be as worthy, if he is redeemed, when he walks with his Redeemer in white.

Value the vicious. Although they wallow in a deep mire to-day, they have fallen from a high estate, and may yet regain it. If one who had been a king's son should, in the frequent revolutions of these days, be cast a naked and penniless wanderer on our shores, we would not think of him as of a common beggar. If he should come in want to your door, you would look with a kind of awe on him who is the heir of a sovereign house, and may yet sit upon a throne. Under his piteous condition you would recognize what he has been, and may yet be.

When an abandoned woman passes you on the street, do not despise her. Perhaps beneath that bold look shame begins to swell, and would burst into repentance if it could get an outlet. She is human; Christ is human; and therefore she may yet be partaker of the divine nature. A jewel most precious lies under these loathsome incrustations. That is a precious soul. If she were snatched from the burning, she might be on earth yet a sister beloved, and in heaven a daughter of the Lord Almighty. Despise her not as you pass. Let your heart glue itself to hers; and if you must pass, unable to draw her from the pit, let it be such a passing as will leave your own heart torn and bleeding for the outcast whom you cannot save. Let not the frequency of such a contact rub your heart hard and smooth, so that other victims passing to perdition shall slip easily over, getting no grip, and leaving no pain within you. Never learn to pass the lost without a sigh, for she is human, immortal. If she is lost, the loss is eternal; if she were won, the gain would be unspeakable, to your Lord and you.

It is time that the brotherhood in Christ were aroused to estimate aright the value of a drunkard, and the peculiar danger of his state. They who spurn him away in disgust, and they who make merry with his weakness, are alike out of their reckoning. We should not lightly laugh at him on the one hand; we should not hopelessly give him up on the other. The saddest feature of the drunkard's sad case is the tendency that may be observed, even among earnest Christians, to give him up as beyond the reach of human help. I see that some, even of those who are girding themselves for saving work upon the world, without saying that the inveterate inebriate is absolutely irreclaimable, are deliberately passing by the class, in order that they may quarry in other veins where experience holds out greater hope of success. The peculiar hopelessness of the advanced stage in this form of sin gives peculiar force to the maxim, " Prevention is better than cure."

That poor staggering drunkard is worth more than worlds, if he were won. If you could win him, he would be a crown of joy to you in the great day. " Of some have compassion, making a difference : and others save with fear, pulling them out of the fire " (Jude 22, 23). They who hope in Christ should not count any case hopeless.

Value yourself. Do not hold yourself cheap, ye who may have Christ for your brother, and heaven for your home. This body the Lord has cleansed, that he may make it his own dwelling-place ; and why should these loathsome lusts be permitted to possess and defile it ? These lips are needed to support a part in the new song of the redeemed out of all nations ; and why should they be lent out as instruments of sin ? I shall not lightly accord my company to every comer, for the King is courting it : " Lo, I am with you alway, even to the end of the world."

In estimating the value of yourself, for all the practical purposes of life, adopt the standard of the King Eternal ; and the value which he attached to the subject may be seen in the price which he paid—" Who loved me, and gave himself for me."

Brotherly Love
(1 Peter 2:17)

"Honour all men. Love the brotherhood. Fear God. Honour the king."

I N this letter Peter teaches the scattered Christians that in the lowest sphere they should highly value human beings as such, and in the highest sphere reverently worship the Supreme. Between these two he recognizes a brotherhood to whom a different species of regard is due: "Love the brotherhood." Distinct, on the one hand, from the respect due to immortal man as the Creator's greatest work, and, on the other hand, from the worship due to Deity, brotherly love, pure and fervent, should be cherished towards all who have been redeemed by the Saviour's blood and renewed into the Saviour's likeness. The "brotherhood" here manifestly means, not those who have been born into the same family on earth, but those who have been born again into the family of God.

The obvious order here is, the object first, and then the emotion; the brotherhood whom Christians love, and the love with which they regard the brotherhood.

The brotherhood is a winsome word. It falls kindly on one's wearied ear in the intervals of the world's strife. Like the term in the preceding clause, it is universal. It includes a whole class without exception, although the class is less numerous than the other. As the whole is greater than a part, the brotherhood is a group indefinitely smaller than the " all men " of the first clause.

When we say " honour all men," it is as if we should say " all waters," comprehending those that are in the sea, on the earth, and in the air; comprehending the salt and the fresh, the pure and the impure,—absolutely and universally all waters. When we speak of the smaller class, "the brotherhood," it is as if we should say the waters that float in the air,—the clouds. These are waters too. These waters once lay in the sea, lashing themselves into fury there, or seething, putrifying under the sun in hollows of the earth's surface. But they have been sublimed thence; they are now in their regenerated state, and their impurity has been left behind. These waters float now in the atmosphere, far above the defilements of the earth and the tumults of the sea. Although they remain essentially of the same nature with that which stagnates on the earth or rages in the ocean, they are sustained aloft by the soft, strong grasp of a secret universal law. No hand is seen to hold them, yet they are held on high. Their Maker has given them the command, " Come out from among them, and be ye separate, and I will receive you."

As the clouds which soar in the air are to the universal mass of waters, so are the *brotherhood* of God's renewed children to the whole human family. Of mankind these brothers are in origin and nature; but they have been drawn out and up from the rest by an unseen omnipotent law. Their nature remains the same, and yet it is a new nature. They are men of flesh and blood, yet they have been elevated in station and purified in character. They are nearer God in place, and liker him in holiness. They have been " washed and justified and sanctified in the name of the Lord Jesus, and by the Spirit of our God." The command, " Come out from among them," having been obeyed, the promise has also been fulfilled to them,—" Ye shall be my sons and daughters, saith the Lord Almighty."

Let none think that the expressions employed to designate this change are extravagant. The language is not too strong, but too feeble. When a guilty man has been forgiven and reconciled to God through the death of Christ, the change of condition is greater than can be expressed in human language. No formula can adequately express the distance between the carnal mind, which is enmity against God, and the spirit of adoption, that cries, Abba, Father. In the nature of the case, those who have experienced only one of these conditions cannot compute the distance between them. Only they who have passed from the one to the other can appreciate the magnitude of the transition. To pass spiritually from death unto life is a great passage. From the sullen enmity of the guilty to the glad confidence of the forgiven, is as far as from east to west, or from earth to heaven.

This whole class in the spiritual sphere is, by a figure borrowed from human life, designated the brotherhood. It is one of the relations by which human creatures are bound into one. The conjugal, parental, and fraternal bonds constitute the strands of the three-fold cord by which our Creator, in the constitution of our nature, has knit his intelligent offspring in groups for their mutual support and comfort. The brotherhood are those who have been born together into the same family. They have one Father, a pervading likeness, and a common home.

This human relation is a great and good thing. It is one of the wonderful works of God. It is a contrivance in the system of the universe for binding a number of feeble rods into one, so that each of the fragile offshoots may, in the period of its weakness, enjoy all the strength of a tree. The natural affections of brothers and sisters in a family are stronger than the general affinities of man to man in the world. All history testifies that attempts to substitute artificial communism for the natural divinely-appointed constitution of the family, only torture the individual and dislocate the machinery of society.

But this precious earthly thing is not introduced here merely for its own sake ; it is borrowed as a term to express a spiritual and heavenly relation. The brotherhood in Peter's pointed precept means that great company on earth, of every nation and kindred and tongue, who are in the regeneration sons and daughters of the Lord Almighty. It is by comparison with the first of the three precepts that the import of the second may be most certainly ascertained. Honour—that is, count precious, value highly —" all men : " these terms include all of humankind born. But two births are possible for man. Many learners, like Nicodemus, find this lesson hard,—" How can a man be born when he is old ? " But those who simply sit at Jesus' feet, and ask for the Spirit, will surmount the difficulty. Those who are born again believe in the new birth. All men are born, and the brotherhood are born again. They have become new creatures in Christ Jesus. Their life now is hid with Christ in God. The two connected precepts point to these two births and these two lives. We should highly value the generation—all human-kind; but we should fondly love the regeneration—those who are forgiven and reconciled and renewed. Clasp fellow-disciples to your bosom; walk hand in hand with them across the pilgrimage of life, expecting to enter with them at length into the joy of the Lord.

Love One Another
(1 Peter 2:17)

"Love the brotherhood."

CONSIDER now the precise species of affection which is due by Christians to those who are fellow-members with themselves in the family of God: it is *Love*. There is a sense in which we ought to love the whole human race; but the love which is due to man as such is different from that which we owe to the disciples of Christ. Love, indeed, is a generic emotion, comprehending several distinct species; and, as often happens in natural history, one of the species bears the same name with the genus. The generic love to mankind branches into pity for those that are without, and love, specifically so called, to those who are within.

1. Love to the brotherhood is an instinctive emotion. It is not an accident, but a nature. It springs in renewed hearts, as love of her offspring springs in a mother's breast. It is the result not of an artificial policy, but of a natural law. The new creature owns and exercises instincts as well as the old. The members of Christ cannot but love their fellow-members. In as far as they have drunk into the Master's spirit, they will follow the Master's steps.

2. The Lord Jesus was not satisfied with the measure of this affection which existed among his followers during his personal ministry. He desired that it should be increased. For its increase he pleaded alternately with God and with man. "That they all may be one," was his prayer ; "Love one another," was his command.

3. Those who are destitute of this affection themselves are acute enough to observe the want or weakness of it in Christians. The bitterness, malice, and envy which defile and disturb the Church, afford to scoffers a foundation all too solid for their railing. Among Christians the state of matters is bad, and among those who are not Christians it is counted and called worse than it is. We give some, and they take more, occasion to blaspheme.

4. Brotherly love among Christians, when it really exists, honours the Lord and propagates the gospel. Like the blood of the martyrs, it is the seed of the Church. It has convinced many who resisted harder arguments.

5. It is the most pleasant of all emotions to the person who exercises it. Other passions may in certain circumstances be right and useful, but none generate so much joy as they flow. You may be "angry and sin not ;" but you cannot be angry and suffer not. As a great gun recoils violently, and is heated and defiled within by every discharge, a human spirit is shaken and perhaps soiled by discharges of anger, even when it does well to be angry against evil deeds. But love is delightful in the exercise, both to the lover and the loved. It leaves behind no sourness and no sediment. "Love is of God," and its character corresponds to its origin. It constitutes the atmosphere of heaven, where there are no pain and no defilement. At home, in the Father's house, when the whole

brotherhood finally assemble, there will be no anger and no fear,—only love.

Love of the brotherhood is the command of God, and, consequently, the duty of men; but another thing goes before it to prepare its way—lies beneath it to bear its weight. Before you can love the brotherhood, you must be a brother. It is the new creature that experiences this hallowed affection. These pulses do not throb through severed limbs; these beautiful blossoms do not open on withered branches. Those who are one with Christ in faith, are in spiritual communion with "the whole family in heaven and on earth." When you and I are, and know that we are, members of Christ, we shall love one another as he loved us. Like draws to like. Although the gates of a lost paradise were opened again on earth, and you admitted within the long-forbidden precincts, if there were only, on the one hand, angel-spirits flitting to and fro as flames of fire on their Maker's errands, never encumbered by a body of flesh; and, on the other hand, the dumb creatures, all tame and all submissive and affectionate according to their powers,—if there were these, and only these, for company, the place would be no paradise for you. You would long to go forth again. You would rather contend with thorns and thistles outside, but in company of your kind. Man is not made for solitude. He must have a brother on whom he can lavish a brother's love. Hence in Paul's esteem heaven was desirable, because the Elder Brother's presence is enjoyed there.

LIFE IN CHRIST

Life in Christ
(Philippians 1:21)

"To me to live is Christ, and to die is gain."

I SUPPOSE the chief reason why Christianity does not yet pervade the world, is that Christ does not pervade the life of Christians. We speak of "the Christian world." The picture is truer than most people deem. It is a world with a Christian tinge upon it, but still a world. It is not a new heaven and a new earth, wherein righteousness dwells.

Among the many shortcomings of disciples, perhaps the chief is this : that to a large extent their life and spirit seem to intimate that they count Christ an unfortunate necessity, instead of exulting and boasting in him as their joy and their life. Christians seem to sigh because they cannot do without him, rather than welcome with glad songs the Sun of Righteousness as he rises upon a dark world with healing in his beams.

Oh for a step forward, a leap higher! Forgetting the things behind, let us bend forward mightily, and endeavour to apprehend the Christ, who has apprehended us. Arise, blind beggar on the highway-side! arise, lo, he calleth thee into light and joy!

To live beneath our privilege is to dishonour the Lord. The same act of advancement, which would be gladness to the Christian, would be glory to Christ.

I do not come here to preach a gloomy gospel: I proclaim glad tidings of great joy. I do not wield a spiritual terror to wrench human beings away from their only joys, and compel them to accept Christ lest they should drop into hell. I come to bid you retain and enjoy all the gifts of providence, and to enjoy them a thousand-fold more by enjoying them in the light of your Redeemer's countenance, as you enjoy a thousand-fold more the landscape when the sun is up.

The life and the death of which Paul speaks here are the ordinary life and death of human creatures. The terms are employed in no figurative or emblematic sense. To live is simply to live as you or I lived yesterday and live to-day. And to die means to depart from life, in the act of putting off this mortal. We do not need to search here for any hidden or mysterious meaning. The language is used in a simple and natural sense.

To live, for this man, now that he has been redeemed and forgiven and renewed,—to live is something great and sublime. Life for this man is not like the life of the beasts that perish—let us eat and drink, for to-morrow we die.

For him to live is not to eat and drink and be clothed. It is not the mere struggle for existence, or the chase after luxuries when the necessities of nature have been satisfied. Some men make this their life. They change the end for the means. Food and drink and raiment are necessary, are sweet, are God's good gifts to his children. It is the duty even of these children to labour for them, to use them, to enjoy them. Without them there cannot be life, and consequently none of life's highest ends. These are the means of preserving life; but these are not the objects for which we live. A disciple of Christ and heir of glory lives *on* these as long as he is here; but no child of God lives *for* these. They who seek their life *there* shall lose it.

Life for him is not gain. The aim and end of living is not to acquire a great property. Property is useful in fulfilling some of the more important ends of life; but whenever it comes to be itself an end, its nature is changed. It is no longer a blessing. It is then like a bag of gold hung round the neck of a shipwrecked miser, to drag him down, down to death. He who knows what human life is, who knows its deepest need and highest destiny, has said, " A man's life consisteth not in the abundance of the things which he possesseth."

Life for this man does not consist in pleasure. He will not occupy his day in chasing tufts of thistle-down as they float on the breeze. He is a grown man, and has put away childish things; he is a new man, and has put away the old man with his deeds.

Life for this man is not honour—the highest place among his fellows. He has gotten the favour of God as a dear child, and he sets less value on the honours that the world bestows. Life for Paul does not consist in the chase after these things or in the enjoyment of them; so far all is clear.

But further: his life does not consist in refusing and avoiding these things. Suppose you should strip all these off, and deny yourself all comforts, you would be no nearer a true life in the Lord and for the Lord. Life consists neither in having them nor in wanting them. The truly living may have them to-day and want them to-morrow.

This is a new life of which Paul speaks. He did not always possess it. Formerly he lived without Christ in the world, and now he lives with him. Before the Lord met him, he lived a sort of life. While he was in it he thought it good. It was a vigorous, active life. It burned like fire; but the sparks sprang from earth—they were not sunbeams out of heaven. As soon as he escaped from that life, he counted it vile. He thought with a shudder of his previous life. From the moment that the life of Christ was revealed to him, he was a new man.

But even this is not what he says in our text. It is not a life with Christ, or even a life in Christ; but his very life is Christ. This extraordinary expression conveys an extraordinary thought. It behoves us to search and see what it means. Life is now to him another thing: his former life he remembers as a horrid dream. And the bound over is extreme. It is not that his life is like Christ, for it *is* Christ. He is a new creature. His former self is lost. It is not I that live, but Christ that liveth in me.

A vine is growing; it grows in good ground; it grows strong. It draws the sap of the ground, and bears much fruit; but the fruit is bad. It is bitter to the taste, and poisonous. Another vine grows near it—a good vine—all good. They take a branch of the good vine, and bend it gently towards the wild vine; and they lay a strong hand on the wild vine, and bend it towards the good vine. They touch. They are fastened—the branch of the good vine to the stem of the evil. As yet this produces no change on the wild vine; but it is some needful preparatory work. They now make an opening in the stem of the wild vine, and another in the branch of the good vine. They place them into each other at the wound, and bind them up. The wounds heal, and the two have grown into each other. The next step in the process is to cut off the head of the wild vine, and leave instead the now en-grafted branch of the good. Then the branch of the good is severed from its parent stem. The root of the evil tree remains; but its head now is the new and the good tree.

"I live," murmurs the root and stem of the old evil tree far below. *I live*—you live; you have no leaf, no flower, no fruit: all the life is in the new tree. "I live," still humbly murmurs the old root out of the ground; "never-theless not I, but the new good tree liveth in me; and the life that I now live in the ground, I live through the new and good tree, which loved me, and gave itself for me."

This cutting, and bleeding, and binding, and grafting process took place while the patient was prostrate and blind outside the gate of Damascus.

Thus is Paul's life a new thing; for to him to live is Christ.

Suppose he had said, To me to pray is Christ; it would have been true—a precious truth. Not only that he needs Christ when he draws near to God, but that to pray is all Christ. He comes not himself. He says, Look not on me, but on the Beloved; for worthy is the Lamb. He comes not in the filthy rags of his own righteousness. It is the righteousness of the Redeemer that is presented to the eye of God. The suppliant commands, because he stands on the right of the Son.

But it is not when he prays—when he comes to the communion, leaving the world outside—that he and the

Saviour are one ; but it is his common life—when he lies down and rises up, when he buys and sells, when he labours and when he rests, when he is in the bosom of his family and in public.

The Father loveth the Son. From everlasting the Son is in the bosom of the Father. This is the original and perfect idea of sonship. All that we know yet on earth is but a shadow, projected and dimly outlined upon the ground from the one perfect and substantial Sonship in heaven. In the eternal covenant man was designed as God's son : the Eternal Son was the ideal—the perfect man. When Adam was made, he was made on the model, in the image of God. But he was sent into life free—he was not upheld by Divine power ; and he fell. But when man, as he lived on earth, became corrupt, the perfect manhood was not lost. God did not risk all on one stake. The original remained, the type off which Adam in innocence was cast. Of him the Father will yet make a great nation.

Sometimes, after an engraven steel-plate has given forth some pictures it is destroyed, in order to enhance the value of the copies thrown off. If the copies were all destroyed, then the ideal would be lost. But when one type was thrown off and planted in Paradise, the original remained when the copy was spoiled. Man still remained—the Eternal Son remained.

Next time it was not another mould taken, and a holy man sent into the world to make another trial. This time it was the Eternal Pattern himself—the God-man—that came into the world, and took hold of us, and made himself one with his people.

" Saul, Saul, why persecutest thou me ? " These words

were spoken to Saul as an enemy of Christ. But I think the words were very precious to Paul when he came into Christ. These words were burned into his memory, and taught him that Christ and his people are one. Thus those words of God that are against the wicked become the very bread that the children live on when they are children. I think Paul would roll those awful words as a sweet morsel under his tongue. *Me!*—not only on my side, but they are *me*.

Paul was thus acting, when Festus cried out, "Paul, thou art beside thyself." Right, Festus. You may trust the governor for the mere observation of the fact. He knew what a *Saul* in himself would be—a Hebrew of the Hebrews — a Pharisee — "touching the law blameless." But he made a mistake when he attempted to give the reason. Paul is not here—he is put off: another stands in his stead—"To live is Christ"—"*to die is gain.*" I do not think these two are different in kind; it is only in degree. You might say: Here is a man who is very rich; he owns vast estates in his own right; this wealth he enjoys in his father's lifetime, and his father's death will be gain—that is, he will retain all he had, and get it multiplied manifold. All his wealth he retains, and gets more. So here: it is not that in life Paul had Christ, and that at death he would lose that and obtain something else instead. "To me to live is Christ." And what will death be to you when it comes? It will be Christ, and more.

The substance of the inheritance beyond we know, from verse 23, is the same Christ—"To depart, and to be with Christ." But there will be something more—"To die is gain." What are the gains? Peace instead of war. Here Christ and conflict: there Christ and peace. Here

Christ and ignorance, seeing in part through a glass darkly: there Christ and light—we shall know, even as we are known. Here Christ and sins, vexing his Spirit, and polluting his dwelling-place: there Christ and purity—nothing shall enter that defileth.

Some people count their gains very carefully when they have got them. Some count the gains before they are won; they calculate the expected profit, and enjoy it by anticipation. Christian winners do likewise. Paul counts his gains before he gets them; he enjoys the expected wealth. It does no harm to gloat thus over the true riches. Your real money-makers never despise small winnings. This is their art—they despise nothing because of its smallness. It is thus that careful souls grow rich in grace.

Here we have Christ and pain. A dying girl said to her mother, "There will be no sore heads in heaven." To her to live was Christ and to die was gain. And she counted her gains beforehand on her bed of languishing, and cheered her aching heart with the glitter of expected fortune. There will be no evil-speaking there: that is a gain awaiting us. There will be no envy swelling in our own breasts: what a gain! There we shall have Christ and the company of Christians in all the beauty of holiness: how ravishing!—those bodies glorified like Christ's glorious body; souls perfect in purity shining through those beautiful countenances. "Thou art all fair, my love;"

> "Thy beauty to the King
> Shall then delightful be."

"*To die.*" In the original it is "*to have died*," a past tense; whereas "to live" is a present. *Not* death is pleasant; it is a dark passage, and the child shudders as he goes down. Not the narrow gate, but the life it leads to, is a gain. He will be richer too; he will rejoice over every one that returns. And oh! his joy will be great over the multitude that no man can number.

God was not taken aback and defeated when man his child was drawn into rebellion and death. He had a grander scheme in reserve prepared beforehand. The very fall of man touched a spring that set the greater plan in motion—a motion which will not cease till his many sons have been brought into glory. When the first Adam fell, the second Adam stood. The second Adam came—the Lord from heaven; the Man who should restore humanity, and make a glory that excelleth to encircle the brow of ransomed men. Men redeemed by Christ are higher up and closer in than angels unfallen. Will he have room for us all, and a beam of light from his countenance for each? Look up into the heavens. "Who hath created these things, that bringeth out their host by number? He calleth them all by names, by the greatness of his might, for that he is strong in power: not one faileth." "Lo, I am with you alway." *That is life: after life* that, and more. Christ the man—eternal, everywhere present God; yet transfused through every ransomed man. Every one in Christ; Christ in every one.

Christic and the Ordinances
(2 Corinthians 3:17)

"Now the Lord is that Spirit: and where the Spirit of the Lord is, there is liberty."

THE ministry of Moses was glorious in comparison with the utter darkness of the heathen world, and with the feebler light of earlier revelation; but much more glorious is the ministry whereby the Spirit now takes of the things of Christ and shows them unto us. While he was receiving the message from God, and uttering it to the people, a supernatural light illumined the countenance of the lawgiver; but as soon as he had delivered the prophecy, he veiled his face, so that the people did not see its brightness long or continuously. Only glimpses of the light were shown; and then the revelation stopped short—the rest hidden by a veil.

But this was not the only obstacle: a veil, opposite, and yet corresponding, was spread over the hearers' minds and hearts. When it was no longer a speaker's voice to be heard, but the Scriptures of the Old Testament to be read, the veil remained on the readers' hearts. The hardening of their heart constituted the blinding veil that prevented them from fully comprehending the Scriptures, and their testimony to Christ. Their descendants remained in the same state at the date of this epistle; and until this day the same veil, at the reading of the Old Testament, remains, not apocalypsed, not revealed, when it (Old Testament ritual) is done away in Christ. The veil that then hid the speaker's countenance, has now been put on the readers' hearts. They cannot, when they read the Old Testament, perceive how the outward ordinances pass away, and leave Christ the substance and inner spirit of them all. This veil prevents them from seeing the glory that shines in the Old Testament—its prophetic word, and prophetic sacrifices. They cannot discover that the letter is done away, by the full unfolding of the spirit; that the promises, however rich and precious, fall away of their own accord, when the Promised One has come.

Even unto this day, says Paul, the veil is upon their heart, when Moses is read; when that heart of theirs shall turn to the Lord, the veil shall be taken away. It is when they behold in living faith the Lamb of God, that they understand the meaning of the appointed sacrifices. "We have found him, of whom Moses in the law, and the prophets, did write, Jesus of Nazareth" (John i. 45).

The shell, hard and encompassing, holds firm in spite of influences from without, until the kernel within comes to its time, and, affected by prepared conditions, swells and bursts out into manifestation and life.

The Lord is the spirit that lies in the Old Testament, under the folds of its sacrifices, giving them life. When the eye of the soul is opened to behold the beauty of the Lord, the observer comes to understand aright, both the spirit that animates the body, and the body that clothes the spirit—to understand both the Christ whom the sacrifices promised, and the sacrifices that promised Christ.

When it is intimated that Christ is the spirit of all ordinances, the intimation is not meant to disparage these ordinances, which constituted for him a body until the fulness of time. The period of his ministry on earth was brief. He manifested himself the Saviour before he be-became incarnate, and after he had ascended to heaven. On both sides of the cross were sinners suffering, and love from the face of Christ crucified beamed in gracious offer either way, reaching earth's utmost ends—penetrating to Adam backward, and down to his latest child. In order that Christ, before and after his sojourn on earth, might make himself known to men, it behoved him to adopt a body palpable to human sense. Accordingly, before he was born in Bethlehem, and after he ascended from Olivet, he presented himself to faith clothed in certain forms and symbols, that touched human senses, and so made way into human souls.

He knows what we are, and what we need. He not only filled the fountain of grace on high ; he also prepared suitable channels through which it might flow to the needy. Divine truth revealed must have respect to its *objects* as well as to its *Author*. It must, in its nature, be like God ; but it must also be, in its form, like man. People object to certain details in the Bible, averring that they seem far below the Divine : they are ; and that because it was necessary to bring them down to the human. Our knowledge comes to us in the first instance through the bodily senses ; and how shall God, a Spirit, be made known to us? The method adopted in the covenant, and manifested in the Scriptures, is—in order to bring us up to his nature he bowed down to ours. In order that we might know and receive the Lord, the spirit, God has from the beginning prepared for that spirit a body, which brings saving truth within the reach of embodied men.

While God in his ordinances condescends to our low estate, a tendency is always manifest in the divine dispensations to advance from the lower to the higher. The more carnal ordinances came first; afterwards, the more spiritual. The New Testament is an advance upon the Old; and a yet greater advancement awaits the Church. Things are prepared for them that love God—things which eye hath not seen yet, nor ear heard. In the meantime, however, it is only what the eye can see or the ear hear that can be made known to us. Revelation must assume some bodily shape ere it can be intelligible to men in the body.

Such, accordingly, were all the ordinances of the Ancient Church, and such all the revelations that were made under the earlier dispensations. Christ, their spirit and life, was in them; but those things in which the life was lying were bodily things.

The bondage in Egypt, and the redemption thence by the blood of the lamb; the open way through the Red Sea to Israel, and the burying of their oppressors beneath its flood; the journey through the wilderness, and the rest that lay beyond; the manna from heaven, and the water from the rock; the deadly wound by the bite of a serpent, and the healing by a look,—all these had Christ in them, and all were employed to make Christ known. The permanent institutes, as well as the passing events, were bodies prepared for containing and conveying that one blessed spirit. The unblemished lamb, and its blood on the doorposts; the one fair mitre on the high priest's brow, and the twelve precious stones on his breast,—that signifying Christ's holiness before God, and this Christ's imperishable love to his people ; all the sacrifices and types that were written in the laws of Moses, and reverently observed throughout the generations of Israel, were *bodies* prepared for bringing Christ near to men. All these were handles let down from heaven, whereby the perishing might grasp their Saviour. Christ put these garments on in those ancient days, that his people, when bowed down by disease, might be enabled to touch their hem, and so live. Christ was within those bodies, their quickening spirit. Believers like Abraham saw him thereby long before he came in the flesh. It was his delight thus to reach them, and *give* them life ; it was their delight thus to reach him, and *get* life. The song, " My beloved is mine, and I am his," is an old, old song, and a very sweet one to those who have an ear to hear what the Spirit, out of the ordinances, saith unto the Churches. But though these bodies were precious, as vehicles for containing and presenting Christ, they were worthless wanting him. A body with the life is good. When the spirit animates the body, the body clothes the spirit, and enables it to reach its object. But a body when the spirit has fled is useless, and worse. Itself is dead, and it kills others. Such are ordinances, even those of divine appointment, when Christ, their spirit, is not in them, or is not owned.

It is no disparagement to God's wisdom in the construction of the human body, that it becomes corrupt and corrupting when the soul has fled. The human body is a wonderful work ; but it is most wonderful as the home of a human soul. When the soul has departed, it is of no further use ; we are fain to bury it out of sight, God's work though it be. Such are the ordinances of religion when Christ is not in them. Their deadness and loathsomeness, when their life is lost, is no reflection on the wisdom that ordained them. They were never meant to be, in themselves and for their own sakes, either beautiful or good; they are obedient and loyal, and so they part with all their glory when the King goes away.

There is a strong tendency in us to cling to the mere body of a religious ordinance and let its spirit go. This error appeared early in the Churches of Galatia. They turned from Christ, who is the spirit of the ordinances, to the old ordinances destitute of Christ. Returning to the elements of the world, they distrusted Christ, and leant on circumcision. How vehemently Paul cried out to them: " O foolish Galatians, who hath bewitched you ?......Having begun in the Spirit, are ye now made perfect in the flesh?" They were leaving the animating Spirit, and going back to the dry bones of the dead.

As sensible ordinances were appointed for communicating Christ to faith before the incarnation, so also after the Lord had ascended into heaven, he has appointed ordinances in which he their spirit will dwell, and where his people will find him. The Scriptures of the New Testament, like those of the Old, are bodily things, suited to bodily senses. They are words and letters. If they have not a spirit in them they are dead; and the dead cannot give life. Christ is the soul that animates them; and if we do not find him in the Bible, we find nothing there. As a human body with the life in it is the most beautiful object in nature, and a human body when the life has gone the most forbidding, so I suppose the Bible is to one class the most attractive of all books, and to another the most forbidding; because to the one it is a dead letter, and to the other it is a body all glowing with Christ its life. The Jewish scribes of our Lord's day spent much time in handling the Scriptures, but the letter in their hands was a body dead, and their schools had the thick noisome air of a dissecting-room. " Ye search the Scriptures," said the Lord to those learned Jews, " for in them ye think ye have eternal life; and they are they which testify of me. And ye will not come to me, that ye might have life." They stolidly manipulated the carcass, and rejected him who came to be its spirit and life. They embraced the dead because the look of the living reproved them.

But the ordinance of the Supper is in a peculiar manner and in an eminent degree the body whereof Christ is the inner living spirit. As men often missed the spirit of the old dispensation, so they miss the spirit of the Lord's Supper now. If we do not by faith realize Christ at his table, it will be no more to us than a Jewish passover would be.

In the remarkable discourse which is reported in the sixth chapter of John's Gospel, Jesus taught clearly and fully that himself is the bread on which a soul must live. That discourse does not contain the institution of the Lord's Supper. It is an exposition by the Lord himself, while he stood among the disciples, of the central saving doctrine which the Supper afterwards expressed and commemorated. It is not his body but himself that he represents as the bread of life. At the beginning he said, " I am that bread of life;" and at the close he repeated, " He that eateth me shall live by me."

In the light of that discourse observe the relation between our text and the ordinance of the Supper. " This is my body...this is my blood;...take; eat...drink ye all of it;... this do in remembrance of me." In all this you have the body; but to eat bread and drink wine will not save, will not profit a soul. Where is the spirit of the body? The Lord is that spirit. The Supper is indeed a body,—a sort of channel appointed for conveying Christ to the believing,— but it cannot by itself contribute an atom of influence to the procuring of pardon, or the purifying of the heart. The Lord is the spirit; and if they who come to the body do not seek and find by faith that spirit, the body will profit them nothing, divine institute though it be.

This question is entirely independent of that which concerns the right administration of the **ordinance**. Suppose it to be administered by apostles, and in exact conformity with the Lord's will, still it can impart nothing to the unworthy receiver. His evil heart of unbelief has refused Christ, and there is none other who can be the spirit of the ordinance. The bread and wine are but beggarly elements. As the lead of a water-pipe, although most perfectly fitted for conveying water from the fountain to the lips of the needy, cannot in any measure contribute to allay his thirst, so the Supper, although divinely ordained and purely administered, can do nothing for a sinner who closes the door of his heart against the Saviour Christ.

We do not deny to the Supper a place when we refuse to give it the place of the Saviour. The body, which is nothing when dead, is a great thing when living. It is not only that the soul inhabiting the body is great: the body is great when a soul inhabits it. In like manner, it is not enough to say that, though a Christless ordinance is nothing, Christ himself is great. That is true; but more than that is true. While the ordinance is dead and worthless, if Christ its spirit be not apprehended, the ordinance is most precious when the believing partaker seeks through it communion with the Lord. When he makes himself known to a longing heart, that heart loves him; and loves, too, in its own place, the channel through which he comes.

Recall to mind the design of Christ's departure from the disciples, and the process of weaning through which they were put. They loved the Master, with a fond, adoring love. When they were tossed on a stormy sea and ready to perish, the only want they felt was the absence of their Lord: "It was now dark, and Jesus was not come to them." But while their love was grateful to his heart, he knew that sense with them was growing too rank, and was choking the more feeble, more precious faith. Carried away in a flood of personal love that lay in the senses, Peter passionately opposed the dying of the Lord: "Far be this from thee." There Satan got an advantage over Peter. But Peter's love to the person of the Lord, as seen by the bodily eyes, was the cover under which the old serpent lurked while he dealt this blow.

Knowing what was in man, the Lord prepared to go out of his people's sight as soon as his atoning work was done. The faith of these Galileans would have been smothered outright under the ample folds of their love to the man Christ Jesus, their personal friend. When he departed, they remained glued to the ground and gazing up to heaven. The ministry of angels was needed and employed to tear them from the spot, and turn their minds another way. But the ministry of angels, though fitted to take them away from their needless looking into the sky over Olivet, was not fitted positively to lead them to the perception and enjoyment of Christ, the spirit of word and ordinances. The ministry of angels ceased, and a more glorious ministry succeeded it. The Holy Ghost came upon them; and his mission was to glorify Christ. They were wrenched away from sensible, human companionship with Jesus, as infants are torn from their mother's breast. They were led by the Spirit to Christ; and although Christ was now bodily removed, he was still manifested to them under bodily forms. In the ordinance of the Supper they found Christ with less of tumult and distraction than they would have experienced if he had again appeared in the flesh.

As the result of the Lord's ascension and the Spirit's ministry, we learn that in mutual love and ordinamental communion they did eat their meat with gladness and singleness of heart. "This is my body...this do in remembrance of me"—"Lo, I am with you." The Lord became the *spirit* in the body of their ordinance. They lived on the same Saviour; but now their life in him was more purely a life of faith. This body which he has left is as fit to nourish us as his personal, visible presence on earth would be. We may now praise him for having weaned his Church in those days: he has given us food convenient for us; he hath done all things well. Let the Lord be the spirit of our ordinance, and we shall feed on him by faith, with less distraction than if he should return to show us either the marks of former suffering on his hands, or the signs of present glory on his countenance. By his reappearing in bodily form, we should be flooded by tumults of human passion;—either crying out, "Depart from me; for I am a sinful man, O Lord," or "falling at his feet as dead." In these tumults flickering faith would be overlaid and quenched.

He gives us the sensible sign, that in it we may receive himself by faith as our Saviour, with less distraction than if his eyes as a flame of fire were opened and bent upon our company. We should gladly accept any body wherein he pleases to present himself ; and if there be less in these symbols themselves to carry us away than there would have been in the transfigured presence of the Lord descending on our mount, all the more complete should be the inner worship of the soul, while we cleave to the Lord the spirit in these bodily memorials of his death.

Tell me the sweetest scene of mingled moral and material beauty that may be seen on earth. It is an infant satisfying itself abundantly from a living mother's breast. Tell me now the saddest sight that eye hath seen or ear hath heard of. It is that which they say has sometimes been seen in the wake of war or of pestilence—-an infant unconsciously sucking a mother dead. If that process continue long, the child will draw death from that which was formed to be a well of life.

The letter of the ordinance is dead if Christ be not known and tasted. The letter, when the spirit has departed, is not only dead, but deadly : " The letter killeth." But the same letter, when the Lord is its spirit, is life, and gives life.

The tendency to go back to the dead letter in the ordinance of the Supper is, of course, seen in its grossest form in modern Rome. But even that deepest error of the Romish superstition has a more terrible meaning to us at this day than formerly, because of a movement—broad, deep, and rapid—in the Church of England to follow in the wake of Rome. Opposite and equal to the revival movements upward to the Lord that have been experienced in our day, other movements have emerged,—movements of men's spirits gravitating downwards like lead, from Christ the spirit of the Supper to the form from which Christ has departed. This gravitation downwards affects us all, except in as far as the Holy Spirit is given to quicken and elevate. Whereas all the sacrifices of the Old Testament, being symbols, ceased when the one Sacrifice was offered, they multiply their sacrifice of the Mass, as they call it, to ten thousand times ten thousand—thus returning to the shadows again. Their wafer and their wine-cup, they say, have become the body and blood of Christ—the very body that was nailed to the cross, and the blood that flowed from his wounds. It is the most adventurous imposture that ever human heart invented. But even although it were true, what gain would accrue from it ? Although the wafer and wine which the devotee swallows were the body and blood of Christ—which they are not—what better would he be of swallowing them ? It is the spirit that giveth life ; bodily service profiteth little. The Lord, the spirit, is not there ; he has gone away offended, leaving the dead letter for the dead worshipper.

The second clause of the verse intimates that "Where the Spirit of the Lord is, there is liberty."

I know not a shorter or surer method of illustrating the liberty that prevails wherever the Lord, the spirit, is recognized by faith, than to point out the bondage which crushes the people wherever the spirit of the ordinance is lost, and its body resorted to as a charm. The converse of the clause is strictly true and eminently appropriate to the times,—" Where the Spirit of the Lord is not, there is slavery." Human spirits are too high in nature and too capacious for worshipping any other than God. When men, as individuals or as communities, let Christ slip from the grasp of their faith, and fasten on some corporeal thing, whether a superstitious ceremonial or a human priesthood, farewell to liberty. It becomes, on the one side, an iron tyranny; and, on the other, the cringing of a slave. The Pharisee would lose peace of conscience if he should eat with unwashen hands. A modern bondsman, a sincere worshipper in his way, will count that he has committed a sin against God, which must be atoned for by a painful or degrading penance, if by some accident he has tasted a kind of food on one day of the week which he might eat lawfully on any other. A man of education and refinement in this country will eat meat with peace of conscience at a certain season of the year if an aged priest at Rome shall give permission, but would count that he had incurred the displeasure of God if he should eat meat at that season without such permission. There is no imaginable depth of degradation which the master of a soul may not impose— which a soul enslaved will not endure. Woe to human spirits when they let go Christ and submit to a carnal ordinance or a fellow-man!

Take all the advantage that can be obtained—and it is great—from the union and organization of Christians, as a brotherhood of God's children; take instruction and accept fellowship wherever you can obtain them pure and useful, —but subject your soul to none but Christ. When in reading the Scriptures, in prayer secret or social, in the worship of the great assembly, or in the act of showing forth the Lord's death, you seek and get communion in spirit with the living Saviour ever present, you enjoy a sublime freedom. You walk at liberty before God as a dear child, consciously reconciled through the blood of the covenant; you will walk at liberty through life, calling no man master, and not trembling before shifting shadows or rustling leaves; you will walk at liberty through the swelling Jordan, when you approach the border line, and get an abundant entrance into the rest that remaineth.

If the Son make you free, you shall be free indeed ;— free from the fear of man ; free from the snares of the devil ; free from the condemnation for sin ; free from the terrors of conscience ; free from the sting of death ; free from the clog of a mortal body ; free from the confusion of a consuming world : freed *by* the Lord ; free *with* the Lord.

Faith and a Good Conscience
1 Timothy 1:19)

" Holding faith, and a good conscience ; which some having put away, concerning faith have made shipwreck."

CHRISTIANS in this country are at present [1874] more than usually happy and hopeful. Both the constituents of apostolic cheerfulness are present, " a wide door," and " many adversaries." So wide is the door, and so great the spiritual enlargement, that the " adversaries," instead of depressing, tend rather to stimulate and elevate the hearts of believers. The shout of a King is in the camp, and he is leading many captive.

As in ancient times, so now, " This is the victory that overcometh the world, even your faith." " Justified by faith," is the key-note of the hymn that is now rising heavenward like the voice of many waters from a revived and united Church. Christ the substitute—the just dying for the unjust—is the distinguishing feature of the preaching which at present is accompanied with power. This is as it should be ; it is under this standard only that the Christian host will conquer. This gospel of free grace must be always and everywhere proclaimed. The evil spirit that possesses human hearts goeth not out by any other adjuration.

But while this should be done, there is another thing which ought not to be left undone. A watchful, energetic effort personally to turn from all evil, and to practise all good, must be made by every one who trusts in Christ for pardon and peace. Work *from* peace and pardon as energetically as if you were working *for* peace and pardon. There is not safety for an hour in any other attitude. If the upper side of true religion, pointing heavenward, be, " Believe on the Lord Jesus Christ, and thou shalt be saved;" the under side, pointing earthward, is, " To visit the widows and the fatherless in their affliction, and to keep himself unspotted from the world." If the upper side of the seal which binds a believer to the sure foundation bear the inscription, " The Lord knoweth them that are his ; " the legend on the under side must be kept clear and legible by constant rubbing, " Let every one that nameth the name of Christ depart from iniquity " (2 Tim. ii. 19). Actual holiness is as necessary to the life of faith as the left side of a man's body is to the life of the right.

In these circumstances I think I shall contribute a word for the times, if, for the special use of young converts, rejoicing in a free and full salvation, I set forth the two sides of the Christian life in their union and relations.

These I shall present as given by that great master of logical connections, the Apostle Paul.

" *Holding faith, and a good conscience ; which some having put away, concerning faith have made shipwreck* " (1 Tim. i. 19).

The two subjects here are *faith,* and *a good conscience.* We must inquire first, What they severally are, and next, How they are reciprocally connected. Their *nature* first, and then their *relations.*

I. *What they are.*

1. *Faith.*—The term is in the Scriptures applied both to the revealed truth which a disciple believes, and to his act in believing it. Faith is objective, or subjective. It is at one time the truth which you grasp, and at another time your grasp of the truth.

Both of these senses occur in the text, distinguished (in the original, though not in the English) by the presence or absence of the article. " Faith," in the first clause, is the soul's act of believing ; " the faith," in the second clause, is the gospel which the soul believes.

Both in the Scriptures and in their own nature these two are closely interwoven together. It is impossible everywhere to preserve and mark the distinction between the light that I look on, and my looking on that light. True, my looking on it does not create the light, but it makes the light mine. Unless I look on it, the light is nothing to me. If I am blind, it is the same to me as if there had not been light.

In some such way are *faith* and *the faith* connected and combined. It is quite true that the gospel remains, although I should reject it : my unbelief cannot make God's promise of none effect. Yet my unbelief makes the gospel nothing to me—the same to me as if it had not been. *The* faith stands in heaven, although *faith* be wanting on earth ; but if *faith* is wanting, *the* faith does not save the lost : as the sun continues his course through the sky although I were blind ; but my blindness blots out the sun for me.

2. *A good conscience.*—It is not necessary to explain what conscience is: my readers know what it is better than I can tell. What is meant by conscience is a thing to be experienced rather than to be taught ; but what is meant

by a " good conscience " is not so obvious. Here the principal question is, Whether does the epithet " good " refer to
the conscience that gives the testimony, or to the testimony
that the conscience gives. The term " good " here belongs
not to the testifier, but to the testimony.

In one sense that might be called a good conscience, that
tells the truth even though the truth torment you. When
the conscience, like an ambassador from God in a man's
breast, refuses to be silent in the presence of sin, and disturbs the pleasure of the guilty by uttering warnings of
doom, that conscience is good, in the sense of being watchful and useful ; but it is not the good conscience of this
text, and of ordinary language. Both here, and in common
conversation, a good conscience is a conscience that does
not accuse and disturb. It is the same as peace of conscience. It is no doubt true that in an evil world, and
through the deceitfulness of an evil heart, the conscience
may sometimes be so drugged or seared that it may leave
the soul undisturbed, although the soul is steeped in sin.
It sometimes says " Peace, peace," when there is no peace.
" There is no peace, saith my God, to the wicked ;" but the
conscience sometimes contradicts God, and says that there
is peace to the wicked. This is, however, an abnormal
state of things ; as when an ambassador at a foreign court
turns traitor to the king who commissioned him, and
refuses to deliver his lord's commands to the court where
he has been accredited. Although this state of rebellion
is in point of fact common among men, it is in its own
nature a contradiction and an anomaly. Although it
abounds in this fallen world, it is an exception and a rarity
in the universal dominion of the supreme God. It may
for our present purpose be set aside. The conscience in

man is intended to be God's witness, and to speak to the man all the truth. Taking conscience, not as twisted and seared by sin, but as constituted by God in the conception and creation of humanity, then a good conscience is peace of conscience. You have and hold a good conscience when that present representative of God in your bosom does not charge you with sin. When it accuses it is an evil, when it approves it is a good, conscience. The one is an inward sense of guilt, the other an inward sense of righteousness.

By the light of Scripture we know that, as matters go among the fallen, a good conscience, if real and lawfully attained, implies these two things :—(1) The application of the blood of sprinkling for the pardon of sin; and (2). Actual abstinence from known sin in the life through the ministry of the Holy Spirit. A good conscience—if it is not a cheat—implies a righteousness *on* you and a righteousness *in* you. There is the washing away of guilt in the fountain open; and there is the actual turning from all filthiness of the flesh and spirit. There is a righteousness which you get, and there is a righteousness which you perform. The one is the justification, and the other the sanctification, of a believer. The one is an act of God's free grace; the other is the work of God the Spirit. The one, as being an act, is completed when it is begun; the other, as being a work, drags its slow length along—alas, through corruptions within and temptations without—along the whole line of a disciple's life, until he escape from the body and depart to be with Christ. Pardon and renewing combine to constitute, under the gospel, a good conscience. What God hath joined, let not man put asunder. The first dissociated from the second is antinomianism; the second dissociated from the first is legalism. The hope of pardon through grace, without actual newness of life, tramples under foot God's holy law. The effort to lead a holy life, without looking for pardon through the blood of Christ, parades the filthy rags of a sinner's righteousness, as if they were fit to constitute the wedding garment of the King's guests when the King cometh in. The conscience is then really good when your trust is in the blood and righteousness of your Redeemer, and your life is practically dedicated to the Lord that bought you. The conscience is good when it truly testifies that God is at peace with you, and you are at peace with God. For all practical purposes, the good conscience here may be taken as synonymous with well-doing.

II. *Their relations.*—The text consists of two parts. The first is a command, the second is an example. The example, as is usual both in human teaching and divine, is adduced for the purpose of enforcing the precept. An illustrative case, taken from actual life to explain or apply a prescribed duty, may be in its form positive or negative; that is, it may either directly show how good it is to obey, or how evil it is to transgress. The case which is employed in this text is negative. It exhibits, in concrete form, not the good that results from obedience, but the evil that results from transgression. Doubtless, Paul could have called up from his own experience many examples to show how good it is to hold both faith and a good conscience; but it suited his purpose better, in this instance, to adduce an example which shows the dread consequence of attempting to separate them. In point of fact, an example of these two rent asunder is more effective in proving the necessity of their union than a hundred examples in which the union remains intact. Thus, if proof were necessary, to divide a living child in two with Solomon's sword would constitute more vivid evidence that in a human being the left side is necessary to the life of the right, and the right to the life of the left, than the sight of a hundred unharmed children. When one side is wrenched off, the other side also dies : this is shorter and surer proof that the two are mutually necessary to each other's existence than a hundred examples of positive, perfect life.

Besides, it is easier to find a foundation for a negative than for a positive example. In buoying a channel, they cannot well set up a mark where the ship ought to go ; they set up a beacon on the sunken rock which the ship ought to avoid.

On this principle, the apostle selects a negative rather than a positive example to enforce his point. A case in which death resulted from severance suits his purpose better than a case in which life is preserved through continued union. In this case, one of the related pair is severed, and the other, as a necessary consequence, perishes. Holding faith and a good conscience, which some—and he immediately names two men who had actually passed through the course which he describes—which some having put away, concerning faith have made shipwreck ; that is, when they put away the good conscience, the faith also was lost.

Here a question of the deepest interest crosses our path and claims our regard. Granted that faith and a good conscience are linked so intimately together that the one cannot live without its consort, what is the specific character of the relation ? Whether of these two is first in nature as cause, and whether follows as effect ? Looking to the form of expression in the text, which is exact and definite, we find that in the case adduced it was not the dissolution of faith that destroyed the good conscience, but the failing of the good conscience that destroyed faith. These men put away the good conscience ; then and therefore, they lost the faith. What then ? As the continued possession of the faith depended on maintaining the good conscience, is it through prior possession of a good conscience that one may attain faith ?

No. The converse is the truth, fully and clearly taught in the Scriptures. You do not reach faith through a good conscience, but a good conscience through faith. A good conscience grows on faith, like fruit on a tree, not faith on a good conscience.

A good conscience in both its aspects, as already explained, is the fruit of faith. Without faith it is impossible to please God, either by the righteousness of Christ in justifying, or the new obedience in sanctifying. God is pleased with both righteousnesses, each in its own place, and after its own kind. The righteousness which a believing man receives satisfies his justice, and the obedience which a converted man renders adorns his doctrine. God is well pleased, for his 'righteousness' sake, when he sees his Son accepted in your heart and his law honoured in your life. But both of these are attained through faith. It is faith that justifies the man before God's judgment, and establishes the law in the life-course of the man.

Now this specific relation is not reciprocal. The good conscience does not produce faith, as faith produces a good conscience. What then ? If faith goes first as the cause, and a good conscience follows as the fruit, the good conscience obviously cannot subsist without faith ; but may faith subsist without a good conscience ? No. As to production at first, the relation is not reciprocal; but as to maintenance it is. We cannot say, as a good conscience springs from faith, faith also springs from a good conscience; but we can say, as the want of faith makes a good conscience impossible, so, also, the loss of a good conscience is fatal to faith.

Some species of trees retain life in the roots although the head and stem are cut away. A young tree may spring from the old stump, and grow to maturity. But other species, such as the pine, will not thus spring a second time. When the mature tree is cut off, although the root, with a portion of the stem, is left, the tree does not revive. The root dies when the head is severed.* There is an interesting analogy between a pine-tree and the pair which are joined in the text. It is not the tree's towering head that produces the root; the root produces the towering head. We can, therefore, safely say, If the root is killed, the head cannot live; but we may also say, If the head is severed, the root will die. Precisely such is the relation between faith and a good conscience. Faith is the producing, sustaining root, and a good conscience the stem that it sustains. Consequently, cut off faith, and a good conscience falls to the ground. Yes, this is the truth; but it is not the whole truth. We can also say, Destroy the good conscience, and faith cannot stand.

---

* The emigrant, in clearing his lot in the American forest, does not at first dig each tree out by the root. This process would occupy too much time. He cuts the tree four or five feet above the ground, and the root rots away in a few years. Hence, a common feature of the landscape in newly-reclaimed territories—fields studded all over with the stumps of trees, and the corn growing around them. Hence the coinage of a new word in the English language as used in America. A candidate for office is said "to stump the state"—that is, he goes through it addressing meetings and soliciting votes. One of these stumps constitutes a convenient platform for the political orator.

Thus in one way only may the good conscience be obtained; but in either of two ways both may be lost. Let faith fail, and the good conscience goes with it; let the good conscience be polluted, and the faith itself gives way.

In the first place, then, speculative error undermines practical righteousness. As belief of the truth purifies the heart and rectifies the conduct, so a false belief leads the life astray. Let it suffice to have enunciated the relation on this side; we shall turn for practical lessons chiefly to another aspect of the case. The example given in the text, and oftenest found in experience, is not false faith leading to an incorrect conduct, but impure conduct undermining faith. I suppose, in the experience of human life, if the speculative error producing practical wickedness slays its thousands, the practical wickedness perverting the creed slays its ten thousands.

The backsliding begins more frequently on the side of conduct than on the side of opinion: the good conscience is lost in most cases, not by adopting a heretical creed, but by indulging in the pleasures of sin.

" A good conscience, which some having *put away*." When a man who has known the gospel and professed to be a disciple of Christ yields to temptation, and indulges in a course of sin—knowing the right, but doing the wrong—he forthwith loses the good conscience. His peace is disturbed; the witness in his bosom accuses him, and he is tormented by the fear of divine wrath. To this wicked man there is now no peace, and that by the word and decree of God. His heart is a house divided against itself, and it is wretched. Now, will this man who has fallen into sin, and so lost his good conscience, continue still sound in the faith ? When his conduct is polluted, will his opinion continue true ?

No, verily. As in the case of the text, when the good conscience is thus forced out, the sound creed will soon follow. Having put away a good conscience, concerning the faith they have made shipwreck. It is true indeed that pure conduct depends on sound doctrine ; but it is also true that sound doctrine depends on pure conduct. And, in point of fact, it is much more common to find the faith perverted by loose practice, than practice perverted by a loose creed. The wicked one knows that a soul may be undone by a successful assault either on his faith or his practice. But in seeking whom he may devour, he finds the side of a holy life more easily reached and pierced than the side of orthodox views. Our enemy finds it easier to persuade us to do what is evil than to believe what is false. The conscience is more exposed in the battle of life than the intellect. And it is on the weak point that a skilful adversary will concentrate his attack.

For our instruction and reproof, the Spirit, by the apostle, adduces a case in which, while all the beliefs remained sound, the heart and life glided into impurity. In such a case there is strife in a man's own bosom. The doctrines of grace entertained in the mind wage war against the vices indulged in the life, and the vices indulged in the life wage war against the doctrines still retained in the mind. This battle cannot last very long. One or other combatant must give way. Either sound doctrine, maintaining its ground, will drive out the vile indulgence, or the vile indulgence, growing, like an appetite, by what it feeds on, will put to flight the faith.

In the case of our text the bad conscience prevailed and

cast out the good belief. There is another case recorded in the same epistle—ch. vi. 9, 10. Here are some who erred from the faith. How came that? They first gave themselves over to covetousness; then and therefore they erred from the faith. In truth, a man cannot make both money and Christ his portion. A double-minded man is unstable in all his ways; and in some turn of the way the unstable traveller will stumble and fall.

While the calamity is substantially in all cases the same, the faith may be shipwrecked in any of three distinct forms,—a dead faith, an erroneous faith, and no faith. In the first a form of sound words remains, but they are a dead letter; in the second, false views of Christ and his work are entertained; and in the third, the backslider sits down in the chair of the scorner, and says, No God, with his lips as well as in his heart.

Among ourselves, perhaps a dead faith is the most common form of soul shipwreck. Through the indulgence of various vanities and lusts, although the name of Christ and the salvation which it brings remain as words, they are words of no meaning, no power. It is difficult to tear the stump right out of the ground at once. The same end is gained by leaving it standing dead; it will gradually rot away.

Faith and covetousness, faith and any impurity, cannot dwell together in the same breast. These cannot be in the same room with living faith. As well might you expect fire and water to agree. The cares of this life and the deceitfulness of riches choke the word. What then? In order that faith in us should not be choked and die, we must crucify the flesh, with its affections and lusts. Does this savour of legal teaching? See how Paul, the preacher of the Cross, acted in his own experience—Acts xxiv. 15, 16: "And have hope toward God...And herein do I exercise myself, to have always a conscience void of offence toward God and toward men." You have faith in Christ; well, this is the way to keep it—to keep it living. Let not one of us suppose that his faith will remain fresh and full without watching and striving, when we see that even Paul found it necessary to exercise himself every day to keep his conscience clean.

Young men are, in the present day, peculiarly exposed to the danger of speculative error or unbelief. They hear many arguments against either certain doctrines of the gospel, or the gospel itself; they must listen to many sneers against men who profess the faith. I do not deny that there is danger on that side. There is danger: a process of sapping and mining goes on, which may in time overthrow the faith of some. I confess there is danger of false opinions insinuating themselves into men's minds. All I contend for is, that the danger is greater on the other side. Faith is easier and oftener reached and undermined by stains that eat through the conscience.

I knew a young man once who became what was called a Socialist. He attained a great degree of boldness in the profession of ungodliness. No God, or no God that cares for me, was his short, cold creed. But I knew him and his communications before he had made shipwreck concerning faith. The second table of the law had, by indulgence of sinful pleasure, been rusted out of his heart before the first table was discarded from his creed. He had cruelly dishonoured his father and his mother, before he learned to blaspheme God. It cannot be comfortable to a young man in his strength to come day by day to open his heart to God, if day by day he is deliberately disowning and dishonouring his parents in the weakness of their age. The dishonourer of his parents finds it necessary to his own comfort to cast off God. This man put away his good conscience, and therefore his faith was wrecked.*

I knew another, who had in youth made higher attainments, and who, on that account, made a more terrible fall. He had experienced religious impressions, and taken a side with the disciples of Christ. I lost sight of him for some years. When I met him again, I was surprised to find that he had neither modesty before men nor reverence before God. He was free and easy. He announced plainly that he did not now believe in the terrors spiritual that had frightened him in his youth. I made another discovery at the same time regarding him. He had deceived, ruined, and deserted one whom he falsely pretended to love. Through vile and cruel affections he had put his good conscience away ; and, to pacify an evil conscience, he had denied the faith. The belief of the truth and the practice of wickedness could not dwell together in the same breast. The torment caused by their conflict could not be endured. He must be rid of one of the two. Unwilling to part with his sin at the command of his faith, he parted with his faith at the command of his sin.

But though the shipwreck of faith is often, it is not always, the issue of the struggle. When the conscience of one who tried to be Christ's disciple is defiled by admitted, indulged sin, the struggle inevitably, immediately begins. The Spirit striveth against the flesh, and the flesh against

---

* The man ultimately recovered his faith. The stress of life was too heavy for an empty heart to bear ; and he was fain to return, like the prodigal, to his Father.

the Spirit. The sin often casts out the faith ; but the faith also often casts out the sin. The outcome is often, through grace, the discomfiture of the adversary. "Thanks be to God, who giveth us the victory." " The steps of a good man are ordered by the Lord. Though he fall, he shall not be utterly cast down ; for the Lord upholdeth him with his hand."

David put away his good conscience. His conscience was deeply stained by great, grievous, deliberate sin. The sword of the Spirit, glancing from a prophet's lips, pierced through the searing, in the short and awful word, " Thou art the man." Then began the conflict to rage in his breast. This battle cannot last long. One or other combatant, in such a fast and furious struggle, must soon succumb. Angels desire to look into it. Here is a fight for the life of a soul ! Now, or never ! Either his faith will triumph over his sin, or his sin will triumph over his faith. These two cannot divide the kingdom and reign in concert. Repentance or Atheism will gain the day, and possess the man. It must either be the cry of Repentance, " I have sinned against the Lord ; " or the cry of Atheism, " There is no Lord to sin against."

The struggle closed in the confession of the penitent ; and the Lord also put away his sin.

The Prodigal
(Luke 15:11-24)

" And he said, A certain man had two sons : and the younger of them said
to his father, Father, give me the portion of goods that falleth to me. And he
divided unto them his living. And not many days after, the younger son
gathered all together, and took his journey into a far country, and there wasted
his substance with riotous living. And when he had spent all, there arose a
mighty famine in that land; and he began to be in want. And he went and
joined himself to a citizen of that country ; and he sent him into his fields to
feed swine," etc.

Part 1 — His Departure

THE young man goes away.   Why ?   What drives
or drags him from that sweet home—the home
that might be sweet to him, if he would open
his heart and drink in its pure enjoyments ?
Within the man are the " seven devils " that hold the reins
and direct his course, and urge him to his ruin.   " The pleasures of sin for a season" have been long secretly nursed in
his heart : now they have obtained the mastery, and can no
longer be restrained.   The impure passion which he has cherished and not crucified now lords it over him ; and under
the tyranny of his own lusts the way of this transgressor
is hard.   Like the centurion among his soldiers, the will of
this possessing foul spirit is supreme over all the powers of
the victim's mind, and all the members of his body.   To
the right hand appetite says, Do this ; and the right hand

doeth it. So with all the rest of the faculties : they do the bidding of their master, even to the maiming and mutilating of themselves.

These imperious lusts drove the young man from his home, because they could not completely get their own way in his father's presence. " Out of my father's sight," he thought, " and then no longer any bridle on my passions ; no longer any limit to my pleasures." The wretched dupe was photographed long ago, for warning to all generations : " With her much fair speech she caused him to yield, with the flattering of her lips she forced him. He goeth after her straightway, as an ox goeth to the slaughter, or as a fool to the correction of the stocks ; till a dart strike through his liver ; as a bird hasteth to the snare, and knoweth not that it is for his life" (Prov. vii. 21–23).

The fugitive could not halt or look behind him till he had crossed the borders of his native country, and found shelter among foreigners, as a tree is hidden by the wood. Nobody knows me here ! I have here no character to keep ; I shall give rein to passion, and have pleasures without stint.

Very soon, however, his substance is wasted. The English word " substance" is ambiguous. It may mean the pith and marrow of a man's body, or the contents of his purse. It may be taken both ways at once ; for these two kinds of substance generally melt away together, in the bitter experience of the prodigal. His fortune is lost ; his health has failed ; and his pleasures, such as they were, have fled. The pleasures, when they flee, leave behind them stings and terrors in the conscience. The youth begins to be in want ;—in want of food, and clothing, and home ; in want of friends, in want of peace—in want of all

things.   A. waif drifting towards the eternal shore—a lost
soul.

Such is the track of a prodigal.   The footprints are
thick on that path.   A multitude tread it.   The way
down to death is thronged.   As the saved tread their path
in daily life, they are jostled at every step by a crowd
hastening the opposite way.   Oh, it is a solemn thing even
for the saved to tread our streets, for they are rubbing
every hour on fellow-immortals hastening on their own feet
to their own destruction !

But yet there is hope.   If these pages meet the eyes of
any prodigal, turning his back on God and all the good—
chasing the pleasure that is fleeing from his grasp, in order
to lead him over a precipice to the death that does not die,
—we have two pieces of good news for him.   Pause, prodigal, and listen !

1. God is angry with you.   How do you know that ?
I read it in his Word : "And the Lord was angry with
Solomon, because his heart departed from the Lord God of
Israel" (1 Kings xi. 9).   But you promised to give us good
news, and you announce the most dreadful message that can
reach human ears,—the anger of the Almighty God !   The
message I bring is good tidings : nay, it is, in your circumstances, the best news that could possibly be sent to
you from God or man.   If God were not angry, but pleased
with you, in your sin, it would mean that there is neither
holiness nor happiness in heaven or on earth—in time or
eternity ; which would be folly and blasphemy either to
think or to say.   If God were not angry with you, prodigal, for going away, he would not be glad when you
return.   I shall give you here a note of my experience.
I have learned to love and delight in the anger of my

Father in heaven. His anger against my departing, when I depart, means that he loves to feel me near. If he were pleased when I go away, I could not expect him to welcome me back.

Think of it: as the central sun would miss this world, if this world should burst its bonds and wander away into the darkness of space; so God, the Father of the spirits of all flesh, misses a single wandering soul, and is angry. Anger here is but the other side of love. It proves that "he careth for you."

If I were a runaway child of an earthly father, and if the conviction could be conveyed to my weary, despairing heart, in the land of the stranger, that my father was angry with me for going away, hope would beam again into my dark soul; for the fact would lead me to expect a welcome, and no upbraiding, if I should return.

2. Christ himself, by the word of his own lips, in the parable, marked and made a path for the prodigal's return. As they said to the blind man at Jericho, " Be of good comfort; rise, he calleth thee,"—so, with the Bible open in our hands, we can address every prodigal child: " Rise, he calleth thee." Why did he paint the picture? Why did he leave on record for all generations this most tender and melting story? It was to make and leave open a way from the place where the prodigal lies, on the very brink of the pit, back and up to the Father's home and the Father's bosom. He traced every step of that way with his own hand. The way leadeth unto life, and the gate stands open now.

Poor worn-out wreck, at war with yourself and with all the world; torn with remorse, and freezing under the dark shadow of despair; lonely, desolate, lost;—there is One that cares for you. Read the parable of the Prodigal Son once more. Though father and mother forsake you, He who spoke that word will not give you up. If he had been willing to let you go, and content to leave you lost, he would not have left on record that wonderful word. The lines of the parable are like beams of light from heaven, streaming towards the dark region round the sides of the pit—the outgoings of the heart of Jesus in unchanged compassion towards those self-destroyers who have put themselves beyond the reach of human help. He who wept over Jerusalem is still the same.

That departure, in its results, is now grieving you: there is another One whom it grieves. Christ weeps for want of you: he will not frown on you when you return.

> " Just as I am, without one plea
> But that thy blood was shed for me,
> And that thou bidd'st me come to thee,
> O Lamb of God, I come !"

Make that plea your own, and you will feel the arms of the Father's love clasped around you. " This man receiveth sinners."

Part 2 — His Return

" Out of the depths have I cried unto thee." I suppose it will be found, when the books are opened, that most of the cries that have reached to heaven rose from the depths. When all was lost, when he was on the point of perishing, the prodigal came first to himself, and then to his father.

The word that marks the turning-point is very suggestive: " He came to himself." Had he then been beside himself, had he not been in his right mind, when he left his home and wasted himself among strangers ? The word makes it clear that the man was not himself in his prodigal course. His act was madness, as well as sin. It was the act of the evil spirit in him, and yet it was his own act. Jesus rebukes Peter when he says, " Get thee behind me, Satan." The madness of a prodigal's act does not make it any the less his own. It is a great point when the deceived soul discovers his deceiver and denounces him. The tide of battle is already turned when the ruined soul finds out that himself is his destroyer, and turns against the enemy within his own heart.

As soon as he comes to himself, he resolves to return to his father. But the picture, as drawn by the Master in the parable, speaks for itself. It does not need explanation. The point in hand for us is its application. When the prodigal comes to himself, is convinced that he is lost by his own sin, he returns to God, and is accepted.

To show how this blessed word operates, I shall describe a case that came under my own observation long ago—a case from which I learned a good deal of the Lord's way when I was young, and which has been a mine of wealth to me ever since.

When I was sixteen years of age, a youth very dear to me, two years older than myself, was seized with paralysis of the limbs. He was handsome and amiable and well-conducted—no prodigal, but the delight of the family circle, and a favourite throughout a wider sphere. The ailment advanced by very slow degrees ; but it advanced, and he died before he was twenty-two years of age. In the earliest stages he was pleasant, but reserved. Afterwards, for a while, he became sad. At the next stage he opened like a flower in spring, and blossomed into the most

attractive beauty, both of person and spirit. He manifested peace and joy in believing. His society was sought
even by aged and experienced Christians.

After his soul's burden was removed, his face lighted up
and his lips opened ; he told me fully the history of his
spiritual course, which he had kept secret at the time. It
was this : When he found himself a cripple, although otherwise enjoying a considerable measure of health, he saw that
the world had for him lost its charm. The happiness he
had promised himself was blasted. His former portion
was gone, and he had none other. After the first sadness
passed, he thought of turning towards Christ for comfort ;
but he was met and precipitously stopped at the very
entrance on this path by the reflection : " Christ knows
that as long as I had other pleasures I did not care for
him ; he knows that if I come to him now, it is because I
have nothing else—that I am making a do-no-better of
him. He will spurn me away. If I had chosen him
while the world was bright before me, he might, perhaps,
have received me ; but as I never turned to him till I had
lost the portion I preferred, I can expect nothing but upbraiding."

This thought kept him long back. It was like a barrier
reared across the path—the path that leadeth unto life—
and he could not surmount it. By degrees, however, as he
studied the Scriptures in his enforced leisure, he began to
perceive that, although he deserved to be so treated, Christ
would not treat him so. He discovered that " this man
receiveth sinners" when they come, without asking what it
was that brought them. Further, he learned that whether
one come when the world is smiling, or when it is shrouded
in darkness—whether he come in health or in disease—it

is in every case the love of Christ that draws him ; and that no sinner saved will have any credit in the end. All and all alike will attribute their salvation to the free mercy of God. At first his thought was, " If I had the recommendation of having come when my fortune was at the full, I could have entertained a hope." But at last he learned that whosoever will may come, and that he who cometh will in no wise be cast out.

On these grounds he came at Christ's command, was accepted, and redeemed. For the remainder of the journey he went on his way rejoicing.

It is possible that some who read these pages may have fallen into that " slough of despond" in which that young man for a short time lay, and the story of his experience may help them out. But by far the best help in such a case is the parable of the prodigal. The Physician who wrote this prescription knows both the ailment and the cure. He is mighty to save.

You have sinned away your soul, prodigal, and perhaps sinned away also the health of your body. You begin to be in want, and in your want your poor desolate heart tries to turn to Christ. But the consciousness that your own wickedness has wasted all that you had rises up before you, and seems to drive you away from the Redeemer's presence. He seems to say, " When your vice has so wasted you that you can no longer get any enjoyment in it, will you come with your ' blemished' body as an offering to me ?"—he seems to say these forbidding words ; but though you hear these words, Christ has not spoken them. " An enemy hath done this ;" the same who sows tares among the wheat. When the tempter cannot get you to go any deeper into vice, he tries to persuade you that Christ will reject you for having gone so deep. But be of good cheer; answer this fear with a "Get thee behind me, Satan." These things savour of man, but not of God, my Redeemer. His terms are, "Him that cometh." He has left that brief blessed word behind him, and nothing has been added to it since.

And look to the prodigal in the mirror that He holds up, until the prodigal's latter end be yours. What did that youth deserve from his father? The fellow was out and out worthless. He could not enjoy prosperity while his father was near; he would not remain with his riches even in the same territory. In the land of the stranger, when he began to be in want, he thought not of home. This young gentleman, reared in ease and honour, will serve a stranger rather than come home. He consents to be a "field hand," toiling and associating with the meaner class of slaves. Nor is it merely to till the stranger's ground that the Hebrew freeman is reduced, but he must accept the most detested of all employments—must feed the foreigner's swine. The wretch submits to all this, and plods on through his dreary task with no tender relentings towards home. When hunger comes, if he can succeed in sharing the swine's food, he will live on that rather than cast himself on his father. It was only when even swine's food was not to be had, and death by starvation was staring him in the face, that he said, "I will arise and go to my father." And how did the father receive him? Look again to that divinely drawn picture: "His father *ran*, and fell on his neck, and kissed him."

Young man, far from Christ, and fearing that he would forbid your approach because of your provocations, look once more into this picture. Remember, it is not the history of an actual case. It is a story made by Christ, and so made in every feature as best to serve his purpose. And his purpose is to show that he receives sinners, even the chief ; that no possible or conceivable degree of provocation has any effect in closing his heart against him that cometh.

No Cross, No Crown
(John 19:19)

*"And Pilate wrote a title, and put it on the cross. And the writing was,
JESUS OF NAZARETH THE KING OF THE JEWS."*

NO cross, no crown: how deep and broad is the
principle expressed in these words! It belongs
to the Master as well as to the servants; to the
covenant of God as well as to the experience
of men. Christ's title of royalty is written on his cross;
this blessed fruit grows only on that cursed tree. Our
Redeemer is made perfect through suffering. In the
Apocalyptic prophecy a Lamb as it had been slain is seen
in the midst of the throne. It is the cross that bears the
crown.

Worthy of notice here is the machinery by which the
Redeemer's royal title was engraved and his royal dignity
proclaimed. The human instrument acted blindly, and
knew not what he did; all the more fitted therefore was
he for doing the necessary work. You may observe that
in nature those operations that are performed by blind
unintelligent instinct are most surely and most perfectly
performed. The creatures that act without intelligence
keep their time and execute their tasks far more perfectly
after their kind than man. The reason is, that they are
only instruments in their Maker's hands. The Omniscient

forms the design, and employs suitable instruments. The execution is correspondingly perfect. But when a creature intervenes, with a determining will of its own, irregularities occur of every kind and degree.

Even in human affairs, those operations that are performed by machinery proceed with greater uniformity and exactitude than those that depend on the worker's will. The worker may be distracted, or idle, or ignorant, or malicious, and corresponding flaws appear in the product; but beams and wheels, having no purpose of their own, simply work their owner's will. Thus Nebuchadnezzar, king of Babylon, became a rod in Jehovah's hand for chastening backsliding Israel. He did not intend and desire to inflict paternal chastisement upon his neighbours for their good. If the plan had been his, it would not have been executed so well. Nebuchadnezzar gave rein to his own cruel ambition. The Father of wayward Israel lifted the ambition of the heathen king, and employed it as a rod to chasten his child.

In like manner, Pilate was employed to proclaim Messiah's kingdom. He did it better, or rather it was better done by him, than it could have been done by any disciple of Jesus. If Pilate had planned this coronation, he would have greatly erred; nor would Peter, or James, or John have done it better. For this work friends and foes were equally unfit. Some of his followers attempted by force to place him prematurely upon an earthly throne. And Peter ventured to rebuke his Master for intimating that the cross must come before the crown.

When the Lord would have his own sovereignty at length proclaimed, he did not employ a herald whose will entered into the transaction. Had he desired to use the

will of a man in the matter, he must have chosen one of
his own disciples, for his enemies refused to own his sovereignty. But none of his disciples at that period understood the nature of his reign or knew the date of its
beginning. They would not have proclaimed the kingdom
at the right time, nor would they have proclaimed the
right kingdom. Even after the Lord had offered himself
a sacrifice, and risen again, their eyes were still blinded on
this point; we find, accordingly, that the promise runs in
this form: "Ye shall receive power after that the Holy
Ghost is come upon you, and ye shall be witnesses unto
me."

They erred on both sides: they attempted to establish
the kingdom before the time had come, and when the time
had come they did not acknowledge it. They would fain
have set the crown on the Lord's head while he was living
and working miracles. In presence of a fickle Jewish mob
on the one hand, and of armed Roman legions on the other,
they thought they would be safe as subjects of one who
could raise the dead by his word, or summon fire from
heaven to consume his enemies. They would have crowned
Christ at the wrong time; and when the right time came,
they had lost confidence in his power.

In a tone of the most forlorn despondency, the two with
whom the Lord conversed on the way to Emmaus said,
"We trusted that it had been he which should have redeemed Israel." They trusted once, when they saw his
power; but they abandoned hope when they knew he
was crucified. They were not the men to write "King"
upon the cross of Jesus. They would have crowned him
when his raiment glistened on Tabor; but when his bleeding head drooped on his breast on Calvary, their fond

anticipation of a kingdom vanished like a dream. " O fools, and slow of heart to believe all that the prophets have spoken! Ought not Christ to have suffered these things, and to enter into his glory ? "

With the precision and punctuality of an unconscious machine, blindly executing its author's will, Pilate composed the regal title of the Redeemer, and fastened it aloft upon the cross. Thus the dumb Roman preached Christ crucified before the burning lips of Paul were baptized by the Spirit for taking up and continuing the theme. With equal ignorance in the instrument, and therefore with equal exactness in the performance, the priesthood of Emmanuel was proclaimed by Caiaphas, " It is expedient that one man should die for the people." Pilate, the supreme civil ruler for the time, meant in revenge to pillory the Jewish leaders aloft before the world as the subjects of the crucified Nazarene ; but this wrath of man was by God's unseen hand intercepted in its flow, and compelled to publish the Redeemer's praise.

" My kingdom," said Jesus, in his ministry—" my kingdom is not of this world." In origin, nature, object, and end it is wholly diverse from other kingdoms. As in other features it is peculiar, so especially in this, that the King's glory lies in the shame which he endured. The King's power sprang from his weakness ; the King's authority rested on the King's death. The crown of the kingdom hangs on the cross of its King. This kingdom that springs from the cross is a new thing. Hitherto it had not been known among the works of God.

Not that then the divine sovereignty over the world began first to be exercised. There was a kingdom of God before the cross ; but the kingdom that rose from the cross was a new manifestation of the divine attributes, more glorious than any that had been previously made. From the beginning the divine sovereignty was exercised both in the material and spiritual departments without the suffering of a divine person.

In nature the Lord reigneth; his throne is from everlasting to everlasting. The heavens declare his glory, and obedient earth echoes back the witness to the sky. How exquisitely perfect is the divine government over matter! How beautiful the laws of that kingdom, and how uniform the obedience which its subjects yield! These stars never wander from their paths; that sun never forgets to rise. Every tree produces its own kind of seed, and every seed reproduces its own kind of tree. How manifold, O Lord, are thy works; in wisdom hast thou made them all!

This kingdom is governed by wisdom and power, infinite and eternal. No cross is needed to sustain this throne. The Son of God does not need to become a man and die that the stars may be kept in their courses, and the sea within its bed.

Nor would a sacrifice be necessary to restore the kingdom to its beauty, if it were reduced to chaos by a universal flood. Again, as at the beginning, might God say, " Let there be light," and light would be. Again, internal heat might be employed to upheave new mountain ranges, and leave another hollow for another sea. Other races of living creatures might be called into being, more or less closely resembling those that had been destroyed, and the earth might be commanded to produce fruit for their food. In all this there would be nothing new under the sun; it would be only a repetition with minor variations of what had previously been done. There would, indeed, be a new heaven and a new earth ; but no new exercise of divine wisdom and power would be put forth in calling them into being. In regard to the character and kind of sovereignty exercised, it might be proclaimed over the new creation, " All things continue as they were." The heavenly hosts might in such a case continue the praises they had learned at their birth, but no new song would have burst from their lips.

In the moral department, too, there was a kingdom before Christ was crucified, a rule that did not demand for its exercise the crucifying of Christ. Sovereign rule on this side did not require that the Ruler should suffer even unto death. The kingdom in this department parts, like a stream interrupted by an island, into two diverging channels. The Lord reigneth over the *good* and the *evil*.

He reigns over all holy, unfallen intelligences. The sovereignty on this side consists of one unbroken course of holy love from the King, and a corresponding course of holy obedience from the subjects. It is difficult for us to form a distinct conception of this species of rule ; for we have no experience of it. The will of the King is the law of his subjects ; and yet their service is free. There is no disobedience ; and yet there is no constraint. What a mystery is here ! A lordship absolute over the highest kind of created beings ; and these beings with all their faculties absolutely free. The kind of sovereignty which the holy God exercises over holy creatures, is perhaps as widely distinguished from his moral government of fallen humanity as it is from his control over material nature. A perfect moral supremacy over intelligent beings, who yield a perfectly willing and delighted obedience, must constitute a happiness in kind and degree far above our capacity of conception. Eye hath not seen, nor ear heard, neither have entered into the heart of man, the things which God hath prepared for them that love him, when in them perfect love has cast out fear.

A government exercised over beings perfectly intelligent and completely free, and that government as absolute as the control of matter by the natural laws, constitutes, as I apprehend, a main element in the happiness of heaven. When we shall be as free as we now are in sinning, and yet with that free will shall render to God an obedience as perfect as the elements of nature, we shall have in our hearts the joy of the Redeemer, and that joy will be full. If the stars in their courses possessed our intelligence, how happy should they be in the sweet willingness of their perfect obedience ; if we, with our intelligence, were like the stars in the perfection of our obedience, how happy should we be in knowing and doing God's will, without a distracting thought or a rebellious desire !

But there is another and opposite department of God's moral government. The same holy Sovereign rules also over unholy intelligent creatures, distinct from man and created before him. Here, too, the relations between the Governor and the governed are short and simple. On one side it is all holiness ; and on the other all sin. As in the case of holy creatures in their relation to God, the agreement is perfect ; so here is the disagreement. On that side there is no jar ; on this, no harmony. On the part of the King, it is justice executed ; on the part of the subject, it is judgment endured. The lines of relation here between the throne and the prison are terribly short and straight. Righteousness pure and bright, and straight like sunlight, streams from the judgment-seat ; and no mediator stands in the way to receive its piercing, or deflect its course.

Such were the departments of Jehovah's kingdom, and such the kinds of government which he exercised, before man made in his image disobeyed his law. The authority in these several departments was in species various, but in all of them alike it was single, short, direct. No mediator intervened. Towards matter, it was omnipotence ; towards moral intelligence, righteousness, diverging practically into two channels; towards the good, complacent love,—towards the evil, holy anger. In none of these kingdoms did it behove the King to die.

But when human creatures fell, a new thing happened in the universe. The exercises of divine sovereignty hitherto put forth did not apply to the case, and contained not a cure for the ailment. The laws of nature do not reach it, for they are spiritual, intelligent beings who have rebelled. The law of gravity would grasp a falling star and raise it—would seize a wandering world and restore it to the circle of the planets in the sky, as a good shepherd bears back a strayed sheep to the fold ; but the law of gravity has no power over a prodigal soul. It has no sense to perceive the departure, and no faculty to arrest the fugitive. Even all-comprehending omnipotence does not keep a soul from sinning,—does not win back a soul that has sinned. Spirits escape from the grasp of power, even though that power be divine, as water escapes through the net which encloses and brings to land the fishes great and small that lie within its sweep. This is not a defect in the attributes or government of God. He hath done all things well. It is no more a disparagement to the wisdom and power of God that the laws of nature do not control spirits, than it is a disparagement to the skill of man that a net does not hold water. The net was not made for holding water : neither were the natural laws intended to rule spirits. It was God's plan to leave meshes wide enough in the circumference of his providential government for spirits to escape into rebellion, if they should so will. To arrest and win back these fugitives he has instituted a new kingdom, and in it now exercises a new and unique species of sovereignty. When power and wisdom and holiness, in their simple and direct exercise, are no longer adequate to meet the creature's need and accomplish the Creator's purpose, the Infinite and Omniscient will call in another principle of government, foreseen and predetermined by himself from eternity, but never exercised till now.

The problem is deeper now ; more glorious, therefore, will be the display of wisdom and love by which its secrets shall be searched, and its difficulties overcome. Hitherto, in exercising sovereignty over moral and intelligent beings, God had only visited the good with simple approval, and the bad with simple condemnation. In the one direction no displeasure radiated from his face, and in the other no favour. Upward, it was all and only paternal love ; downward, it was all and only judicial condemnation. But now, in accordance with the divine counsel from eternity, his love and his justice will be more gloriously manifested by being joined in one. The love of the Holy One will now be seen to flow full on spirits that have rebelled. To make this possible, the Son of God becomes a man and dies. This new exercise of sovereignty can be put forth only through a suffering Sovereign. The title of this King can be written nowhere but on his cross.

Christ crucified, and none other, is the power of God that can control the course, and renew the character, and make blessed the destiny, of fallen men.

With the awful exactitude and irresistible force of machinery, whose iron arms are destitute of thought and feeling, and therefore only execute the designer's will, the kingly dignity of Jesus is held in reserve until Jesus himself is nailed to the cross; then it is emblazoned over his head, and proclaimed in three languages to the world.

Fix your regard now on the great central and fundamental fact, that Christ's reign rests on Christ's suffering. In the shedding of his blood lies the essence of his power to save. This kingdom is a new kingdom. Its power is as great, and its control in its own sphere as complete, as the divine sovereignty over matter and over good and bad spirits; but it is a sovereignty different in essentials from all that the Supreme has hitherto put forth. The newness, the peculiarity lies in this, that the power which the King wields rests on the death which the King endured. From the cross a kingly power goes forth, to heaven above, and hell beneath, and earth around. It is the blood of the Lamb that satisfies God, silences the adversary, and wins a human soul.

It was this sovereignty which Jesus desired to obtain and delights to wield. For this hope that was set before him he endured the cross, despising the shame. He refused to permit himself to be proclaimed King prematurely, because a crown before the cross would not have possessed power to save sinners. When the people were bent on elevating him to the throne of David, he conveyed himself away. When the Greeks sought to be introduced to him before he suffered, he intimated that unless he should die he could not put forth in their behalf the power which they needed—" Unless a corn of wheat fall into the earth and die, it abideth alone." Without the suffering he could not obtain the power to win back and rule a multitude of alienated, condemned creatures; but if he should suffer death according to the covenant with the Father, he would thereby acquire power to ransom and renew a people unto himself manifold as the grains of wheat in the fields of harvest. If the corn of wheat die, it bringeth forth much fruit. When he made a similar intimation to his disciples, and Peter officiously interposed with, " Far be this from thee, Lord," he resented Peter's advice as the suggestion of Satan to subvert his throne.

Thus uniformly and peremptorily did Jesus repudiate a kingdom, until by his suffering he had acquired the right to reign and the power of reigning; but as soon as the cross was planted on Calvary, and his body was nailed to the cross, he permitted the regalia to be displayed above his bleeding brow. For, mark, if he had not permitted it, the thing would not have been done. Expressly on that very day this Jesus had said to Pilate, " Thou couldest have no power at all against me, except it were given thee from above." He who so long refused the title of royalty will not let it lie idle when he has accepted it at last. He had not power to act in his new kingdom until he suffered; but now that by suffering he has obtained the power, he will certainly wield it. He is a crowned King now; whatsoever he does as Mediator, he does in a kingly way. Kiss ye the Son, lest he be angry. Blessed are all they that put their trust in him.

Christ crucified satisfies divine justice, and forgives his people's sin. In a royal way he cancels the sentence of death, although it was righteously pronounced and recorded. The handwriting that constituted a soul's death-warrant, duly signed and sealed by the King of righteousness, he wrenches from the executioner's hand and cancels; but observe, it is by nailing it to his cross that he can blot out that dread handwriting.

On the cross the work was finished,—the Father's work which the Son loved to perform. There is now no condemnation to them that are in Christ Jesus. The death of Jesus perfects for ever all his own. The truth and the power of God are pledged here. An omnipotent sovereignty shields the disciples of Jesus. " Father, I will that they also, whom thou hast given me, be with me where I am." After the manner of a king, the Saviour of sinners speaks. He knows his own power, and we may safely trust it. A half-hesitating faith dishonours the Lord, and mars the happiness of his servant. What pains he took that his work should be complete, and that its completeness might be manifest! There is sovereign power in this shed blood! " The blood of Jesus Christ God's Son cleanseth us from all sin "—" Who shall lay any thing to the charge of God's elect? It is Christ that died"—" I saw in the midst of the throne a Lamb as it had been slain." Righteous Abel,—that blood of the Sacrifice washed his sin away, and made him just with God. The sprinkled blood on the door-posts kept the Hebrew households safe from the angel of death on the eve of the exodus in Egypt. Let that blood be on my conscience, and I shall be safe from the second death. Christ crucified has all power in heaven and in earth. Count him a King. Treat him as a King. Confide in the royal power of his sacrifice,—he shields all his own from condemnation. " The sufferings of Christ

and the glory that should follow:" as the flowers and
fruit spring from the living root that spreads darkly
under ground, so the blossom of hope here and the fruit
of eternal life hereafter, for all Christ's members, spring
from the suffering of Christ in his people's stead.

The dying of the Lord Jesus has a sovereign power to
win us to obedience, as well as to shield us from wrath.

It is the power that lies in the cross to which we must
look for arresting, controlling, moulding human hearts.
Our spirits are not made for yielding to any other kind of
power. The forces in nature that have raised the mountains, have no efficacy to rend a stony heart. The force
that shook the jail at Philippi could not have shaken the
jailer. God was not in that sense in the earthquake. It
was a still, small voice, accompanying or following the
shock of nature, that reached and melted the man. "No
man can come unto me, except the Father *which hath sent
me* draw him." It is the new kingdom—the kingdom
whose throne is occupied by a Lamb as it had been slain,
that reaches and leads them captive.

Bear in mind that if you are ever grasped and held for
saving, that you may not go down to the pit, it is the
power of the dying of Christ that will do it. There is
power in the blood that he shed to hold you—and hold
you up, when the power which keeps the stars in their
courses would fail to arrest your fall. Brother, a power
is sent out from heaven, and softly thrown around you,
greater than the power that sends angels forth on their
errands, and casts the wicked into their own place.
Abandon yourselves to its drawing, and you will be
borne safely home. "I, if I be lifted up, will draw all
men unto me." But why so few drawn to Jesus—drawn

by the power of his dying, whithersoever he will? Yonder
ship lying on the water has all her sails spread, and a great
steady breeze filling them; yet she moves not. Why?
She is in secret unseen depths touching the earth. She
is aground. It must be a similar cause—it must be some
secret cleaving to the dust that keeps us from being
won by Christ, so as to run the way of his commandments.

Saved men, from righteous Abel to the last saved man,
are like one long procession marching across the world.
The head of the column appeared at the gate of Eden;
while the rear rank will pass only before the flame in
which the earth shall be burned up. It is one company,
and there is no break in the line. The shout of a King is
in the camp all through; but the King personally marches
neither with the first nor with the last. Jesus is in the
midst. But his kingly power—the sovereign sway of his
dying, covers the foremost and covers the last, shields the
earliest and shields the latest; and gives to all, at the
journey's end, an abundant entrance into the joy of their
Lord.

Two lessons at the close hang on two IFS :—

1. *If* Christ had not died. If his patience had given
way when he had wept over Jerusalem, and Jerusalem
still laughed him to scorn; if he had dashed the cup from
his lips in anger, refusing to drink it for a thankless world;
if he had taken the scoffers at their word, on Calvary, and
come down from the cross to save himself,—what then?
Ah! the kingdom's power would have been all employed
to cast into outer darkness a wicked world. No sacrifice
for sin! but a fearful looking for of judgment. He was

faithful unto death. " I am the Lord, I change not; therefore ye sons of Jacob are not consumed."

2. Now that the price is paid and redemption completed; now that Christ crucified is King, and has all power in heaven and in earth; now that the shelter of Omnipotence is spread open towards time,—if any one of us pass over time and across the border into eternity without taking shelter under this sprinkled blood—what then ? No MORE sacrifice for sin; but a fearful looking for of judgment.

Christian Doctrine and Life
(Romans 12:1)

"I beseech you therefore, brethren, by the mercies of God, that ye present your bodies a living sacrifice, holy, acceptable unto God, which is your reasonable service."

OUR object in this paper is to feel for the connection between Christian doctrine and Christian life. The link which unites doctrine and duty in the Christian system is neither an imaginary line nor an iron rod: it is like the Word of God, "both quick [living] and powerful." It is like the great artery that joins the heart to the members in a living body—both the channel of life and the bond of union. If that link is severed in the animal, the life departs; there remains neither heart nor members. So in the Christian system, if doctrine and duty are not united, both are dead; there remains neither the sound creed nor the holy life.

Here, then, we shall find *a logical argument and a practical lesson*. Inquirers should know the truth on this point, and believers should practise it.

A common street cry of the day is, Give us plenty of charity, but none of your dogmas: in other words, Give us plenty of sweet fruit, but don't bother us with your hidden mysteries about roots and engrafting. For our part, we join heartily in the cry for more fruit; but we are not content to tie oranges with tape on dead branches lighted with small tapers, and dance round them on a winter evening. This may serve to amuse children; but we are grown men, and life is earnest. We too desire plenty of good fruit, and therefore we busy ourselves in making the tree good, and then cherish its roots with all our means and all our might.

In the transition from the eleventh to the twelfth chapter of the Epistle to the Romans, the knot is tied that binds together doctrine and duty in a human life. Speaking generally, with the eleventh chapter the apostle concludes his exposition of doctrines, and with the twelfth he begins his inculcation of duties. At the beginning of his great treatise he plunged into the deep things of God, and at ch. xi. 33 he emerges from his exploration with a passionate cry of adoring wonder at what he has seen and heard— " O the depth of the riches both of the wisdom and knowledge of God !" After relieving his overcharged spirit with that grand anthem which constitutes the close of the doctrinal section, he addresses himself (xii. 1) to the business of directing and stimulating an obedient and holy life in believers; and this theme he prosecutes to the close. At the point of contact between the doctrinal and practical divisions of his treatise he defines and exhibits the relations established in the laws of the Eternal between the gifts which flow from God to men, and the service rendered by men to God. Hitherto he has been opening the treasures of the kingdom, and permitting the divine goodness to flow freely into the lap of the needy; but here is the turning-point : henceforth he will urge that tribute should stream upward, like a column of incense, from man to God.

Who hath first given to God, and it shall be given to

him again? None. No man first gives to God, and then gets back an equivalent. But though no man gives first to God, all renewed men give to him second; that is, the disciples of Christ, having gotten all from God first and free, then and thereby are constrained to render back to him themselves and all that they possess. This apostle knows human nature too well to expect that men will render fit service to God first and spontaneously. He puts the matter on another footing. He expects that the mercy of God, first freely poured out, will press until it press out and press up whatever the little vessel of a redeemed man contains, in thankofferings to the giving God.

Here is a leaden pipe concealed under the plaster, stretching perpendicularly from the bottom to the top of the house. What is the use of it? It is placed there as a channel through which water for the supply of the family may flow up to a cistern on the roof. "Water flow up? Don't mock us. That would be contrary to its nature. Water flows down, not up. How should it change its nature when it gets into your pipe?" Place your ear near the wall, and listen. What do you hear? "I hear water rushing." In what direction? "Upward." Precisely; water left to itself outside of the pipe, flows down; but water left to itself inside, flows up. "Why?" Because there it is pressed by the water that flows from the fountain on the mountain's side. It is the weight of water flowing down that forces this water to flow up.

It is thus that living sacrifices, holy and acceptable, ascend from a human life to God, when that life is in Christ. When a human soul is within the well-ordered covenant, it is constrained, by the pressure of divine mercy flowing through Christ, to rise in responsive love.

"I beseech you therefore, brethren, by the mercies of God, that ye yield yourselves," etc. The word "therefore" is the link of connection between doctrine and life. Here it unites the *product* to the *power*. The whole epistle consists of two parts, united together by this word. The first portion is occupied with truth revealed, and the second with obedience rendered; and the truth is in point of fact the force which generates the obedience.

Much mischief is done in the world by a wanton or ignorant divorce of this divinely united pair. There are two errors, equal and opposite. Those who teach high doctrine, and wink at slippery practice in themselves and others, fall into a pit on the right hand; those who preach up all the charities, and ignore or denounce the truth and the faith that grasps it, fall into a pit on the left. Let not one man say, I have roots, and another, I have fruits. If you have roots, let us see what fruit they bear; if you would have fruits, cherish the roots whereon they grow.

Beginning his course of practical lessons with the twelfth chapter, this rigidly logical author binds the motive firmly to the act, and the act to the motive. He tells us what we ought to do, and what will induce us to do it. For power to propel his heavy train, he depends on "the mercies of God," as these have been set forth in the preceding portion of the treatise; and the train which by this power he expects to propel is, "Present your bodies a living sacrifice," etc.

The mercies of God constitute the motive force.

A consecrated life is the expected result.

Consider carefully now the power employed in constant view of the effect which it is expected to produce. "I beseech you, brethren, by the mercies of God." Up to this point the epistle is occupied with the enunciation, elucidation, and defence of doctrine. The writer started with the set purpose of directing and stimulating human life in the way of holiness and love; yet he expends the greater part of his time and strength in the exposition of abstract dogma. Paul has made no mistake here. Although his aim was to get human hearts and lives filled with love to God and man, he devotes his attention first to truth revealed.

This is a scientific operator. He knows what he is about. He is especially skilful in adapting means to ends. To provide the water-power may be a much more lengthened and laborious process than to set the mill agoing; but without the reservoir and its impounded supply, the mill would never go round at all. Paul goes forward with a firm step and a straight course towards his aim in a sanctified and useful human life; but he takes every step on the assumption that a devoted and charitable life cannot be attained, unless the person and work of Christ be made clear to the understanding and accepted with the heart. Hence the time he has occupied and the pains he has bestowed in exhibiting and commending at the outset a complete theology.

A class of men is springing and pressing to the front in our day, who laud charity at the expense of truth. The truth, exterior to the human mind, which God has presented in his Word, they ignore as unnecessary rather than denounce as false. Doctrine, as truth fixed and independent, they seem to think a hindrance rather than a help towards their expected millennium of charity. In their view, a man may indeed become a model of goodness although he believe sincerely all the doctrines of the gospel; but he may reach that blessed state as quickly and as well although he believe none of them. Their creed is that a man may attain the one grand object of life—practical goodness— equally well with or without belief in the Christian system. That there may be no mistake in the transmission of their opinion, they take care to illustrate it by notable examples. John Bunyan, who received all the doctrines of the gospel, and Spinoza, who rejected them all, attain equally to the odour of sanctity in this modern church of charity. This representation is publicly made by men who profess the faith, and hold the preferments, and draw the emoluments of the Established Church in England.

In order to elevate love, they depress faith. For our convenience, they have compressed the essence of their system into a phrase that is compact and portable—" A grain of charity is worth a ton of dogma." The maxim is well constructed, and its meaning is by no means obscure. If it were true, I should have no fault to find with it. But, as I have seen a mechanic, after the rule applied to his work gave unequivocal decision in its favour, turning the rule round and trying it the other way, lest some mistake should occur; so, in the important matter before us, it may be of use to express the same maxim in another form, lest any fallacy should be left lurking unobserved in its folds— thus: " A small stream flowing on the ground is worth acres of clouds careering in the sky." In this form the maxim is arrant nonsense; but the two forms express an identical meaning, like the opposite terms of an algebraic equation. Wanting clouds above us, there could be no streams, great or small, flowing at our feet; so, wanting dogma—that is, doctrine revealed by God and received by man—there could be no charity. They scorn dogma, and laud charity—that is, they vilify the clouds, and sing pæans to running streams.

There is an aspect of childishness in the methods at present in fashion for undermining evangelical faith. When I was a little child I thought the clouds were accumulations of smoke from the chimneys. I also thought that, while the barren atmosphere above our heads was filled with stacks of dry thick smoke, the earth beneath our feet was rich and beneficent, seeing that from its bowels spring up all the waters that feed the rivers and fill the sea. Foolish child! The clouds are the storehouses in which the water is laid up, ready to be poured on the earth. From these treasures the wells obtain all their supply. We have streams on the ground because we have clouds in the sky. As the clouds create the rivers, the love of Christ exhibited in the gospel causes streams of charity to circulate in human life. The Bible teaches this, and history proves it. " God so loved the world, that he gave his only begotten Son, that whosoever believeth in him should not perish, but have everlasting life." This is a dogma ; and before that dogma came, how much charity was in the world ?

Our latest reformers, I suppose, came easily by their discoveries. I am not aware that they have passed through any preparatory agonies, like those which Luther endured at Erfurth. Your philosophic regenerator of the world dispenses with a long search and a hard battle. When he brings forward for my acceptance his savoury dish, like poor old blind Isaac, when his slippery son presented the forged venison, I am disposed to ask, " How hast thou found it so quickly, my son ?" Ah, it is easy for those who have never been deeply exercised about sin to denounce dogma and cry up charity in its stead; but whence shall I obtain charity if I abjure truth ? " Beloved, if God so loved us, we ought also to love one another." The Apostle John got his charity from the bosom of the Master whereon he lay. Where do the modern apostles obtain theirs ? How can you move the world if you have nothing but the world to lean your lever on ?

The Scriptures present the case of a man who was as free of dogma as the most advanced Secularist could desire, and who was notwithstanding wofully lacking in charity. " What is truth ?" said Pilate; and he did not wait for an answer, for he had made up his mind that no answer could be given. Pilate was not burdened with a ton, with even an ounce, of dogma; yet he crucified Christ—crucified Christ, believing and confessing him innocent—that he might save his own skin, endangered by the accusations of the Jewish priests at the court of Rome.

Those who, in this age, lead the crusade against dogma, are forward to profess the utmost reverence for the life and teaching of Jesus Christ. But he did not despise dogma. " Thou art the Christ, the Son of the living God." Nothing more completely and abstractly dogmatical can be found in all the creeds of the Church than that short and fervid exclamation of Peter in answer to the Master's articulate demand for a confession of his faith upon the point. And how did the Master receive it ? He not only acquiesced in the doctrine and the expression of it by his servant, but, departing in some measure from his usual habit of calm, unimpassioned speech, he broke into an elevated and exult-ant commendation : " Blessed art thou, Simon Barjona ; for flesh and blood hath not revealed it unto thee, but my

Father which is in heaven." Let men keep congenial company, and let things be called by their right names. Either doctrine—truth revealed by God and accepted by man—either doctrine is decisive and fundamental for the salvation of sinners and the regeneration of the world, or Jesus Christ was a weakling. You must make your choice. The divinity of Christ, as confessed by Peter, is a dogma : for that dogma Jesus witnessed ; for that dogma Jesus died. For it was because he made himself the Son of God that the Jewish priesthood hunted him down. Did he give his life for a dogma that is divine and necessary to the salvation of sinners, or did he fling his life away by a mistake ? Men must make their choice. Those who are not for Christ are against him.

If you do not receive Jesus Christ as God your Redeemer, you cannot have him as the beautiful example of a perfect humanity. He claimed to be divine, and died in support of the claim. Therefore, if he be not the true God, he must be a false man. Thus the Holy Spirit in the Scriptures has presciently rendered it impossible for modern Secularists to reject the great dogma of the gospel, and yet retain the life of Jesus as the highest pattern of human character. Both or none : Christ cannot be so divided.

The word " therefore," destitute of any moral character in itself, and deriving all its importance from the things which it unites, is like the steel point set on a strong foundation which constitutes the fulcrum of the balance. To one extremity of the beam is fixed, by a long plummet-line, a consecrated benevolent human life ; but that life itself lies unseen in the dark at the bottom of a deep well, a possibility only as yet, and not an actual entity. No human arm has power to bring it up and set it in motion—power to bring it into being.   Here is a skilful engineer, who has undertaken the task.   What is he doing ?   We expected that he would stand at the well's mouth, and draw with all his might by the depending line, in the hope of drawing up that precious Charity from the deep.   But no ; he is busy at the opposite extremity of the beam.   He is making fast to it some immense weight.   Who is he, and what is the burden that he is zealously tying to the beam ; and what does he expect to get by his pains ?   The operator, diminutive in bodily presence, but mighty in spirit, is the Apostle of the Gentiles ; the weight that he is making fast to the beam is nothing less than *the mercies of God* as they are exhibited in Christ,—all the love of God ; nay, God himself, who is love.   He has fastened it now, and he stands back—does not put a hand to the work in its second stage.   What follows ?   They come ! they come ! the deeds of Charity—they ascend like clouds to the sky, at once an incense rising up to heaven, and a mighty stream of beneficence rolling along its channel on the surface of the earth, and converting the desert into a garden.

Ask those great lovers who have done and suffered most for men—who have taken up their abode in dungeons in order to soothe the spirits and relieve the wants of the wretched inmates—who have braved pestilential climates to Christianize and civilize the long-degraded negro ; ask the whole band of flesh-and-blood angels who, by sacrificing themselves, have sought to heal the sores of humanity, what motive urged them on and held them up.   They will answer with a voice like the sound of many waters, *The love of Christ constraineth us.*   Those who have done most of the charity that has told on the ills of life do not think, and do not say, that this fruit grows as well on all doctrines, or no doctrines, as on the truth of the gospel. They tell us that the force which sent them into the field and kept them there was the mercy of God in Christ, pardoning their sin and sealing them as children. They are bought with a price, and therefore they glorify God in their lives.

In the scheme of doctrine set forth in the first half of the epistle, we behold the reservoir where the power is stored; and in the opening verses of the second section the engineer opens the sluice, so that the whole force of the treasured waters may flow out on human life, and impel it onward in active benevolence. Let the memory of God's goodness, in the unspeakable gift, bear down upon our hearts, as the volume of a river bears down upon a mill-wheel, until its accumulating weight overcome the inertia of an earthly mind, and the interlacing entanglements of a pleasure-seeking society, so sending the life spinning round in an endless circle of work to abate the sins and sorrows of the world.

The mercies of God being the power that sends out the product, the product so sent consists of two distinct yet vitally connected parts, as soul and body in the natural life. These are, devotion in spirit to God our Saviour, and substantial kindness to man our brother.

The constituents of a true devotion are, a living sacrifice and a reasonable service. Whatever is rendered in sacrifice to God is rendered whole. The phraseology is in a high degree typical, but by reference to the Old Testament institutions it is easily understood. The distinguishing features of the New Testament sacrifice are, that it is the offerer's own body, not the body of a substitute; and that it is presented not dead but living. It is not a carcass laid on the altar to be burned; it is a life devoted to God. Love is the fire that consumes the sacrifice; and in this case, too, the fire came down from heaven. The body is specially demanded as an offering : the body is for the Lord ; it bears the mark of his hand. We are fearfully and wonderfully made.

Stand in awe and sin not : give not that which is holy unto the dogs. Your body is another Bible : read it with reverence. Its precepts, like those of the Decalogue, are written by the finger of God. Show me, not a penny, but a man ; for this is the only coin which the great King will accept as tribute. Whose image and superscription hath he ? God's. Render therefore unto God the thing that is God's.

As the sacrifice is living, the service is reasonable— rational. It is not the arbitrary though loving command addressed by a father to his infant son—burn the fat upon the altar—that he may be trained to habits of unquestion- ing obedience ; it is rather the work prescribed by the father to an adult son—a work which the son understands, and a purpose in which he intelligently acquiesces. The burning of incense, practised in the Romish community for ages, and now resumed by those who should have known better, is not a reasonable service. It is a going back from the attainments of the gospel to the beggarly elements of a past dispensation.

The second constituent of Christian duty is reciprocal justice and kindness between man and man, like the har- mony and helpfulness which the Creator has established between the several members of a living body. Mark how the hand comes to the defence of the eye in its weakness; and how the eye with its sight, and from its elevated posi- tion, keeps watch for the welfare of the lowly, blind, but laborious and useful foot. The mutual helpfulness of these members is absolutely perfect. Such should be the charity between brother and brother of God's family on earth ; such it shall be when all the sons and daughters are assembled in the many mansions of the heavenly home. In the remaining portion of the epistle Paul labours with all his might to stimulate practical charity—in one place reducing the whole law to one precept, to one word—love. After devoting so much attention to the roots, he will not neglect to gather the fruit. After so much care in obtaining the power, he looks sharply to the product, lest it should turn out that he had laboured in vain.

We must look well to our helm as we traverse this ocean of life, where we can feel no bottom and see no shore—we must handle well our helm, lest we miss our harbour-home. Such seems to be the counsel given for the guidance of life to those who count that all religion and all duty lie in subjective care and diligence, while they ignore, as unattainable or useless, all objective revealed truth. But careful management of the helm, though necessary, is not enough on our voyage. By it alone we cannot bring our ship safe to land. We must look to the lights in heaven. The seaman does not look to the stars *instead* of handling his helm. This would be as great folly as to handle his helm vigorously and never look to the stars. Not this one nor that one, to the neglect of the other. Both, and each in its own place : the stars, to show us the path in which we ought to go ; and the helm, to keep us in the path which the stars have shown to be right. Not turn to the contemplation of dogma, instead of labouring in the works of charity ; but looking to the truth as the light which shows us the way of life, and walking in that way with all diligence.

It is interesting to notice how the spiritual instincts of

the Lord's immediate followers led them in the right way, at a time when their intellectual comprehension of the gospel was very defective. On one occasion the Master taught the twelve a lesson on this subject—charity—which seemed to them very hard. The point in hand was the forgiving of injuries, and how far it could or should be carried. " Master," they inquired, " how often shall a man sin against me, and I forgive him ? Seven times ?" That, they thought, was as great a stretch of loving forbearance with a neighbour as could reasonably be required of any man. But what is the word of the Lord in this case ? " I say not unto thee, till seven times, but until seventy times seven." That is, he refused to set any limit to the charity of his disciples. Charity in his Church must be like the atmosphere wrapped round the world—no mountain-top can pierce through it to touch another element beyond. Charity shall surround life so high and so deep that all life shall float in it always, as the globe of earth in the circumfluent air.

The poor men were taken aback by this great demand. It cut their breath. They had been educated in a narrow school, and could not at first take in the conception of a love that should know no other limit than the life and capacity of the lover. But on recovering from their first surprise, and becoming aware of their own short-coming, a true instinct directed them to the source of supply. Then the disciples said unto the Lord, " Increase our *faith.*" Faith ! O ye simple Galileans, it is not in faith that ye come short; it is in charity ! How foolish, at such a moment, to give chase to the ignis fatuus of *dogma*, when it is *life* that you need—more of love in your life ! If our secular philosophers had been there, such would have been their patronizing reproof of those simple, unlettered fishermen. But the fishermen, taught of the Spirit, possessed a sounder philosophy as well as a truer religion than their modern reprovers. I could imagine that Peter, in such circumstances, would have stood up as spokesman for the whole college, and made short work with the logic of the Secularists. Although blind, like old Jacob, to objects outside, like him Peter was endowed with an inner light. When Joseph brought his two sons to the patriarch for his blessing, he led them forward so that the elder should stand opposite the right hand of his grandfather, and the younger opposite the left. But Jacob crossed his hands in bestowing the blessing, so as to lay the right hand on the head of the younger child. When Joseph interfered to correct what he supposed to be a mistake, his father persisted in his own plan, saying, " I know it, my son ; I know it." He guided his hands wittingly. So would the simple but courageous fisherman answer the philosophic Joseph of our day—" I know it, my son ; I know it." He guided his lips wittingly, when, in lack of charity, he prayed for faith ; for faith is the only efficient of charity. He would fain yield himself a living sacrifice for behoof of his fellows; but if he is ever impelled forward in this arduous course, he will be impelled, as Paul teaches, by the mercies of God. The instincts of the new creature in Peter taught him that if he should ever *do* more in forgiving love for his neighbours, he must *get* more through faith from his Lord.

A miller, while he watches the operations of his mill, observes that the machinery is moving slower and slower, and that at last it stands altogether still. On searching for the cause, he discovers that some small hard pebbles have insinuated themselves between the millstones, first impeding the celerity of their motion, and then stopping it altogether. What will the miller do? Put in his hand, and try to remove the obstruction? No; he is not such a fool. He goes quietly to a corner of the mill, and touches a simple wooden lever that protrudes at that spot through the wall. What is the miller doing there? He is letting on more water: impelled by more weight of water, the millstones easily overcome the obstacle, and go forward on their course. The demand of unlimited forgiving was the obstacle that stuck on the heart of those poor Galileans, and brought its beating to a stand; and they wisely applied for a greater gush of the impelling power—more faith. When the circulation of the spiritual life was impeded by that hard ingredient, they gasped for a widening of the channel through which the mercies of God flow from the covenant to the needy. More faith meant getting more of forgiving grace from God to their own souls; and they knew that when the vessel was full, it would flow over. The best of the argument, as well as of the sentiment, remains with the fishermen.

It is now time, however, that we should turn to the other side, and gather there a very needful lesson for Christians ere we close. We have been showing that it is faith accepting the mercies of God that produces a devout and charitable life; but what shall we say of those who have faith, or seem to have it, and yet lack charity?

Here a very interesting question arises. Want of faith, it is granted, among evangelical Christians, is followed by want of goodness, as a blighting of the root destroys the stem and branches of a tree. But does the converse also hold good? Will a languid life weaken faith, and an entire cessation of Christian activity make shipwreck of the faith? As a metaphysical speculation, we do not touch this question; but on its practical side a useful warning may be given. Of all trees it may be said, destroy the root, and the stem will wither; but you cannot predicate of all trees that the destruction of the stem in turn destroys the root. Many trees when cut down to the ground retain life and grow great again. But some species— pines, for example—die outright when the main stem is severed. Here lies a sharp reproof for all who bear Christ's name. True it is that your faith in Christ is the root which sustains the tree of your active life, and insures its fruitfulness; but true it is also that, like the pines, if from any cause the life cease to act, the faith, or what seemed faith, will rot away under ground. It was in this manner that Hymenæus and Alexander fell away. They first lost the good conscience; then and therefore they made shipwreck of the faith. They gave way in the sphere of duty, and then dogma melted away from their hearts. (1 Tim. i. 19.) The stem of the tree was cut off or withered, and the root rotted in the ground.

Thus, as the roots nourish the tree, and the growth of the tree in turn keeps the roots living, so is it with the trees of righteousness, the planting of the Lord that he may be glorified. While faith, by drawing from the fulness of Christ, makes a fruitful life; reciprocally, the exercise of all the charities mightily increases even the faith from which they sprang.

While, on one side, the necessity of the day is to maintain the faith as the fountain and root of practical goodness in the life; on the other side, especially for all within the

Church, the necessity of the day is to lead and exhibit a life corresponding to the faith it grows upon. Here it is safe to join full cry with the Secularists—more charity— charity in its largest sense, a self-sacrificing, brother-saving love, that counts nothing alien which belongs to man, and spares nothing to make the world purer and happier. A pure, holy, loving, active, effective life,—this is the first, and the second, and the third requisite for the regeneration of the world. It is quite true that those who bear Christ's name fail to walk in his steps; and to this defect it is owing that so little of the desert has yet been converted into a garden. It is life, it is love, it is living sacrifices that are wanted; this is the cure for the sores of humanity. But how shall we get that life of mighty doing and suffering charity, which we confess is lacking, and which, if we had it, would flow like a stream over the world and heal its barrenness? How and where shall we obtain this heaven-born charity?

Enter into thy closet, and shut the door, and seek it there. Seek, and ye shall find. Copy literally the simple request of the amazed disciples. Say unto the Lord, Increase our faith.

That means that your very soul should open to Christ, and accept him as all your salvation. It is not to have a faith printed in your creed-book about one Jesus; it is to clasp him to your heart as your Redeemer, your Friend, your Portion. It is to taste and see that he is good, and to bear about with you the dying of the Lord Jesus. This will be a force sufficient to impel all your life forward, so as to please God and benefit your brother. " I beseech you therefore, brethren, by the mercies of God, that ye present your bodies a living sacrifice."

Ultimately, we must look to the sovereign Lord God for a baptism of the Spirit, greater than that of the Pentecost, to produce a revival that will usher in the glory of the latter day; but mediately and instrumentally that revival will come through the MERCIES OF GOD, manifested to the world in the incarnation and sacrifice of the eternal Son, accepted, realized, and felt, in new and greatly increased intensity by the members of the Christian Church.